THE JESUIT POST

THE JESUIT POST

#Faith #God #Frontiers
#Culture #Mystery #Love

Edited by
Patrick Gilger, S.J.

Maryknoll, New York 10545

Founded in 1970, Orbis Books endeavors to publish works that enlighten the mind, nourish the spirit, and challenge the conscience. The publishing arm of the Maryknoll Fathers and Brothers, Orbis seeks to explore the global dimensions of the Christian faith and mission, to invite dialogue with diverse cultures and religious traditions, and to serve the cause of reconciliation and peace. The books published reflect the views of their authors and do not represent the official position of the Maryknoll Society. To learn more about Maryknoll and Orbis Books, please visit our website at www.maryknollsociety.org.

Published by Orbis Books, Maryknoll, New York 10545-0302.
Manufactured in the United States of America.

Library of Congress Cataloging-in-Publication Data

The Jesuit post : faith, God, frontiers, culture, mystery, love / edited by Patrick Gilger, S.J.
pages cm
ISBN 978-1-62698-076-1 (pbk.)
1. Jesuits. 2. Theology. I. Gilger, Patrick, editor of compilation.
BX3701.3.J47 2014
255'.53—dc23

2013038610

To all our readers
online and offline

Contents

Acknowledgments

It is always good to say thank you, if for no other reason than that it redirects anxious attention away from what the future may hold toward the good things that have already happened. It's in that spirit of gratitude for the good that has already happened that I want to say thank you, not only to the people who have helped make this book possible but to all those who have helped *The Jesuit Post* since its conception.

To all of you who read TJP, or watch our videos, or laugh at our memes, thank you. We would like to dedicate this book dually to you and God, because it is that relationship that occupies all our attention. Thank you for allowing us any access at all to such a sacred relationship—especially when you never have to do so, especially because it is a vulnerable thing to allow—and for letting us focus on the new and holy things God is already doing in our world. We are very grateful for the ways that you allow us to be who we are becoming as Jesuits.

Thank you, Tim O'Brien, for co-editing this book with me. If not for your humor and depth and support the whole process would have made me even balder than I already am.

Sam Sawyer and Eric Sundrup: Thanks, guys. I'm convinced that God is still building upon the foundation of our friendship something larger than any of our imaginings—this book is just a part of that larger dream. I am proud to be your companion in the Lord.

Thank you also to Jim Keane and Michael Rozier and Jim Martin. When TJP was still an idea and I was still unsure of it, your interest and support gave me the courage to keep going. Thank you for saying yes. And to all the folks at Orbis Books, thanks for this opportunity; I hope it's only the first of many.

To the TJP staff, from the most hidden (Konzman?) to the most visible, thank you. It has made me very happy to work with you and, especially, to see so many of you succeed within the forum that is TJP through both your own talents and God's grace.

To our superiors in the Society of Jesus, especially Tom Smolich, Dave Godleski, Tom Lawler, and Tim Kesicki, thank you for taking a risk.

Stephan Salinas and Tim Luecke, who did the interior and cover artwork respectively, thank you both for your talent and for being so good to work with.

Thank you also to those who know us best, our families and friends. Your support before and after we added "S.J." to our names has been a *sine qua non*, and we are grateful (and love you, too).

Lastly, thank you to Pope Francis, whose continual effort to refocus our church, to help us come out of ourselves, and to train our eyes on the margins and the marginalized has been a source of energy, tears, and great joy. Although TJP began fifteen months before the first Jesuit pope took office, his pre-conclave intervention serves as a mission statement for us as well. To his then-fellow cardinals, he said, "Evangelizing presupposes a desire in the Church to come out of herself. The Church is called to come out of herself and to go to the peripheries, not only geographically, but also the existential peripheries: the mystery of sin, of pain, of injustice, of ignorance and indifference to religion, of intellectual currents."

It is the desire to do just this, to be attentive to a God who is already at work in our world in many and confusing places, that gave birth to and sustains *The Jesuit Post.* Thank you all for reading, for forgiving us when we make mistakes, and for supporting us as we continue to seek alongside you a God who may "show Himself more in deeds than in words," but still, we hope, does indeed show Himself in words as well.

In Christ,

Paddy Gilger, S.J.
November 5, 2013
Feast of All Saints and Blesseds of the Society of Jesus

Foreword

James Martin, S.J.

Not long ago, a group of young Jesuits told me about an exciting new venture they were planning on starting. It would be a Website that looked at the intersection of faith and culture, and which would be specifically designed to appeal to the young (i.e., *real* young people: in their teens, twenties, and thirties) who might be otherwise bored with organized religion, confused about faith, but still curious about God.

The Website would be called, they told me, *The Jesuit Post.* It would be run and staffed entirely by Jesuits in training (aka "formation"), and all the articles and videos, and anything else that showed up on the site, would be created by them. They would write on any topic that interested them, and more importantly, that they hoped would interest their young readers. The young Jesuits were particularly interested in looking at issues not normally considered "religious" or even "spiritual." Edgy, it sounded.

Fantastic idea, I thought, and catchy name, but I had my doubts about whether they could succeed.

To begin with, this wasn't an "official" Jesuit work, or, as we say in the trade, an official Jesuit "ministry" (even tradier, "apostolate"). Wouldn't it be hard for Jesuits still in training to get the approval of their religious superiors for what they posted on a public Website? Wouldn't that limit what they could say?

No problem, they told me, they had already received that approval. The editor-in-chief, Paddy Gilger, S.J., a young Jesuit who's just been ordained and was then beginning theology studies at the Jesuit School of Theology in Berkeley, California, would oversee the content. If anything seemed too controversial he could pass it along to his superior.

"Really?" I said, somewhat dumbfounded. "You mean that you can basically write what you like?"

"Yup," said Paddy.

"What about all the technical expertise? Here at *America* magazine we have a full-time editor who does nothing but manage the ins and outs of our Website."

"No problem," said Paddy. "We have several Jesuits who are quite adept at that sort of thing."

"But what about getting guys to write for you?" I asked. "Would they be hard to find?"

"Not at all," said Paddy. "They're already lining up to do so."

A final concern. Weren't they concerned, as they aged, that the site wouldn't be written by young Jesuits? Again, no problem. They already planned to hand it on to the next generation when they had finished with their Jesuit training. In this way the site would be forever young, to quote a cheesy song I liked in my own youth.

The more I heard about the venture, the more my enthusiasm grew. Young Jesuits writing about such a wide variety of topics for young people (and most likely curious middle-aged and senior readers) seemed just the thing for the "New Evangelization," the church's effort to use any and every media available to attract people to Jesus Christ. Frankly, it wasn't such a bad approach to the "Old Evangelization" either, that is, just spreading the gospel. And it was the perfect way to speak to youth in a language that they could understand.

As the "launch date" drew near, I kept checking my email for an official announcement. One night, Sam Sawyer, S.J., and Eric Sundrup, S.J., the other founders of the site, told me that the site was up and running. Could I take a look at it to see what I thought? I surfed over and was amazed at how well they had achieved their goals. It was clean, exciting, and as far as this fifty-year-old Jesuit could tell, young. Enthusiastically, I posted a link to my public Facebook page and tweeted out the news, and posted a link on the *America* magazine blog.

A few minutes later all three—Paddy, Sam, and Eric—emailed me ("High Priority!") to say that the site was not "live" but only in a testing mode. No matter though, it was too late. People were already enthusiastically reading what the *The Jesuit Post* guys had to say, and their new ministry had begun. As they now like to tease me, "You launched us!"

This new book is a compendium of not only a few of the best pieces from what has (inevitably) come to be known as TJP over the last few years, but also more than twenty newly written chapters—all done by some of the best young Jesuits around. As on the TJP Website, the essays in this book range widely in subject, style, and sensibility. From a look at medicine, prayer, and poetry to the hidden spiritual benefits brought to us by, um, crazy people on the Internet; from why Catholic teaching on economics might be particularly relevant after a financial collapse, to why the Jesuit superior general's discussion of the "globalization of superficiality" (great phrase) might actually overlook what is "deep" in pop culture. (I vow not to tell the author's superior general about a young Jesuit writing that his superior might have overlooked something.)

TJP already has a recognizable, distinctive, and clear voice. It is the voice of a faithful Catholic who looks at the world as a place alive with God's spirit. Only this time, the "world" isn't simply a church or a theology class or a formal ministerial setting like a campus ministry office. Rather, it means, as those topics listed above imply, that the Spirit is alive while you're surfing the Web, cheering on your favorite team, listening to the radio, partying with friends, and even watching TV. "Finding God in all things" is probably the most popular shorthand for Jesuit spirituality, and the guys at TJP do that with energy, enthusiasm, and a lot of wit. I know this sounds a bit fatherly, but I'm proud of them.

These writers are absolutely alive to the Spirit at work in the world. They don't quail before what might seem confusing or even offensive to people who want to keep God in a little box. (As in: "The Web? What does *that* have to do with the Holy Spirit?") Their firm grounding in faith means that they can proclaim the Good News in new ways with an old virtue: zeal. These guys are zealous for the reign of God, zealous about using any means necessary to spread the gospel, and zealous to help you find God everywhere.

So get ready to find faith in a new way, thanks to the zeal of my Jesuit brothers, who saw an opportunity that no one else had, and took it, or rather gave it, to God—and to us.

1. An Ontological Change

Patrick Gilger, S.J.

I was ordained a priest forty days ago.

For whatever reason, and despite the remarkable sameness of the days before and after the bishop of Youngstown, Ohio, laid his hands on the crown of my head, the word "priest" feels a bit stiff to me, over-starched. Not yet worn-in. Maybe that's why, after writing that first, stand-alone sentence, I feel tempted to find some way to lighten the expectation the words contain, cut across them somehow. That last sentence will have to do, I suppose.

In the run-up to the day, my friends, being friends, would ask questions like "How do you feel?" or, "What does it feel like to be so close to being a priest?" I was almost invariably stumped. Not because I didn't know what I was feeling—many will readily testify that emotion does not so much need to be wrung from me as sopped up from the floor near my feet—but because I felt . . . completely normal.

I felt, more or less, exactly the same as I had the day before, or the week before that. Or this is how I felt: I felt completely the same, except that every four or whatever hours this bolt of adrenaline would thunder-storm-warning itself through me, waking me up from a pre-sleep stupor, and an alert would sound in my head: "Patrick, you are about to be ordained a priest." Or this is how I felt: I felt like a guy who'd been just, you know, living his life. And then this.

These first forty days have, more or less, preserved that same sense of normalcy. And yet you might've noticed that I keep using that phrase "more or less." I thought about just deleting it, but I left it in because it's those words that give me some kind of a grip, soapy though it may be, on the slow shift in meaning the word "normal" is undergoing on this, the far side of commitment.

Still, despite having been ontologically changed—received "an indelible spiritual character," marked permanently by the "vocation and mission received on the day of [my] ordination"[1]—they have felt remarkably normal. These days I mean. More or less.

1. *Catechism of the Catholic Church* (CCC), numbers 1582 and 1583. http://www.vatican.va. Accessed September 3, 2013.

But now I've gone and skipped right over the best moment, haven't I?

#

The best moment wasn't actually one moment at all. It was more a string of moments, wooden pins on a clothesline.

The first came about fifteen or so minutes into the ordination Mass. I was ordained along with a friend, a fellow Jesuit named Jayme, and by this time in the Mass, he and I had already donned our albs of not-quite-matching whites, and pinned closed our two stoles and hung them diagonally from shoulder to hip to show that we were deacons, ready to be ordained. And we had already made our first (immensely relieving) mistake when we failed to take the correct place in the entrance procession. I had already sat (safe between my parents, almost anonymous for those few minutes within the warmth of the congregation) through the Liturgy of the Word. And the bishop had, just seconds before, asked our superiors and the people filling the church that most loaded of questions: "Do you know them to be worthy?"

Jayme and I stood in a gap between the front pews and the steps leading up into the sanctuary waiting for the answer. I held a breath. Then our superiors said "Yes." And the bishop, too, said "Yes." I let out the breath. And then we were asked to turn and face the assembled church that had chosen us.

They responded by applauding. Wave after wave of applause.

It felt like acceptance, that applause; the dam of affection accumulated over many years suddenly bursting to soak into us. For many seconds that torrent of sound, and the relentless, exuberantly honest love it made physical, pounded us.

Within it I felt two things in quick succession. The first was the briefer and the less surprising: I felt great. Ravenous for praise as I often am, I felt great. I looked out at my loved ones, those whose patience had slowly worn away the roughest of my ego's edges. I saw them standing hip-to-hip, in their nicest of clothes, heads tilting to find sightlines. I sought their faces, caught their eyes. I listened and I stood and I accepted and I felt filled, filled, filled.

And then, I wanted it to stop. I wanted to ask everyone to please stop, please. Or, failing that, I wanted to step to the side and gesture with my hands toward an other at whom the remainder could be directed. Or slip away. Or deploy some sort of emotional umbrella so that I could breathe in the midst of the downpour.

I don't mean that I got cold feet or that I didn't want to be priest anymore or anything. It wasn't like that. It was more like remembering—not remembering like a scene in my mind but remembering like a sensation, like the way a long-healed scar all of a sudden digs up another slice of pain. And what

I remembered in the midst of that applause was all the ways I'd failed to deserve it. What I remembered said, and accurately, "Your applause is misplaced. I am not worthy and we all know it."

Looking back on that moment now from the dry height of the future, that second reaction seems a normal thing, another example of how routine, how absolutely banal it is for human beings to recoil from acceptance. As if we are living deserts only able to accept so much water at once, and no more. Or, even when able, unwilling.

It's not as if there is no reason for our avoidance of such acceptance, either. In fact, I think there are two that are quite good. The first is that we are, actually, unworthy of it—unworthy because in the face of such affection our own pettiness and persistent self-mismanagement seem all the more unacceptable. The second is simply because we are unable to live up to the desires such acceptance holds—unable because all our finite capacities shrink from the towering hopes that grow within the womb of such endless approval.

So, no, it wasn't cold feet. And it wasn't that I didn't want to be a priest. It was just an utterly human reaction. It's what we do when we're shown by those we love how accepted we are, with what affection we are held, and—in the exact same moment, because we are so accepted—how unworthy. It's what humans do when, after being known for years, we are then swaddled by forgiveness and desire. It's what we do when all of that is staccatoed into life by hundreds of hands, like the falling of a thousand thousand raindrops. If we are allowed to, we turn away.

It took only a few seconds more—long seconds of pride and remembered fear and refusal to accept such acceptance—for my resistance to be proven weaker than their love.

#

I'd spent years on the way to that first moment, nearly eleven of them to be exact. This is the time we Jesuits call "formation," during which we study (philosophy and theology), we teach (high school or catechism), and, in our twenty-first century at least, we do at least one other thing: We practice asking a question. And we spend hours and weeks and years practicing the asking of this question, and the question is some version of this: Will you let me be a minister for you?

People react in all kinds of ways to a question like this, and rightly so. Some bristle, raise their quills and, verbally or otherwise, make it clear *they are just fine, thank you*, regardless of whether that is deeply true or not. Which is fine. Others are almost over-eager, their "yes" overlapping the tag end of the question as they melt and the tears come. Which is also fine. And others hem and haw, put their eye to the keyhole and peer out; these leave the chain on even after the deadbolt is thrown and the door cracked. And this, too, is fine.

It's fine because in our day and age there is no other way for one person to become a minister (a doorless frame, a paneless window for God) than by being given permission, than for another person to say, verbally or otherwise, *yes, you can be for me a pathway to God.*

I can't tell you how many times I've asked people if they are willing to let me be this kind of minister for them and been turned down. It always hurts. But when it works, when the initial question is true, it also forms a kind of discipline, like whatever the opposite of a callus is, inside of those of us who keep asking, keep allowing the rejections to deepen the desire to become even more transparent, even more clean a conduit for the electrons. In this way rejection is also a gift.

But the pain of having that question rebuffed and our selves refused, that is not an experience foreign to any of us. Which is why I am confident that you, reading this now, can imagine how it feels when, suddenly, one cloudy morning in June on the day of your ordination, everyone around you . . . No. I was going to write, "is saying 'Yes' to my oft-repeated question," but that's not right; it was more than that. It was that all of these people—lined up as they were in the church after the Mass, asking me one after another for my blessing, my priestly blessing—it was as if all of these people suddenly became for me the gentlest of interrogators, putting to me that softest of questions: Will you be a minister for me?

It was, after years—years—of being taught that I have to earn the right to be a minister, like a trap door in a hot carnival booth had suddenly opened and dropped me into cool waters. And I kept hearing it all that morning—in the confusion of the crowd taking pictures at the altar, on the sidewalk outside in the thin rain, in line to get what was left of brunch—"Will you bless me, Father?" It's good to say "Yes."

In case it wasn't clear: That was the second of the best moments.

#

The last came a few hours later in a recently emptied ballroom, steps from the church, where I sat at a plastic foldout table with a handful of my closest friends. These were women and men I'd known for years, the kind you meet early in college and all of whose dance moves you end up knowing (and stealing), the kind with whom you may or may not have watched approximately eight thousand episodes of *Friends.*

On the table where we sat were coffee cups, piles of cards, presents, high-heeled shoes, a necktie; my white-plastic Roman collar. We leaned back in our chairs, draped arms around one another and talked: about the Mass ("What was it like lying on the floor like that?") and our growing families ("I cannot believe this will be kid number five!"), and told funny stories we'd told many times before.

It felt familiar with them; the same as it ever was. But also it was new; things had changed. These friends had married, had gained and lost jobs, bought houses, studied and written and loved and been hurt and triumphed during the eleven years that separated college from the events of that morning. And though we'd kept in touch, we could feel the difference as we talked. One of them, a new mother, was asked what it's like to become a mom. "It takes time to feel the difference," she said. "It had happened—the baby was there—and I had a sense of it already, I think, but it's not like I left the hospital and was suddenly Mom." She talked about how becoming a mother took remembering to put the baby monitor at the bedside, learning to snatch showers between naps, and discovering how a marriage looks inside a family. "It takes time."

Like each species of friend, this kind—the kind who have seen and helped us grow up—has a gift peculiar to itself, one only it can give. Our gift, the one we had been giving one another all through the late morning as we sat in the detritus of reception and told stories, was to ratify the changes that had happened in each of us. And to give each other permission to continue changing. Yes, you used to interrupt every story, but you listen now. You couldn't focus before, but you pay attention now.

It takes time to cut a tomb for our egos from the rock face of old habits, more time for the new actions required of us to build new habits, and more time for those new habits to constitute another sense of self. And then we still must ask our loved ones—our friends, our families, the world—to accept and support and ratify this person we have become.

It wasn't possible when we had met as nineteen-year-olds, but now it was. Now we could be the kind of friends who could certify the great depth that time and commitment, failure and children, marriage and success had carved into us on our ways to adulthood. These were the men and women who had allowed me to become more than I was then, and were now, with great humility, allowing me to be a priest.

#

Near the outset of his career, the great German philosopher Martin Heidegger (who spent a few short months in the Jesuit novitiate before leaving both the Society and Catholicism more or less behind) began writing about ontology, that is, he started thinking about the meaning of being. "What does it mean to be?" he asked, and then spent his life trying to answer that question.

It's early in *Being and Time*, his first major effort to ask these ontological questions at length, that we read, "Every questioning is a seeking. Every seeking takes its direction beforehand from what is sought. . . . As a seeking, questioning needs prior guidance from what it seeks."[2] For Heidegger this meant that in asking what it means to be he was already guided toward an answer.

What do I seek? To know what it means to call ordination an ontological change? To understand what it means that I am now fundamentally ordered to the "unfolding of the baptismal grace of all Christians"?[3] Yes. But it also means that asking is being guided into an answer. The same way that my friend asked her newborn—in getting up every night, in holding her through the tears, in having milk pulled from her body—what does it mean for me to be your mother? For me it means that in asking I am being guided, given direction beforehand, from what I seek, which is God. And how to be a swift aqueduct between God and his people.

Hands have been laid on me. Litanies have been sung. Acceptance in the form of applause has tunneled its way down my spine. For the past forty days I have stood before God and church and said the words. It has happened, and I have a sense of it in the asking, the doing. It's not that I feel so different, I don't. I feel remarkably normal, more or less.

2. Martin Heidegger, *Being and Time* (trans. Joan Stambaugh; Albany, NY: SUNY Press, 1996), 3-4.

3. CCC 1547.

2. Come at Me, Bro! (Why I Love the Crazies)

Eric Sundrup, S.J.

I take a sick pleasure in conversations that involve the question "You know what the Jesuits should be doing . . . ?" In my imagination, I respond by plopping my elbows on the table and resting my chin on my palm. I bat my eyes, gazing up at the all-knowing sage in front of me. "No, I have no absolutely no idea what we should be doing," I begin. "It's funny, but we never thought to ask that question! Shucks, we should've thought of that! Luckily you have, so please, I'm dying to learn what we Jesuits should be doing." Alas, I've been trained to be a caring, loving minister, and so Christian charity (pesky little thing) means this fantasy remains only a daydream. Instead, I smile and listen attentively, even if what I want to do is scream, "Come at me, bro!"

Part of my work for *The Jesuit Post* is administering our social media presence, and let me tell you, in this line of work nearly all of my conversations involve some form of "You know what the Jesuits should be doing?" I like to compare this work to fighting the mythical hydra. If you accomplish something on one social network—that is to say, if you hack off one head of the hydra—two more will sprout up in its place. Behold the nature of virality: if you do your job properly, you are likely to get overwhelmed pretty quickly.

In my time watching our comments and keeping track of who tweets, pins, and posts about TJP, I've seen a whole range of responses to our work. Praise, confusion, and excitement are the easiest ones to deal with. Deep engagement with ideas and sincere conversation about pressing issues both happen and are gratifying. And the honest and open discussion that results is really helpful for our contributors, editors, and readers. It's really easy to love our followers and fans when this happens; I particularly love it when people ask good questions or challenge us to revisit an issue from a new angle.

But by far my personal favorite, what makes me truly love my job, is the absolute lunacy. You know the kind I mean: unsolicited rants, conspiracy theories, and insatiable comment trolls—the people with way too much free

time who stalk the Internet looking for fights—the whole nine yards. Yes, I've discovered that I love the crazies.

Who are the crazies, you ask? Well, at the very least, we can say that they are a species unto themselves. They are the Internet version of the type of folks who end up on *Jerry Springer* or *Jersey Shore*, or whatever sad train wreck of humanity reality television will parade in front of us this season. *Those* people, those other people—right?

Wrong.

Sorry, friend, but "the crazies" probably includes both of us. I know, I know: Surely I am mistaken. Everything you and I think is sane and rational. Wholly reasonable, really. The fruit of calm and careful deliberation. *We* could never be one of the crazies.

Well, I am here to tell you that we are all a little crazy. And that it's OK to be a little crazy.

When we started *The Jesuit Post*, we wanted to provide a place that discussed religion and culture without all the shouting matches we had witnessed elsewhere. We kept wondering what people on the margins must think about religion when most of the discussions they heard about faith were the wars waged in comment sections on religious sites. I know I hardly ever visited those because whenever I did I got the impression that religion was nothing but a war over dogma and doctrine. A whole lot of I'm right and you're wrong; I'm a real Christian and you're a heretic. We wanted to cut out the crazy, wash it out, and clean up the image of religion. We kept saying to ourselves, "There *has* to be a more civil way to talk on the Internet about a serious spiritual life."

We were wrong. But thank God we were wrong!

As I've learned, if you want to have completely reasonable and civil conversation about religion, just give up now. I mean it. Pack up, take your toys, and go home. If we expect people to be completely reasonable about religion, we seem to have missed, oh I don't know, the last three thousand years of human history. And, come to think of it, this loose grip on reasonableness shouldn't really surprise us. Because when you boil it all down, we're asking people to consider a God who loves unconditionally, who sacrificed himself for a group of confused sinners, a God who continues to reach out to us every day. By commonly accepted standards (i.e., ours), God is the crazy one.

There are very few gatekeepers on the Internet. If you set up a comments section, you've just invited everyone into the discussion. Writer Clay Shirky aptly titled his book about Internet-based communities *Here Comes Everybody* (which, fittingly enough, has been offered as a good definition of "Catholic"[1]).

1. The origin of applying this statement to the Catholic Church is (like so much on the Internet) hotly debated. The phrase is James Joyce's, although he almost certainly didn't mean it

As Shirky notes, the cost of creating groups around niche ideas—those outside the mainstream—is significantly lower on the Internet. Thanks to the wonders of technology, each of us can easily connect with people who enjoy the same brand of crazy we ourselves possess. And bolstered by the awareness that there are others who think like us, we become only too happy to share our unfiltered thoughts with the entire universe. Here comes everybody!

So why am I so excited about having everybody around? Because for all the insanity and the moments of great confusion, when everybody (crazies included) jumps into the fray, the ensuing insanity can be a forceful reminder that we are—all of us—mucking around in this world together whether we like it or not. And that we need to make sure we don't take ourselves too seriously as we wade through all that muck.

The Internet gives everyone a soap box and an audience. It's worldwide open mic night. And, just like at a comic we think is bad, if people don't like what we say they have a tendency to boo. Label them whatever you want—crazy, angry, deranged—but they are there, and they aren't going to disappear. Worse still, those labels become an easy way of writing people off, which blinds us from what they have to share with us. If there is anything that teaches me that the world is larger than I am and that I can never hope to fully understand it (let alone control it), it is dealing with some of the crazy comments and interpretations of Jesuits and our work that pop up on the Internet. Paradoxically, this little dose of crazy has gone a long way in keeping me sane.

When I wanted to join the Jesuits, I had to complete a formal application process. This included a full psychological assessment, complete with a battery of tests. I had never seen a shrink before, and I was more than a little nervous at the prospect of having some stranger ask me probing questions about my deepest, darkest secrets. (I'd prefer to have my adolescent years left alone, thank you very much; it was traumatic enough the first time.) Before the big day, I kept picturing myself on a leather couch across from a middle-aged man who smelled of cigars, cognac, and cologne. In perfect Oxford diction, jotting notes on a legal pad, he would say to me, "Tell me about your mother. . . ."

In the days leading up to the appointment, I talked with a few Jesuit friends about the coming evaluation. They reassured me by saying, "Look, they are just checking to make sure you're the right amount of crazy. If you're totally sane, you can't survive Jesuit life, but if you're a complete nut job, well, that's not good either." I'll admit that I have a very active imagination, so while I'd swear I caught a faint waft of cigars, cognac, and cologne, the psychologist I met with had a nasal Chicago accent instead of sounding like

---

the way Shirky does. Regardless, it's certainly true that describing Catholicism as an unruly horde is an idea with deep roots.

a member of the Royal Family. Luckily I had just the right amount of crazy, because he passed me. A year later I entered the Jesuit novitiate.

Throughout my Jesuit formation I've been trained to challenge my assumptions. I've learned that God is always more than I could ever have imagined. Jesuits are constantly seeking to become more free, more open to the continuing call of the Holy Spirit, reaching out to new frontiers, seeking to find God in all things. This can be a slow process, and it requires honest transparency and the courage to face new ideas and new places. The challenges to this process are many, and long standing. We've always faced the temptation to circle the wagons, to close our world into safe, established patterns. Social media is no different. It runs a serious risk of becoming an echo chamber. We too easily follow people who already like us, who think like we do, and who generally have the same interests as we do. As a result, you can end up preaching to the choir, and quickly.

I like to think of the crazies as the Internet's built-in safety valve. Like mutations in evolution, when we take them seriously, these are the people who demand adaptability and change, who teach us new ways of responding to new situations. If the mutation is too much, too insane, too deadly, it won't survive. But maybe, if it's just the right amount of crazy, it can be a game changer—the type of shift that changes the established rules and opens up new possibilities. These are the crazy mutations that show up just when you least expect it, and then our reasonable, sound, and predictable views are suddenly shattered.

The Society of Jesus has always been able to attract a large number of crazy detractors, and that's probably because we are a little crazy ourselves. We are trained to dream big. Really, really big. One of our mottos is *Ite inflammate omnia*, reproduced on greeting cards and kitchen magnets everywhere as "Go and set the world on fire." Legend has it that our founder, St. Ignatius Loyola, sent his close friend (and cofounder of the Jesuits), St. Francis Xavier, to convert the East using those words. And by "the East" he meant, oh, all of Asia and the islands surrounding it. Make no small plans indeed!

Whenever I think I've got it all figured out, I remind myself that I joined a religious order that is almost five hundred years old—we've had plenty of time to make a few serious gaffes. I professed vows of poverty, chastity, and obedience (who's crazy now?), and I am part of a church that in addition to supporting many of the greatest cultural works in Western history also burned witches at the stake and put Galileo on trial for teaching what is today known as basic astronomy. We are plenty crazy. Reasonable is more of a moving target than we like to admit.

I actually keep a folder on my computer with my favorite Jesuit conspiracy videos. On bad days, I open up that folder and have a good laugh. Did you know that we are supposedly responsible for the sinking of the Titanic? (That's right, James Cameron, you owe us. Where would your record blockbuster have been without the Jesuits?) Even better, we apparently run a secret military base in North Korea! When I told the superior general of the Society of Jesus—the head Jesuit, the big cheese, the "Black Pope"—about this secret military base with hundreds of thousands of Jesuits on it, he stopped and, with a wry smile, said, "Where are they? I need them now. Go get them." (So, if this book somehow slips past the North Korean censors and you guys are reading this, please report to Rome immediately. We have work to do.)

It's often tempting to think that the crazies are funny because we aren't like them; we are the sane ones, the ones who understand the world. We are different than the crazies. But, my dear, sweet deluded friend, that is a point of great danger. Because, as I have found, the reason I love the crazies is that they remind me of how very fragile and human we all are, how crazy and insane it is to even believe that we are in charge of this little spinning orb that is hurtling through the cosmos.

Back in the late 1990s, Apple Computer ran a very clever ad campaign called "Think Different." As they played images of Amelia Earhart, Thomas Edison, Albert Einstein, Gandhi, Jim Henson, and Martin Luther King, Jr., the voice over on the ad said, "Here's to *the crazy ones*. The misfits. The rebels. The troublemakers. The round pegs in the square holes. *The ones who see things differently*. . . ." It goes on to say, "You can quote them, disagree with them, glorify or vilify them. About the only thing you can't do is ignore them."[2] The premise is straightforward: the only people who change the world are the ones who are crazy enough to think that they actually can. While it's obviously a well-crafted piece of marketing, it is also profoundly true.

So here's to you, crazies. Here's to you for reminding me that I'm just as insane. And that always playing by the reasonable and rational rules is just another flavor of crazy. So, here's to us, really. Here's to us who still believe this world can be changed, that this world is not what it seems, and that there is so much that we are missing. Here's to those of us who take a good hard look at the mess we're all part of and respond, "Come at me, Bro!"

2. "Apple Think Different ad," YouTube video, 1:01, October 2, 1997, posted by "EveryAppleAds," October 18, 2012, http://youtube.com.

3. Salvation

Joe Hoover, S.J.

The white moon, the quiet goats, the school's tin roof, a candle leading the small single file church lulling chant mary full of grace lord is with thee up the road, stop, turn around, fruit of thy womb jesus plastic beads hot air cooling down . . . I am fairly convinced the world is constantly being saved by eight little boys and two nuns who every night in Lunting walk up and down the mission drive saying the rosary.

And the world is being saved by the meeting of the Porkadoh Self-Help Group—which is organized and run by a whip-thin and vaguely beautiful sister of the Society of the Child Jesus named Delina. Delina, who, in her soft blue habit as it rains outside and we wait for people to show up, cleans off a table with rough green leaves and later carefully sets down a record in speckled goldenrod notebooks provided by the government of India—*the government* of all things.

It is being saved by the host dipped in the small cup, dinner at eight, whiskey hidden from the kitchen girl, dinner moved to nine, home remedies for coughs, honey, milk, egg, and rum, glowing shoots beneath the grass, the magic at the center of the earth or just below the crust, revealing itself for a moment.

And the welcome song I get bored by, bored by the second verse, and yet it's the one place in the universe we are forbidden to get bored—a charming ceremony at a tiny village performed by boys and girls in blue uniforms who have pinned a yellow plastic flower onto my orange Target shirt. But the fact is, by the second verse I am bored with these children, and clearly have the soul of a carp.

And India is loud at night. It is like the earth can be its brash noisy self out here, all the woody harsh trilling sounds they're not allowed to make in the West. The world being saved by the world.

(If you would like objectivity, authorial distance, clear-eyed unsentimental reportage that avoids "romanticizing" the exotic East, the global poor, you will have to go elsewhere. Because this place is nothing if not romantic. The lime green mountains, the perfectly terraced hillsides, the stone-colored cows driven down the road by a boy with a stick. A pure blind romance that also

sweeps up into it my religious order, the Jesuits, and these nuns, who in this article will all come off looking very good.)

I am thirty-three when I arrive in Northeast India, skinny and wired, with short brown hair and an old man's blue hat. It is the summer of 2005, and my superiors have sent me and another American Jesuit to be with our brothers here. It is one of the poorest regions of the country and easily the most forgotten, way out on the edge. A place where India meets Bangladesh and Myanmar and secures a precarious, at times warring, border with a third country, China. We have come here to get a sense of the mission. To watch and see. Case the perimeter. Size things up. We came to this place eagerly. We came with fresh haircuts. We came with Jesus Christ, but without being annoying about it.

#

It seems somehow so . . . naked . . . to speak of things being saved. Worlds, people. Whether by missionaries or praying children or anyone. A mother hears her son cry out and rushes into his room. It is just a video game and his guy has been destroyed. She is naked in her panic, her need to save. Every ounce of her fierce abiding love has been wrenched from the inside to the outside of her body. Her face pale, mouth twisted. He is rolling on the ground in fake agony. She is the fool, the attempted savior. It is just a video game. Who is anyone to be saved? It is outdated fare. We are here, more or less, to companion one another, are we not? To turn nouns into verbs and with these new words do simple and un-intrusive things that bear no edge of panic, need, or fire. We are here to journey.

Even if salvation is necessary, it has gotten murky in the later age. In a document written and ratified by the Catholic bishops of the world fifty years ago, the church made it startlingly clear that one does not need to become Catholic to avoid the white hot fire, the gnawing of the eternal worm. In ways known only to God, a human person can be saved if she is not Catholic. Can be saved even if she does not explicitly know Christ.[1]

When the disciples heard this, they were greatly astonished. Then who

1. There are many nuances and interpretations, leading to many pleasing and lighthearted discussions, surrounding these kinds of church statements and documents. How do you quantify the work of salvation, how does it actually get carried out? Is it only about the afterlife, or really about life right now? Does the Catholic Church have the "fullness of truth," when only God has the fullness of anything? What precisely does "hell" mean? If I have heard of Jesus but don't bow before him, is my soul at risk? What if I didn't hear quite right? Could a God of pure love let anyone fall into a pit beyond saving? Nagging questions, lunches with old high school friends once lawless and chill but now distressingly *apostolic.* Debates at theology schools, the tense clutching of cups of fair trade coffee, the absolute suspension of diaphragm breathing.

shall not be saved, Lord? We have given up everything to follow you. And you say everyone can be redeemed anyway?

In addition, another document of sorts has been written and increasingly ratified in circles of Western society. One that says there really may not be such a thing as salvation at all, because there is nothing to be "saved" from in the first place. The idea that people sin, and so need redemption from sin, is one that does not feel entirely healthy. Nor does the idea anybody could ever be "sent to hell" with no prospect for getting out. Unthinkable. If there is a hell at all. And regardless of what is out there, we don't need some group affiliation to keep us on the right side of things. It is not like it was with Abner Mikva.

In 1948, in Chicago, twenty-two-year-old Abner Mikva stops by the Democratic headquarters in the political ward where he lives. He walks in and tells the ward committeeman he wants to volunteer for Adlai Stevenson and Paul Douglas. The committeeman removes the cigar from his mouth and looks him over. "Who sent you?" he asks. "Nobody sent me," says Mikva. He puts the cigar back in his mouth and says, "We don't want nobody that nobody sent."[2]

Shift this to the spiritual life, and reasonable-minded corners of the world find it ridiculous. God, if there is one, is not a Chicago machine politician. We don't need to be sent by any organization or any creed. God will let us in even if nobody sent us. You just wander down the road, past the Jesus of your parents, or the Jesus you never knew through no fault of your own, or never heard about in the right way. You wander down the road toward whatever end is in sight, and you still get in. The God supposedly barring the door is already on our side and always will be. We are holy as we are. Salvation? We are here to journey. There are only questions to be lived.

#

In a way the Indian Jesuits and religious sisters simply do journey with the people. Jesuit priests go into a village or region and ask the people what they need. Invite them to name their deepest desires. And they help them attain those desires. In thirty-five years of missionary work, the Jesuits and the sisters of Northeast India have waded through disease, gangster violence, catastrophic roads, tribal wars, the muscle flexing of Hindu fundamentalism, and bouts of shuddering loneliness, among other things, to help start dozens of schools and hundreds of self-help groups that facilitate businesses and build homes. They've educated the people about their land rights, lobbied

2. This story can be found in Milton L. Rakove, *We Don't Want Nobody That Nobody Sent: An Oral History of the Daley Years* (Bloomington, IN: Indiana University Press, 1979).

the United Nations, trained local leaders, heard confessions in tiny crowded churches while drums play in the back to drown out everyone's sins. They intend to establish a native clergy of Jesuit priests, and brothers and religious sisters, from the local tribes: Garo, Bodo, Naga, Maw.

They have journeyed with the people as closely as they can be journeyed with. Sister Delina cleaning the table with leaves, cleaning it to prepare it for the arrival of men and women who would be pooling their money together to form a micro–credit union. A union where they would loan one another money for a new ox or a roof or a store that will sell betel nuts and tea and bags of rice. A union that would combat, well, what aren't they combatting? Money lenders who charge 300 percent interest. The insidious forces, in spite of the free, cheery notebooks, of governmental corruption. The brutal edges of a globalized economy that wipes its feet on tiny villages like this one. Frustration! Ignorance! Powerlessness! And they would do this in turquoise shawls or hands just now lifted off the tiller, and babies in slings around their shoulders.

At Good Shepherd School in the North Cachar Hills, where tribal ways are being lost, the Jesuits have done their best to replicate the "bachelor dorms" the tribes used to have. Adolescent boys live together and learn everything about the ancient ways from their elders. A school like this changes everything: roads come, people build their houses nearby, people feel like they have a future. They trust the Jesuits and the nuns and what they do. In the United States, the Lakota chief Red Cloud for years asked for Black Robes to come teach his people, so they could read those damn treaties they kept getting pasted by.

In Maweit, Wilfred is building a giant valley of a soccer field. A Khasi, Wilfred is the first ordained Jesuit priest from one of the local tribes. The Khasis are a matriarchal society in which the women have the important roles, such as owning all the property and raising the children. The boys are often neglected and can sink into a life of drugs, a life without work, a life of feeling a touch worthless. And so to build up their confidence, allow them to do something they are good at, before he builds anything else, he digs out this pitch.

Before Sunday Mass in Assam, hot and spent, I go up to confession at the front of a dark, bamboo church, women on one side, men on the other. A racket of drums in the back as I tell Vital of my usual wretchedness. I tell him how in my travel-weary condition I have no patience for the people I am meeting all the time, their welcome songs, etc. Vital says, "Don't forget, people are boss. You are just here to serve the people." People are boss, we are servants. Later, at the offertory, I watch the poorest bosses on earth bring the best of their food to Father Vital—baskets of squash and capsicum and brinjal, silver plates of rice. He puts the food to the side for now, while I don't quite know where to put any of it.

In one Northeastern village, a domestic worker was kidnapped and missing for six months. The police effort to get her back was unimpressive at best. One hundred women, empowered by their work with the Self-Help Groups, marched on the station and demanded the police begin to trace her immediately. As a priest related to me, the women promised the police that if nothing was done, "You will see how it is for you."

They did not want to see how it would be for them. In four days they had the girl back—rescuing her just before she was going to be sold into the sex trade in Bhutan.

A nun who runs a home for deaf children in Shillong tells us about the time she was traveling back to her village mission for Christmas. She had to walk through an open field to get there and in this open field were a mother elephant and her baby. Her guides said forget it, let's go back, we can't go by this elephant and her baby. They'll trample us. The nun said, I have to get there for Christmas, we'll run. So they ran. They ran through the field, and they were into the forest before the mother elephant knew they were there.

The most gratifying part about this story is that the nun tells it in no way to elicit great admiration for her unbridled missionary spirit. She just wanted to tell us a story about elephants.

They are exquisite, heroic "journeyers with" out here. All of this work is not some ruse, some sort of sly Christian patience lulling the tribes to sleep. Cultivating a friendship, fattening up the torso, ultimately to slip into their softened skin the gleaming knife of Jesus Christ. It's just a being with people. Christ is already there, the church teaches. The people themselves, eventually, ask about this Christ. But the Jesuits and the sisters would do it even if no one became Christian. It is the right thing to do. It is how the work of evangelization should be.

And yet, in the end, in the Northeast, there is evangelization. There is Christ. There is Christ even if he is unveiled by way of this very appropriate and unthreatening new business model. There is conversion, changing, saving souls, people leaving behind old beliefs to take up new ones. Is this OK?

It is one thing to build homes and businesses. Everyone buys this. Everyone agrees. But is it OK to baptize, or even bring up baptizing and salvation? Because it can seem like just not a very nice thing to do to people whose souls are sacred already, blessed by God, just fine as they are.

#

Ignatius of Loyola, former soldier and the founder of the Jesuits, once said to the missionary Francis Xavier, "Go forth and set the world on fire." But the record is unclear whether he actually said that. Francis Xavier bellowed into a raging storm on a sea-tossed ship, "Even more, Lord! Even more!" No one is sure whether he really said these words either. The martyred Salvadoran bishop Oscar Romero was definitely not the one who said, "We are prophets of a future not our own."

But just the fact that people believe they said these things! That they are printed on plaques and cards! That we want someone heroic to say words that cut to the very edge! Declarative sentences! Assertions with no considered latticework of proofs behind them. Simple statements. This is. That will be. Things are this way. I am the way. I am the way, the truth, and the life. Nothing is impossible for God. Come to me, all you who are weary.

Perhaps there is some visceral need for such words. Even in the midst of knowing one's goodness, there is a desire for something to kneel in front of, to crumble before. A clear pool to weep into, a pool into which many, many others have also wept, leaving everything, spent.

If you go to a meeting of alcoholics, or sex addicts, or compulsive gamblers; if you make a spiritual retreat with homeless men; if you enter a federal prison filled with gray-shirted women who tell you that prison was the only thing that woke them up to the rapid death march their life was on, you meet people who know about salvation. You meet people who have been to the very knife's edge of life and are clawing their way back. Or, better stated, have let their Higher Power claw their way back for them. God and salvation feel less and less like an option in rooms such as these.

In the vast sphere of cultures and people that is India, tribal members are just about the least of the least. Their world gives them few cues that they are useful for anything more than plucking leaves in a tea plantation or crouching in orange kerchiefs on a hot road hammering large rocks into smaller rocks to make concrete—for one U.S. dollar a day. It reminds me of what a Jesuit brother told me at a certain bleak and rock-breaking period in my own life, regarding the Son of God. "It's not like he don't know what it's like. It's not like he just stayed up there. He came down here and tried it out."

Discovering that the God of the Universe tried it out, this at least is an interesting thing that tea workers and concrete-makers and all the rest in the Northeast may like to hear about. Hear about and hold on to, and look at now and again, wondering what it means for their own lives. Do they need to be rescued from their own sins? I only have to look at my own sins and say, Yes, who doesn't? To get there, the Jesuits encourage them also to fight the sin that keeps them kneeling in rock piles. Fighting alongside a God who knows what it's like.

Faith and salvation are a simple assertion. The hot knife, the clean single into left, a straight-line wind through the old growth: I believe this, I put everything here. Clipping into sheer rock and dangling with full weight. True, I can learn from other ways! The God of the diamond, reflecting many lights in many angles! I have questions! I even doubt! A lot! All the time! But in the end, I live and die here. The disciples were not wrong to give up all. The mother not a fool for rushing into her son's room. They did what they had to do. They were free, but something compelled them. They couldn't not do this.

And of course this all verges on lunacy, saying any of this. It's just words for something no one ultimately can talk about because talking about God and salvation is kind of like trying to paint oxygen. But sometimes it's nice to talk.

#

Midway through my journey to the Northeast, in a bamboo chapel on rough concrete, surrounded by Jesuit novices, Khasi, Naga, Bodo, Maw, I lay before the host at Sunday night adoration. I don't do this very often back home in the States, but here I am. Jesus reduced to this. As if he put himself through a factory press, or a meat grinder. Christ perfect and round, the raised letters IHS in gold casing. I am not sure if anything has felt more ergonomically proper than being on hands and knees, head low, forehead on the concrete, eyes struck. Has any posture ever matched up? It is silent, and we pray, or we just are silent, and we stay that way in the chapel, and the candles flicker.

4. A Baseball Bat to the Head: Quentin Tarantino and Divine Justice

Jeffrey C. Johnson, S.J.

If we were in need of an addition to the Old Testament, and if we wanted it to match the violence of some of its current sections, and if we wanted our addition not in the form of a book but a film, then I would suggest we look no further than Quentin Tarantino.

Now don't get me wrong, Tarantino is good, but he's not divinely inspired. Plus, we don't need a new book for the Old Testament. Still, though, if we did. Because Tarantino's films share something important with the more violent sections of the Hebrew Scriptures, especially the way that very violence is depicted and in the meaning it has for us who read about or watch it. Allow me to explain.

Tarantino's latest film, *Django Unchained*, was released on Christmas Day in 2012 and kicked up quite the controversy among critics and viewers who were uncomfortable with its treatment of race. Much ink was spilled in popular and intellectual circles about the quality and value of the film. Critics asked: How does it compare to 1970s' blaxploitation films? Is it just revisionist history gone amuck? Should a white man have made this film? And so on. Tarantino was, at the same time, widely praised as a visionary and roundly condemned as an insensitive white man setting out to assuage the guilt of his fellow white Americans.

The controversy over *Django* is not foreign to Tarantino. The film that preceded it, *Inglourious Basterds*, dealt not with race but with Nazi persecution of Jews. In the film a group of American soldiers, all of whom are Jewish, are dropped behind enemy lines. Under the direction of their lieutenant, one Aldo Raine, they methodically surprise small German units. And then execute them. One member of Raine's unit takes particular joy in putting a baseball bat to gruesome use, and Raine encourages his troopers to take the scalps of the dead Nazis. The film ends with the fiery death of the entire Nazi high command, Hitler included. With bats to the head and the taking of scalps, it's easy to see how critics might find in *Inglourious Basterds* something more than

simply another movie about Nazis and World War II. There's a not so subtle hint of revenge being meted out.

It would be impossible to take on all of the criticism and praise Tarantino has received for these two films and digest it in a brief essay. So instead I want to focus on one point, a point about which nearly everyone who has written about the movies agrees. Most writers—whether from *The Atlantic*,[1] *The Huffington Post*,[2] *The Wall Street Journal*,[3] or *The American Conservative*[4]—have unreflectively assumed that *Django Unchained* and its predecessor, *Inglourious Basterds* (or even the *Kill Bill* series), fall in the genres of revenge fantasies. Whether they praise or vilify Tarantino for this, the critics are nearly unanimous that his last two films are fantasies of revenge in which wicked violence is perpetrated against Nazis or white slave owners.

In *Django Unchained*, it is Django (Jamie Foxx) himself, and his mentor, Dr. King Schultz (Christoph Waltz), who inflict most of this spectacular violence, which includes mists of blood, gushing arteries, flesh-ripping packs of dogs, snapped bones, and scores of dead Southerners. It is all meant to be seen, the critic's argument goes, as somehow exacting revenge against the slaveholders of yore. Or perhaps taking revenge against their racist progeny who lurk in the corners of the Internet, in religion, and in other places. It's called fantasy not only because there are no former slave holders from the American nineteenth century around to be whipped like dogs but also because nothing like this ever happened in real life.

Ta-Nehisi Coates, a senior editor at *The Atlantic*, has dismissed Tarantino's project, writing, "I'm not going to see Django. I'm not very interested in watching some black dude slaughter a bunch of white people, so much as I am interested in why that never actually happened, and what that says. I like art that begins in the disturbing truth of things and then proceeds to ask the questions which history can't."[5] Does this mean we can only watch re-runs of *Honey Boo Boo* and *Jersey Shore*? Or, to be a bit fairer about the question, can we only watch documentary films? Is Coates suggesting that art should limit itself to only the possible, probable, or "historical"?

Let's set aside the inherent weirdness of reading an article about a movie written by an author who did not see it, and has no plans to see it. It's even

---

1. Ta-Nehisi Coates, "Toward a More Badass History," *The Atlantic*, January 9, 2013, http://www.theatlantic.com.

2. Leonce Gaiter, "It's Absurd to Associate Django Unchained with Black Culture," *The Huffington Post*, January 6, 2013, http://www.huffingtonpost.com.

3. Don Steinberg, "Tarantino Tackles Slavery," *The Wall Street Journal*, December 14, 2012, http://www.online.wjs.com.

4. Rod Dreher, "Django's Revenge Fantasy," *The American Conservative*, January 11, 2013, http://www.theamericanconservative.com.

5. Coates, "Toward a More Badass History."

weirder to read someone write about art and demand that it be "real" and "truthful." Why? Because nothing like the stories told in *Django* or *Basterds* ever really happened, and so they can't be real or truthful. In my view, art packs the biggest punch when it begins with the fiction of things rather than the truth of things. It's in this way, I think, that we tend to learn more (or, at the very least, to imagine better).

In other words, fiction, when done well, allows us to imagine alternatives, and in these alternatives we might learn more, or more easily, than when we merely recount the facts. Don't get me wrong. The study of history is important and necessary, but fiction, when it presents us with the fruit of an active imagination, allows us to safely dialogue with alternative scenarios. St. Ignatius, himself a big proponent of an active imagination, encourages retreatants to enter imaginatively into Gospel scenes. I don't think that by this he is suggesting that we redo the stories of the Gospels. Instead, through the imagination, we place ourselves in the midst of Jesus and the disciples. Something similar happens with good fiction in movies, novels, and stories. We are imaginatively placed in a new set of circumstances for the purposes of dialogue and learning.

What I'm suggesting is that people—and Coates is not the only one—have forgotten how to read violence on the scale at which we see it in these films not because of any aversion to violence, but because we have forgotten how to read fiction and fictional portrayals of the past. We have forgotten that accepting fiction's invitation to an imaginative world—no matter how violent or unpleasant—can add something just as meaningful and unique to our public conversations as can history. I'm afraid that in our current thirst for the reality of things—whether it's Coates's desire for the truth or another person's penchant for *Duck Dynasty*—we are witnessing an impoverishment of the mind in the ways that literature, art, and music are allowed to make meaning.

These films, *Django* and *Basterds*, are not sloppy revisionist histories of the kind thrown together by filmmakers like Oliver Stone. Stone seems to want us to *believe* his versions of history as presented in movies such as *JFK* (1992). Tarantino not only doesn't expect us to believe that this is "real" history, he asks us not to do so, beginning *Basterds* with an opening title card that reads, "Once upon a time. . . ." He teaches us, in other words, how to "read" his movie. We are to read it like all other stories, not as a documentary approach to history.

We are to read it much like we are to read the Old Testament. That is, we are to "read" these movies like we read myths. By "myth" I am not suggesting that the Old Testament is somehow untrue. I am emphasizing what has become a pretty commonly accepted scholarly point: that the Old Testament is not a documentary-style play-by-play of the history of the people of God, but a cherished collection of stories written in a variety of genres. No doubt these texts were inspired by the Holy Spirit, but that does not mean that they were ever intended to catalog the events of a given people over the course of several thousands of years. Given the similar violence found in the Old Testament and in Tarantino's films, it makes sense to read their violence in similar ways. And what I want to suggest is that Tarantino may be using violence in much the same way as violence is used in the Old Testament.

The Old Testament's main protagonists (God notable among them) are known for their hair-trigger dispositions and for stunning violence. Samson slew thousands of Philistines with the jawbone of an ass. (Not a pretty picture if you really think about it.) And The Lord himself casts Pharaoh's chariots and charioteers back into the crashing waters of the Red Sea. In pop-theological circles, it is common to pit the Old Testament Warrior-Deity God against the more approachable version of God in the New Testament. Is it too much to wonder if Jesus was making a similar point by calling God "daddy"?

In his article "God and Violence in the Old Testament," scripture scholar Terence E. Fretheim encourages us to take a careful look at the catalog of violence perpetrated by humans acting as agents of God and by God himself. He points out that "God's *uses* of violence . . . are associated with two basic purposes: judgment and salvation."[6] God's use of violence against humans—think of the wholesale slaughter of Egyptians on the night of the Passover—is a response to human sin, in this case the enslavement and exploitation of the Hebrews. God's violence leads to the escape of the Hebrew families. Moreover, Fretheim cites Rabbi Abraham Joshua Heschel's observation that "God's sense of injustice"[7] is much more finely tuned than ours and elicits a much stronger response than we are likely to offer in the face of injustice. As Heschel notes, when humans witness injustices against others—especially the exploitation of the poor—we tend to have a lukewarm response, at least when compared with God. In other words, God gets a little put out when it comes to the oppression of widows, orphans, and God's own people.

So, in the collection of stories and episodes that comprise the Old Testament, the inspired authors and editors chose to preserve the tales of God's burning wrath for good reason. We humans can quickly grow tepid in our actions on behalf of the oppressed. Often God even had to remind his own people, who had once been slaves themselves, about the evils of oppression. You wouldn't think that former slaves could forget the horrors of enslavement or the tangible power of evil in the world. But they did. The same goes for us.

6. Terence E. Fretheim, "God and Violence in the Old Testament," *Word & World* 24.1 (2004): 23-24.

7. Ibid., 23.

We can forget or become numb to the punch of evil, even the evil of oppression and exploitation.

There are many reasons for this. In light of the sheer tonnage of evil we see in the world, it becomes easy to do nothing or to take only measured actions. I don't think most of us do this willfully—turn a blind eye to the oppressed, that is. There's just an awful lot of human pain and suffering, and we become desensitized through constant contact with it. Think of the stories we tell of the twentieth century—an era unparalleled in technological advancement. I know that many millions of people were executed, murdered, destroyed, and "disappeared" during this century, but honestly that fact is not foremost on my mind when I hear "twentieth century." Instead, I think of the discovery of flight, near-miraculous advances in medicine, or the Internet. To quote *The Sound of Music* (which came out during that very same century), "I simply remember my favorite things, and then I don't feel so bad!"

In other words, we are hardwired to forget.

And forget we do. But let's be careful and name exactly what we tend to forget. We don't forget the enslavement of Africans in America, nor do we forget the systematic extermination of Jews in Europe. These and other atrocities may enter our consciousness sometimes more and other times less frequently, but we do remember that they happened. In fact, I would venture to guess that it would be really tough to grow up in America and not know that slavery once existed in the "land of the free." The same goes for the Holocaust, despite the continued existence of those who deny that it happened. No, we don't forget the fact that it happened; I think we forget the nature and depth of the evil behind the fact. We forget what we are capable of doing and the efficiency with which we can pull it off.

And this brings us back to *Django Unchained* and *Inglourious Basterds.* I'd like to suggest that one way to interpret the motivation behind Tarantino's penchant for grisly violence is judgment and salvation. In both films, like divine justice in the Old Testament, violence is associated with human sin. If there had been no genocide, then there would be no need for the baseball bat killing extravaganzas of *Basterds.* If there had been no slavery, there would be no need for Dr. Schultz's traveling emporium of assassination in *Django*. Most of the grisliest acts of violence in these films are reserved for the perpetrators of breathtaking oppression, genocide, and murder. The filmmaker's ire has been raised to the level of God's own disgust, the kind we find in many places in the Old Testament. The extermination of the Nazi high command and the execution of many slave owners allows for the liberation of the oppressed Jews and slaves.

But the violence serves another purpose as well. It works against that human tendency to forget the true nature and depth of evil in the world. Films about American slavery and Nazi aggression come along frequently, only to fade into the background noise of our vast culture. Sometimes these films are complicit in the desensitizing tendency in human nature. They are filled with tropes that border on clichés—the tattered yellow stars of David, the claustrophobic and putrid trains to Auschwitz, the jingling leg shackles, the grotesque whelps on the back of a beaten slave, the heartless Southern charmer, the families torn asunder at the auction block. Too often these tropes have lost the ability to communicate the level of evil they identify, and our sense of rightfully earned indignation becomes correspondingly muted and weak.

Thankfully, Tarantino brings a curative baseball bat to the forehead of American culture, dashing our consciences like so much gooey brain matter.

So we must be careful not to call these films revenge fantasies. They are not fantasizing about vengeance, not truly. Nor are they prescribing a cure for the evil of racism in the world. Tarantino is instead helping us to refresh our sense of outrage at injustice. And as the Old Testament, according to the scholar Fretheim, shows, "we will see that, in everything, including the violence, God seeks to accomplish loving purposes."[8] In other words, there is a loving context for the divine violence of the Old Testament that helps us interpret that violence as a part of God's wider mission of justice and salvation.

It makes sense that God gets quite perturbed when his most helpless children are exploited, murdered, raped, and enslaved. Tarantino wants us to get a bit ruffled in the face of the same sorts of evil. Not so that we go and kill everyone out of vengeance ourselves but so that we understand that there really is evil in the world and that we should work against it with all our loving might.

8. Ibid., 18.

5. Finding Joy in Auschwitz

Michael Rozier, S.J.

I stumbled alongside the foundation of a building, my toes occasionally clipping a fallen brick and my mind tripping over just about everything else. I couldn't quite figure out where I ought to look. The heavens might have seemed like a natural place, but here they are impossibly far away. The fields where the bodies were burned and the pond where the ashes were discarded drew my gaze, but looking for serenity feels like betrayal of the dead. So I looked at the bricks, most of them broken and half-buried, like the victims to whose deaths they once bore witness.

There isn't a single gas chamber or crematorium whose walls weren't blown up by the departing Nazis, but somehow they still cast long, dark shadows over all who walk by. I am wandering through one of the major sections of the Auschwitz concentration camp—the section named Auschwitz-Birkenau, a death camp for well over one million human souls. The Auschwitz compound, large enough that the Germans displaced seven Polish villages to create it, may represent the twentieth century more than any other place on earth.

My hope is that it does so not because of what occurred there in the early 1940s. My hope is that in the twentieth century Auschwitz stands for how we respond to what occurred amidst these bricks.

#

I was not alone during my days in Auschwitz. Thank God. I don't know what I would have done without the dozen or so seminarians and medical students who stumbled through it with me.[1] In the evenings, we made meaning of days spent at memorials and death camps. I am not saying we made sense of it—you can't make sense out of something so senseless—but we tried to understand what it meant for our world and for our professions that the Holocaust had occurred. That it had tolled, like a bell humanity can't un-ring.

A version of this essay was published in *The Jesuit Post* on August 20, 2012.

1. We were recipients of the Fellowship at Auschwitz for the Study of Professional Ethics sponsored by the Museum of Jewish Heritage, a shared experience none of us will soon forget.

We had been together for a week or so before arriving at Auschwitz. After that first day of clipping my toes on fallen bricks I shared in my small group that I felt slightly uneasy. Although we had quickly become very comfortable with one another, I felt as if I was walking around in someone else's private space. I, a Roman Catholic seminarian, was walking around an essentially Jewish death camp alongside rabbinical students. And so I shared with my Jewish colleagues that because the Nazis had placed so high a priority on exterminating Jews, I felt, walking through Auschwitz, as if I was eavesdropping on a family tragedy.

Intellectually, I knew there was more to it. Of course the Nazis killed the disabled, and Roma, and homosexuals, and on and on. Of course their actions were not an offense against only Jews but an offense against humanity. Of course it is a reality that everyone, not just Jews, must be aware of. Of course. But just because we know something intellectually does not mean it fully penetrates our hearts. It wasn't until later that the two became more aligned.

#

Maximilian Kolbe, O.F.M. Conv., was imprisoned by the Gestapo for hiding Jews in his friary and was transferred to Auschwitz-I on May 28, 1941. In July, three men escaped the camp, and, as a matter of common practice, the commander of the camp chose ten men to execute in order to deter further attempts. When one of the men chosen cried out, "My wife! My children!" Kolbe offered his own life in place of the man's. So Kolbe was sent with the other nine to the starvation chamber.

I don't want to pass over this too quickly. He was sent to *starve to death*. They wouldn't waste bullets on him. They wouldn't waste poisonous gas. They would just let neglect take its toll. Neglect does that, you know. It doesn't seem like much at first, just a simple passing over. But eventually the depths of neglect twist reality beyond recognition. And that's what the Nazis did so well. Sure, they were active in their hatred. But it was their unwavering neglect of people's humanity that made it all possible.

After the other nine had starved to death, Kolbe was still on his knees praying. His refusal to die on their timeline upset the commanders so much that they injected him with carbolic acid, a favorite of the Nazi euthanasia program. He died on August 14, 1941, and was canonized on October 10, 1982. And I prayed in front of his starvation cell on June 25, 2012.

And, strange as it may seem, my prayer was one of joy.

#

Almost ten years prior, in March 2003, I prayed in the chapel where Archbishop Oscar Romero—considered by many to be a martyr of charity like St. Maximilian Kolbe—was assassinated on March 24, 1980. He was one of seventy thousand people killed in the 1980s during El Salvador's civil war, most of whom were poor. As archbishop he had experienced a few years previously the murder of a good friend, Fr. Rutilio Grande, S.J., and also of many other priests and parishioners in his diocese. I remember him here because it was one of his homilies that I recalled as I prayed in the evening about my day spent at Auschwitz-I and in the starvation cell of St. Kolbe. In the midst of all the killing the Salvadoran civil war wrought he wrote,

> I rejoice, brothers and sisters, that they have murdered priests in this country. . . . For it would be very sad if in a country where so many Salvadorans are murdered, the church could not also count priests among the murdered ones. . . . It is a sign that the church has become incarnate in poverty. . . . A church that does not suffer persecution, that church should be fearful. It is not the true church of Jesus.

These words surfaced many things for me, two of which I would like to share here. First, it helped me make sense of my discomfort, the discomfort of too quickly assuming familiarity with the tender soil of Auschwitz. Second, it helped me see more clearly how this trip, this exploration of the past, ought to inform my future.

#

Although Kolbe is the most well known, the Nazis killed thousands of Catholic priests and hundreds of thousands of Catholics. But their elimination was not systematic in the way Jewish elimination was. Many of them were killed not because they were Catholic, but because they were Polish or a member of some other "inferior" group, ethnic or otherwise.[2] Regardless of the terrible number of Catholic deaths, however, the uncomfortable feeling that I was trespassing on another family's suffering remained.

I believe my discomfort came, most deeply, from the fact that there are so few examples of Catholic clerics who died at the hands of the Nazis because of the courage of their convictions. How many died or were persecuted because their faith compelled them to act in a way that challenged the neglect

2. Although a topic worthy of discussion, the institutional response of the Catholic Church to the Holocaust will not be addressed in this article. I hope readers can tell this reflection is at a more personal level.

of another's humanity? St. Kolbe is one. Blessed Bernhard Lichtenberg is another, but to me it seems a shockingly short list.

This is why my prayer at Kolbe's cell was a prayer of rejoicing. I, like Romero, was filled with strange joy at the murder of a priest because it is a sign the church "had become incarnate in poverty." Because someone realized that the true church of Jesus does not stand aside as others are persecuted. Certainly we ought not seek death for the sake of death, nor persecution for the sake of persecution, but we ought to know by now that the gospel demands more from us than the world is willing to allow us to give. And we ought to celebrate, to rejoice, when one among us gives this more nevertheless.

#

It is never as clear in the moment as it is ten, twenty, seventy years later, at least not to most of us. I'd like to think I would have been as brave as Lichtenberg or Kolbe, but more likely I would have been one of the priests attempting to justify why such a radical position was unnecessary.

. . . *I'm much better at change from within, so I'll bide some time.*
. . . *If we challenge the way things are too much it'll just get worse.*
. . . *One person really can't make a difference in such a big system.*

But one can play it safe in two directions. We can create excuses not to act, but we can also preach to the proverbial choir. I dare to say: if you are mainly getting affirmation for your work then you are probably speaking to people who don't need to hear you. The convictions of our faith do not grow in echo chambers. They only have a chance of helping build something greater if they are brought out to face their challengers. Sometimes those challengers will be fierce. Often it will be easier not to say or do anything.

There is a cost to living the gospel. But if that cost is rooted in prayerful consideration of how best to love God and love neighbor I have faith that the story will not end with suffering. Kolbe's didn't. Romero's didn't. Neither of their deaths stopped the wars raging in their countries, but that's not what God asks of us. God only asks that we do what we can—as inadequate as that may be in the face of great evil—and leave the rest to God.

#

Joy is not the only emotion I felt at the grave of a murdered priest. I felt anger and shame and sadness during the entire trip, especially at Auschwitz. And these were the more natural, the justifiable emotions. And yes, they had their time and their place, and I needed to feel them and not to run. But they were not going to sustain me. It is joy that sustains. It was joy that allowed me to return to Auschwitz the following day.

Isn't that how it is with the rest of our lives? When I confront the health-related challenges of immigrants, the disabled, or the global poor, it is hard not to feel some level of anger or fear or sadness. Think, just now, of something you truly care about, and feel, for an uncensored moment, the roil of emotions that bubble up. Feel the twisting stab of sadness or absence. Feel the lead weight of uncertainty or disbelief. But also feel the leap of joy. Without dismissing any of these others, dwell for a moment in the joy; trust that there is a light that never goes out.

I still don't know where I should have been looking as I walked through the remains of the crematorium that first day. Ultimately it didn't matter. Because where I needed to be looking was at myself. I needed to see what is possible when I—when my church—are for one bright moment courageous; when we do not fear persecution. It may lead to counting cleric and lay alike among the murdered. It's because of these that those who walk through the ruins of our history won't have to look far to find joy in the life of faith.

6. Brian Scalabrine as the Apotheosis of the Human Person

Perry Petrich, S.J.

The following things are true about Brian David Scalabrine of Enumclaw, Washington:

- He was born the day after St. Patrick's Day in 1978.
- In 2001, he was chosen in the second round of the NBA draft, 48th overall.
- He possesses a stunning likeness to journeyman actor Michael Rapaport (of *Boston Public* and *Prison Break* fame).
- He bears the twitter handle @Scalabrine, presumably because he is the G.S.O.A.T.[1]
- He holds a degree in history from the University of Southern California, where, as a sophomore, he led the Trojans in starts, scoring, rebounds, and field goal percentage.
- If you're wondering, it's pronounced *scal-a-breen-ee.*
- He stands 6' 9" and weighs 241 pounds.
- He played, in total, 88 minutes for the Chicago Bulls during the 2010–2011 season. For this hour and a half of work, he was paid $1,229,255. That's 838,128 dollars and 41 cents per hour.[2]
- He went to high school (Enumclaw High, student body 1,700) with NASCAR star Kasey Kahne.[3]
- Over his 11 seasons, he scored 1,594 points, pulled down 1,034 rebounds, and elevated his 109.3 kilograms high enough to reject 121 shots.[4]

---

1. = Greatest Scalabrine of all time.

2. By comparison, league MVP Derrick Rose played 3,026 minutes in exchange for $5,546,160, for an hourly wage of $109,970.13. That same year, then-two-time MVP LeBron James made $14,500,000 over 3,063 minutes, bringing home $284,035.26 an hour.

3. Scal's so far earned $20,126,688 in his career and Kahne $58,565,943. That makes for a combined total nearing $80 million, which allows me to say, with confidence, that these two are the most financially successful children of Enumclaw there will ever be.

4. These numbers put his career on par with Marc Iavaroni and Scott Hastings. Heard of them? That's my point.

- He has, perhaps, the best nickname in the history of the NBA: the White Mamba, a play on the great Kobe Bryant's self-declared moniker, the Black Mamba.[5]
- On his retirement, the league commissioned an official highlight reel to commemorate his career.[6]

You read that right. A player who played fewer minutes last year than it takes to watch the *Mad Men* season premiere received an honor reserved for the likes of Magic Johnson, Larry Bird, or even Tony Kukoč. And this unlikely reel's not exactly lying around collecting dust—it's picked up over 1.3 million YouTube views. As in, the population of Dallas 1.3 million. That's 117 times for each of the 11,000 people who live in Enumclaw. It means that, in total, people have spent three-fourths of a decade watching White Mamba's highlights, highlights that consist of this: three shots of Scalabrine's clothing,[7] ten open threes,[8] two jump shots, two runners, a genuinely sweet reverse lay-in, and—*in toto*—a single dunk.

It is beyond dispute a dull highlight reel. Which begs the obvious question, the answering of which is this essay's *raison d'être*: Why does it exist? And, out of all the things that happen on an NBA court, why is this what I choose to watch over and over again? Why isn't it the legion of Kobe's drop-your-jaw-to-the-floor moves that's got me hunched over my monitor's glow?

Seriously. Kobe's highlights ooze elegance, panache, athletic dynamism, and dominance. And amid this demonstration of virtuosic bodily grace—a grace so extreme that its beauty transcends the context of its sport in a way true only for the world's greatest athletes and so merits contemplation alongside the best of Michael Phelps or Mary Lou Retton or Baryshnikov—there is one particular play that is breathtakingly unforgettable. This highlight is of a young Kobe, all of nineteen years old, in a preseason game against the Washington Wizards.[9] Kobe takes the ball at half court, one-on-one with the unfortunate Jimmy Oliver.[10] Watching, you can feel Oliver's fear as Kobe takes a hard dribble to the hoop. Kobe catches the bounce high with his right hand, elbow

---

5. White Mamba explains his nickname thus: The black mamba is the world's deadliest snake, which makes "the white mamba the world's most dormant snake. It just chills. Watches and chills" (Noah Davis, "Brian Scalabrine Won't Stop: The Ongoing Adventures of a Celtics Fan Favorite," www.bostonglobe.com).

6. If you're in to typing URLs, you can watch it here: http://goo.gl/GqQMiq.

7. #1: Coming off the bus, repping Enumclaw with his flannel; #2: jogging from the locker room tunnel in Bulls warmups; #3: tearing off those same warmups as he takes the floor.

8. Which means that in two minutes we've seen 5 percent of the long-range shots WM's drained in his career.

9. The first year after the team escaped its previous munitions-related moniker.

10. Oliver's career pales in comparison to Scalabrine's, the former only playing 78 games and scoring 331 points over five seasons.

turned outward, ready to drive around Oliver's left. Oliver anticipates, instinctually shifting his weight ever so slightly, and it's all over. Kobe pendulums his shoulders back to the left, his rightward lean turning into a straightforward fall, like a hawk bent on its prey. But instead of falling to the hardwood like a common mortal, Kobe levitates parallel to the floor, the power of his still-skinny left leg propelling him toward the rim, which is incredible enough, except that—remember—he's still dribbling a basketball. And through some kind of bizarre spin or bodily contortion or occult act of telekinesis the ball crosses over and appears securely in his left hand. One more dribble and he plants his right foot and he leaps.[11] The ball is some two feet over the rim, and time has stood still. All 19,522 fans have in fact stopped breathing. All eyes are tracking Kobe's arm, which is now tracing a Vitruvian-man perfect arc to the hoop. Hand meets rim. Ball hisses through net. Kobe glides to the floor. The crowd erupts.

I can't remember the first time I saw Scalabrine's dunk. White Mamba starts *sans* ball on the wing, makes a cut and lumbers toward the hoop. His hands go up to catch a pass, his feet draw under him, and, as if taking a deep breath and calling for the intercession of St. Sebastian,[12] he bends his knees and pushes off with his twin monster hams. And with his body a mere eighteen inches off the floor, with only his thumbs clearing the hoop (here is where the miracle happens), he lifts the ball *just* over the rim and forces it down through the net. The fans exhale a sigh of relief.

Black Mamba's dunk is a feat of pure athleticism and highly developed skill, a honed gift from the gods. White Mamba's is not. But it's still enthralling, maybe even more so: part of you relishes imagining the fiasco that's sure to come; it's impossible to look away. If you've ever watched NASCAR for the crashes, then you know this precise feeling.[13] You can be sure that Scalabrine's defender knows this feeling, because even though he manages to beat the charging ginger to the hoop, he doesn't contest the dunk. Instead he jogs past the baseline and stands with the photographers, as if to join them in savoring the forthcoming epic fail.

Indeed, it's not greatness but surprise that parts the defense and opens the way to the hoop, like Moses does the Red Sea to get to the Promised Land. It's as if the God of the Israelites started this fast break and is determined to see it through to the land of milk and honey. There's a sense shared between

11. He leaps, in fact, over future four-time-defensive-player-of-the-year, Ben Wallace, who foolishly thought his 6' 9" frame would block the lane, but instead finds his upstretched arms rustling like reeds in Black Mamba's wake.

12. Sebas is the patron saint of all athletes. He's famous for being tied to a tree, shot with arrows, and left for dead. Miraculously, he fully recovered from attempt at execution #1 . . . but Emperor Diocletian took a second try and succeeded in beating him to death. Go figure.

13. Is this another similarity between Enumclaw's favorite sons? Their professional propensity to churn fans' stomachs and stop fans' breaths?

casual viewers and players on the floor that Scalabrine just shouldn't be able do these things, and when he defies that sense it's glorious.

And that answers my question. The sense of sharing in the triumph over apparent limitations: that's what has driven those 1.3 million views. Essay over, right?

Oh, would that it were so simple. But as with any truly profound question, answers only lead to more questions. YouTube—in all of her prophetic glory—keeps telling me I should watch all these other Scalabrine videos, and who am I, one who's already invested hours into Scalabrine-related research, to deny her? And when I watch (and watch and watch), I become aware of something more staggering than the mere existence of his highlight reel: Brian Scalabrine is universally adored.

Like, kitten-level adored. Wherever he plays, Scalabrine is welcomed by throngs of fans chanting—ironically, but not sarcastically[14]—"M-V-P! M-V-P! M-V-P!"[15] He surely leads the league in ironic custom t-shirts.[16] And it's not just the fans that dig him. Notoriously surly Celtics star Kevin Garnett once called him "the best teammate I ever had."[17] Since it can't be his play that won KG's love, what was it? What set of qualities and quirks earns adoration from NBA all-stars and overweight hipsters and everyone in between? Who are you, White Mamba?

#

Mediocre[18] athletes are admired for all kinds of reasons. Some are one-of-a-kind physical specimens (think Spud Webb's stature[19] or Anna Kournikova's

14. The difference is this: by chanting, the fans are saying something along the lines of, "Brian Scalabrine is the Most Likable Player in the NBA and the MVP chant highlights this," rather than being a mocking reminder that he only played in eighteen games and scored twenty points—total—all season.

15. Seriously. MVP chant. Note the irony that Scalabrine shared a bench with teammate Derrick Rose, who actually *was* the 2010–2011 MVP and who nevertheless heard those three letters chanted for him far less often. See Scalabrine getting the MVP treatment after entering the game with less than a minute and banking home a two in garbage time: http://goo.gl/MhrGL9 (it's got 391,297 views!). Then compare this with the video of Rose getting the chant (before going on to *actually win the thing*): http://goo.gl/5uOaNk (total: 27,907 views).

16. Including one that features White Mamba's face plastered on a cobra, a shirt that I may or may not own in six colors.

17. Noah Davis, "Brian Scalabrine Won't Stop: The Ongoing Adventures of a Celtics Fan Favorite," www.bostonglobe.com.

18. I use this term very loosely. All professional athletes are better than pretty much everyone else at what they do. It just so happens there were about thirty women better than Anna Kournikova and three hundred men better than the WM.

19. 5'6", 133 lbs., which also happen to be the only characteristics that Mr. Webb shares with yours truly, that is, I have never won an NBA Slam Dunk competition.

beauty[20]). Like Scalabrine, Webb—who stood a mere 5'6"—is famed for throwing down spectacularly unlikely dunks. But unlike Scalabrine, Webb's dunking ability is perfect irony; the shortest player in the NBA is also the best at above-the-rim acrobatics. Webb's fame is a function of his stature; that Scal's a big redhead seems more coincidence than cause. And while Ms. Kournikova's figure kept viewers (tennis fans or no) enthralled, White Mamba's hefty frame somehow fails to captivate.[21]

There are also those second-rate players who gain immortality from a sole defining moment. Take Rudy Ruettiger's single 1975 play for Notre Dame, that blindside sack against Georgia Tech immortalized by that eponymous must-view-for-Roman-Catholics movie. Or Doug Flutie's Hurricane-arresting Hail Mary. Not so for White Mamba. As his seemingly-but-not-actually-ironic highlight reel can attest, his career-best play is a baseline reverse lay-in.

Video after video, however, does reveal one thing about the essence of Scalabrine: his smile never fades. He's always looking for fun. What does he do to celebrate someone else's dunk? Bust out MJ's Billie Jean dance.[22] Do you need a leader for a Boston Celtics Christmas party sing-along?[23] White Mamba's your man. How does he fill up all his post-retirement leisure time? How about challenging any comers to a game of one-on-one?[24] He's such a delight that his famous former teammates relished leading the hometown fans in chanting his name—during an actual game with Scalabrine still on the bench.[25]

But there must be more. His glory has to be more than just a spectacular sense of fun; after all, if playfulness equals glory, Gallagher would be the most glorious man alive. I was puzzled, and then I stumbled on it, hidden in the decaying recesses of the World Wide Web, the Holy Grail of Scalabrine insight: an archived copy of a 2006 blog written by none other than the White Mamba himself. It echoes his highlight reel in two ways: (1) it's something less than a masterpiece, and still (2) I can't stop reading. From January 13:

---

20. Ms. Kournikova spent 2001, 2002, and 2003 on Google's top-ten-most-searched women list, beating the likes of Cameron Diaz and Beyoncé.

21. AK's most enduring legacy might just be poker players adopting her name to describe the Ace-King hand in Texas Hold 'Em. Why? Besides sharing initials, it looks good but seldom wins. And, as if this entire essay weren't homage enough, let me submit that holding a pair of red deuces ought to be called the Scalabrine: not great, but workable in the right circumstance . . . and very, very red.

22. Don't believe me? Watch http://goo.gl/DOBGsD. Also, for some reason, 40,819 have watched him replicate that dance on the playground. See http://goo.gl/2il8gD.

23. Look at it and you, with 1,149,941 others, will never get it out of your head: http://goo.gl/aRGQUr.

24. Four took him up, and when none of them could bring him down, White Mamba offered to take them on three-at-a-time (and still won).

25. Those teammates were Joachim Noah and then-reigning MVP Derrick Rose.

> For me, it was nice to finally get some extended minutes and show all the fans what I can do.[26] I'm one of those guys that can have an impact on a game but not necessarily fill up the box score,[27] and I think we can use some of that. . . .
>
> As far as off the court goes, I recently took in some candlepin bowling, you know the bowling with the little pins and smaller ball, but unfortunately I took the L. It was myself, Raef LaFrentz[28] and Brian Doo (one of the team's strength and conditioning coaches). Raef won the first game and B-Doo[29] took the second. But don't worry about me, I'm going to hide out for a little while and work on my candlepin game, then in a few weeks I'm taking both of those guys down.[30]
>
> I also got a chance to check out the movie "The Chronicles of Narnia" while we were on our last West Coast trip. It's based [*sic*] the books by C.S. Lewis, and I really enjoyed it. I'd have to give it a B+. I was a little disappointed, though, because I wanted to see King Kong but my wife, who joined me on the trip, wouldn't go for that one. She thought it would be a waste of three hours.[31] I guess I'll find out because I'm planning on checking that one out when we fly to Detroit after the Philly game. I'll let you all know what I think in the next blog.[32]

There's a subtle sense of mourning in each of these paragraphs: he realizes how little he contributes to the Celtics, he grieves getting smashed at candlepin bowling, and even admits to losing the movie-selection battle to his better half. Yet these realizations don't bring self-pity or bitterness. Scal's just humbly acknowledging the truth—he knows exactly what he has to offer, which isn't much, and yet this doesn't seem to trouble him.

Remember that time he sat on the bench through the entire 2008 NBA finals? Famously, at the press conference after his Celtics won that series, B-Scal was asked, "How is it for you watching it from the sidelines, not able to play even one little second in the finals?" His response was priceless: "I

---

26. Scal played twenty-eight minutes as the Celtics took down the Hawks in Atlanta.

27. He had only four points, but two of them came with less than a minute to play, and it was his defense that was the difference in the game—he brought down two boards and had a block on all-star Joe Johnson.

28. Who that year started in front of WM and played all eighty-two games.

29. Independent sources could neither confirm nor deny whether this was Mr. Doo's actual nickname.

30. It's unclear if Scalabrine is being ironic.

31. Or twice the minutes Scalabrine played in the 2010–2011 season.

32. Now defunct but an archive copy is accessible at http://goo.gl/OiU9dT and http://goo.gl/cH8prh.

tell you, it's not that difficult to do. Guess what, maybe now you could say, I didn't play a second. But in five years, you guys are going to forget. In ten years I'll still be a champ, in twenty years I'll probably tell my kids that I started, and in thirty years I'll probably tell them I got the MVP. So I'm not too worried about it."[33]

#

The NBA produces an official profile for each player that ends with the answers to a set of beauty-pageant style questions. From the White Mamba's: "Enjoys going to the movies, playing video games, and practicing,[34] lists 'Survivor' as his favorite TV-Show . . . aspired to be a high school teacher and basketball coach before realizing his dream of becoming an NBA player . . . runs several basketball camps throughout New Jersey during the summer."[35]

What kind of pro athlete takes a summer job in Jersey? This bio makes Scal sound like he's settling for a career in the NBA; as if basking proudly in the adoration of thousands of fans is a poor substitute for the nine-to-five he left behind. He covets not glory. After all, what could be less glorious than blogging, sharing your unsolicited opinions and reflections to anonymous, unacknowledged strangers?[36] Maybe he wouldn't mind trading lives with me—his reflected glory for my mediocrity. I mean, doesn't his blog make getting minutes on the floor of an NBA game seem as pedestrian as picking a movie?

Or maybe it's the other way round. What Brian Scalabrine does is make the mundane seem as exalted as professional sports. To him, it seems sincerely to not matter whether he's dunking or bench-warming, teaching high school or schooling strangers. In every activity he carries a sense of gratitude and wonder that is magnetic, more at home in awards-show acceptance speeches than at the front of the classroom. It's like he's tapped into that special vision of beauty reserved for saints, poets, and survivors of childhood cancer; he sees that beauty in everything from NBA hardwood to candlepin bowling.

The NBA didn't put together his highlight reel to glorify on-the-court greatness. The league did better. They've given us an instruction manual on how to see the miraculous among the mundane. Brian Scalabrine personifies in a disarmingly unsentimental way that groan-worthy platitude that there's something to be savored in pretty much everything. Instead of rolling my eyes, I gaze with wonder as White Mamba does even the dullest things with

33. My transcript of this video: http://goo.gl/ekQEa9.
34. Yes, practicing. He prefers practicing to getting minutes.
35. www.scalabrine.com.
36. The irony of this statement is duly recognized by yours truly.

earnest joy. When he engages in what, for me, is the unending drudgery of life[37]—eating breakfast, working out, taking Q.T. with the fam[38]—I suddenly see this mundanity in the same miraculous way I see his spectacularly unexpected dunks.

The simple act of making the perfect pot of coffee in the morning becomes a glorious triumph over limitations, a reason to glorify God. I pause after my first sip and wonder if my life too isn't worthy of highlight-reel canonization. And how can you not love someone for giving you that?

37. And he takes the trouble to (earnestly) share it all on social media.

38. Which, per above, you can see on twitter here (http://goo.gl/1lV7qd), here (http://goo.gl/UlHTk9), and here (http://goo.gl/8dTl6N).

7. Loving the Broken: Or How the Church Becomes Real

Ryan Duns, S.J.

On the second floor of my parents' house where I grew up, there is a closet filled with books. All kinds of books. Old college textbooks, picture books, novels bought for entertainment on vacation, works of literature. Several shelves contain nothing but children's books: *Hardy Boys, Chronicles of Narnia, Lord of the Rings, Berenstain Bears.* Growing up, I loved to read and re-read these books, hiding under my covers at night even though my father had told me to go to bed. In those hours, burrowed under my sheets, I fed my imagination on a steady diet of words.

One of those books, *The Velveteen Rabbit: Or How Toys Become Real,* bears the scars of decades of reading. The heavy cover is battered, its corners long ago worn away; many pages are torn and some even stick together on account of the jelly residue left by little pointer fingers. The book, in short, bears as many traces of wear and tear as does the character about whom it is written.

The story is familiar to many: The Velveteen Rabbit, a Christmas stocking gift, becomes the little boy's favorite plaything. At first, the rabbit is a bit self-conscious; he's not as shiny or intricate as the fancy, metal toys. Nevertheless, the boy comes to love the little rabbit and makes him his constant companion. And it is the boy's love that makes the rabbit real: Where the world would see only a ragged toy, filled with sawdust, gazing out at the world with dingy eyes, the little boy poured in love. And the boy loved not because the velveteen rabbit was the shiniest toy in the toy chest, but because the rabbit was *his.*

What comes next is no surprise: Eventually, after spending constant vigil with the boy during a bout of scarlet fever, the rabbit is judged to be naught but a mass of germs, used up and unsafe, and so is dumped into a sack and slated for incineration. Old, worn, contaminated by its world, the doctor dismissively proclaims: "Get him a new one."

"Get him a new one."

A version of this essay was published in *The Jesuit Post* on March 28, 2013.

3

In recent years, a steady stream of bad news has led many to take the doctor's advice regarding not just stuffed rabbits but the Roman Catholic Church. Very many of us these days—as news reports continue to inform us about the many indiscretions of the church (sexual abuse, financial cover-ups, issues with governance) and to remind us that our church is no longer shiny and new—feel tempted to take the doctor's advice and consign the whole thing to the incinerator. We feel tempted to give up on a church that seems worn and tired, infected with germs, beyond salvaging. Sometimes we just want to get a new one.

And not without reason. Anyone who thought that anger toward the church (particularly over the calamitous issue of child sexual abuse and its cover-up) would simply blow over in time clearly didn't know what to expect. It seems to me—in listening, in talking to others, in feeling my own feelings—that the hurt and rage people feel arises from a sense of betrayal, a sense that the church has failed to live up to its potential.

It hurts so much because so much is at stake. So many of our lives have been tutored by the church; from Baptism to First Holy Communion to Confirmation, the church has been a place where we prayed and played, hoped and feared. The church's women and men—priests and sisters, brothers and committed lay people—worked with us and for us, shaping us to be women and men for others. To learn that this institution, the very institution that encouraged us to be friends of Jesus, had so often and so recklessly betrayed his children . . . this leaves a searing wound.

And a question: How can one be expected to love the church, knowing what we know of it?

I have only one answer: We can love the church because our love makes it real.

#

One night, the Velveteen Rabbit asks an old Skin Horse, "What is REAL?"

"Real," the horse replies, is "a thing that happens to you. When a child loves you for a long, long time, not just to play with, but REALLY loves you, then you become Real."

The church is real because it has been loved for a long, long time. It has been the place where many have learned about love: God's love for us, our love for Jesus Christ, our love for our sisters and brothers. It is the place where the Spirit of love calls us to heal our broken hearts, feeds us at the altar, and encourages us to become what we receive: the Body of Christ.

It's not only believers who admit such. No, the cynic and believer can agree even on this: The church is real. The former might say, "The old girl had her day, now it's time to ditch the old and embrace the new." But even those call the church real. The difference lies not in whether the church is real, but in what reality means. And as for me, I'll cast my lot with the little boy for whom reality was a thing caused by loving, the little boy who loved his rabbit not because he was perfect, but because he was his. Our rabbits are lovable not because they're perfect, but because they're ours. And the church is ours. It's been given to us and yet is held together by that which is more than us, held together, sometimes, in spite of what seem to be our best efforts to tear it apart.

This would all be well and good, apt for a Holy Thursday, if that's all there was. But we ought not forget the remainder of the story. Wriggling free from the sack into which he had been unceremoniously deposited, the rabbit looked out and shivered, having no longer a proper coat of fur. All of his memories rushed back just then, and the rabbit's sawdust heart broke with the question, "Of what use was it to be loved and lose one's beauty and become Real if it all ended like this?"

It's then, the story tells us, that a tear, a real tear, trickled out of the Velveteen Rabbit's eye and fell to the ground. We know this feeling. But the tear isn't barren; in the story it grows into a beautiful flower, and from its blossoms a magic fairy steps. She gathers the old rabbit into her arms and flies with him into the wood. There she kisses him and gives him to other rabbits to play with, live with. After a few moments, the rabbit knows even more fully what it means to be REAL. It means that he can sing and dance with the other rabbits, that at long last he can reach up and scratch his real nose with his real hind foot.

No one ever said loving the church would be easy. Jesus certainly didn't. He promised only that the gates of hell would not prevail (Matt. 16:18). Not a few of us have shed tears, and, I believe, all of us await the coming of the Spirit to breathe into us because we are the church. Without question, to the eyes of the world we have lost much of our beauty. We are worn and tired and ragged. But the church is a gift, our gift, and we receive it most fully when we've been loved and discarded, cried from loss and been given a community again.

We can love the church because it belongs to us, because we belong to one another, because all of us belong together.

#

How will our church's story end? I ought to say, "I don't know." But I believe, in hope, that I do. I believe our own conclusion will be something like that of *The Velveteen Rabbit*, which concludes on a Spring day, when the rabbit creeps out of the wood to have a "look at the child who had first helped him to be Real."

Let us pray for such a Spring within the church, for such a Spirit that can rouse the embers that smolder under scandal and embarrassment. As lovers of a real church, we must decide: Will we allow our church to be judged solely by its tarnished past? Or will we have the courage to live a faith that others can believe in, a faith that washes the feet of prisoners, a faith that loves not perfection but Reality.

The cynic snorts, "Get real, Duns."

I'm trying. Sure, the church is a bit threadbare at the moment. Its gilding has worn away, it's dirty, it's germy. There's no doubt: The church is very much real if, by real, we mean something that is not yet perfect. Just as the Horse told the Rabbit, becoming Real,

> Doesn't happen all at once. You become. It takes a long time. That's why it doesn't happen often to people who break easily, or have sharp edges, or who have to be carefully kept. Generally, by the time you are Real, most of your hair has been loved off, and your eyes drop out and you get loose in the joints and very shabby. But these things don't matter at all, because once you are Real you can't be ugly, except to people who don't understand.

In this I find the courage, the freedom, and challenge to become real as a member of the Catholic Church. I don't have to be perfect.. . . I have to be real.

#

Saint Ignatius, no stranger to the sixteenth-century church's shortcomings, counseled the young Society of Jesus to have just such an attitude. We ought to be those, he wrote, "who love the church, precisely because she is covered with wounds." And this because Ignatius understood that the church was not meant for the perfect, but for the struggling, for those who fall frequently, even scandalously.

Ignatius's words still ring across the centuries, they still challenge: Have we strength enough to dwell within the real church, the wounded church? Have we desire enough to cultivate a real mysticism, one that's able to abide the real rather than trying to flee into the non-existent perfect? Have we courage enough to say, "I believe," in communion with fellow sinners, women and men who daily inflict wounds on the church while still struggling to be conduits of grace in a broken world? Have we hope enough to serve with joy?

A realistic mysticism does not dispel the church's wounds. No, a realistic mysticism peers into the heart of darkness and waits with joyful hope. A realistic mysticism sees the pain in the dismissive advice to "get a new one." A realistic mysticism works by pouring itself out in love not for the perfect, but for the broken. And this for a long, long time, as our pilgrim church continues to become real.

8. *La Virgen* and Fabian Debora: Inculturating the Imagination

James Hooks, S.J.

Amidst an endless stream of photos in a Google search, a slender man with slick black hair, dark eyes, a thin mustache, and earrings dared me not to look him in the eye. The right side of his face was entirely covered in black and white paint, while the left side was left bare. Fabian Debora presented himself in this image as a man merged with the *calavera*, the smiling skull that peeks around every corner during El Día de los Muertos, the annual Mexican festival commemorating the dead.

Debora with Mask

When a half-man, half-skull stares at you, you cannot help but stare back. This is how Fabian Debora found me. A quick search showed that he was from East Los Angeles, that he grew up tough—and that he was an artist. I foraged the Web for his work, and found bright murals that stretched across

A version of this essay was published on *The Jesuit Post* on February 27, 2012.

somber cinder block walls. I found crosses standing high in L.A. neighborhoods and shining rows of corn sprouting from the cement banks of urban canals.

Cross "n" the Hood

What most grabbed me, though, were his depictions of saints, all of whom bore the features of modern Latinos. Like his self-portrait as a quasi-*calavera*, these images offer a reverential nod to tradition while simultaneously bringing that tradition into the present.

His St. Joseph sported a shaved head, Mexican-American features, and tattoos on his neck that read "L.A." One Madonna bore sculpted brows, heavy eye shadow, and an inked shoulder. For Debora, Joseph and Mary were not relegated to some far-off Palestinian past; they were alive here and now.

As striking as this was, Debora's instinct is by no means unprecedented among artists of faith. Even mainstream American Catholicism shows the obvious marks of the inculturation of the imagination. If you search for an image of Mary in an American Catholic church, most likely you will find a mature mother with delicate features, dressed in a long white robe. A veil will flow, unfixed and almost weightless, from her chestnut hair to her sandaled feet. One or another part of her outfit is almost certainly sky blue. Maybe her palms are held gently together in a gesture of prayer, or if the particular Virgin is slightly less introspective, she might extend her arms, as if to express concern and invitation.

Joseph, Depths of Heart

Mary, Mujer Sincera

These women are the Ladies of Lourdes, Fatima, and Knock. They are icons of the spiritual mother of millions of European immigrants who made their way to America's shores in centuries past. We see the Mary whose intercession they sought, whether for protection—for themselves and for the loved ones they left behind—or for blessings on their unknown future in an unknown land. In casting a first-century Palestinian woman this way, these expatriates from European Catholicism advanced a deeply rooted tradition in the artistic history of Christianity: that of imagining central Christian figures as made in our own image and likeness.

Part of this license came from a worldview that, while decidedly premodern, stood firm in popular Western Catholic thought well into the twentieth century. In this framework, time does not operate in disjointed fashion, moving like boxes on a conveyor belt that have no fundamental connection between them. Rather, worldly time is grounded in and surrounded by higher, "eternal" time—the time that pertains to God. And because God's time envelops and embraces our own, human beings do not feel far off from the charged moment of Mary's *fiat*, or the triumphant peace of that first Easter morning, even at a distance of thousands of years. This worldview renders the holy events of ages past accessible to all times, as the porous membrane of secular time only thinly separates "then" from "now."

Given the proximity of past and present, a late medieval or early

Renaissance artist did not have to make a huge conceptual leap to see ancient saints in the dress of his day. Neither, for that matter, did those who beheld his work. Putting St. Joseph, or Roman soldiers, or the Magi in modern vesture was not an instance of "bending time"; it was just "time." For the artist who views time in this way, God's eternal time bound each moment to all others, permitting the saints to draw near to the inhabitants of this age, indeed of every age.

Among the saints, Mary was perhaps felt to be closer than all others. A worldview that cast today and eternity as neighbors, combined with our own visceral, universal experience of being a daughter or son, sealed Mary's place in the Catholic imagination as a tirelessly vigilant and abiding mother. Wherever the Christian faith spread, people felt her close by. Like any mother, she shared in all the features of their lives. For the lost at sea, Mary was their guiding *stella maris* ("star of the sea"). For the plague stricken, she was a healer. When a city fell under threat of invasion, the frightened populous ran to her as protectress, the mediator of divine aid.

My Virgin Mary in Relation to Tonantzín

Mother Mary shared the struggles, joys, and hopes of her children. Little wonder, then, that in many places a mother also shared her children's faces. In the mosaics of Istanbul's Hagia Sophia, Mary sits enthroned as a Byzantine queen. In the statuary of seventeenth-century Macao, she possesses the flowing robes and facial features of Guanyin, the Chinese Bodhisattva of Mercy. And for Fabian Debora, she takes on the faces that populate the streets of East Los Angeles. In *My Virgin Mary in Relation to Tonantzín*, for instance, Debora presents the Virgin as a "homegirl," or a female gang member. She dons hoop earrings and a blue hoodie, and stands gazing over a rich harvest of corn that grows beside the Boyle Heights Bridge. Names cover the bridge's concrete arches—names belonging to Debora's friends who were killed by gang violence. The upper-left hand corner of the painting is colorless and bleak, but the fiery glory of the Virgin fills the vast majority of the frame. Debora's dark past lies behind her while the brightness of his present and future lie within the vitality of the Virgin's gaze. Like a mother, she presides over his life, encouraging him to leave the past behind in favor of a future full of abundance and blessing.

Debora's paintings suggest that for every woeful tale and every memory of decay, he could proffer just as many stories of strength and compassion. He began one such story with a heartbreaking admission: there was a time when he told his mother that she never should have had him. He attempted suicide, and when this failed he fled his mother's house into the city. While crossing a busy highway he injured himself and was almost run down by a passing truck. Coming to his senses, he called his mother and asked her to come find him.

Looking back, Fabian compares his mother's journey to that of the Virgin Mary, who walked to Golgotha to see her dying son on the cross. Both women beheld their sons. They took in the blood and humiliation. The bottomed-out, beaten-down, bare humanity of it all. "All that time," he recalls, "my mother never gave up on me. She always tried to guide me."

Debora at Homeboy Industries

Days later he was in rehab. Within a year, a Jesuit priest came into his life to help him start anew. The priest was Fr. Greg Boyle, the architect and director of Homeboy Industries, a program that gives former gang members job training, education, and a supportive community. With help from his mother, Fr. Boyle, and others, Debora found a way to pull other gang members out of the dregs. Today Fabian himself works at Homeboy Industries as a substance abuse counselor and art instructor.

Given their shared experiences, it is no surprise that Debora regularly names his mother as a constant anchor in his life. Women indeed feature prominently in his story. He describes his grandmother as the spine of his family, and credits her with introducing him to yet another lady who has held immense power in Mexico for almost six centuries, the Virgin of Guadalupe.

Get to know Mexican culture in any measure, and you will know her in turn. Her image and story have a force for Mexicans and Mexican-Americans rivaled by no other figure. Fabian remembers being a boy and hearing his grandmother promise that the Virgin would always watch over him. When we look at his painting entitled *Mi Madre de Los Angeles*, there can be no doubt that, as a grown man, he fully believes it.

Mi Madre de Los Angeles

Debora's painting depicts a young, troubled man leaning on his mother for help. His tattoos and scars tell the tale of a rough life. As for *La Virgen*, she presents herself in the grit of the city—not on canvas, but on a cinder block wall. The young man's forehead rests on her clasped hands. The open fold of her blue mantle gives the impression that she is about to enfold him in it as well. By doing so, she would be enacting an ancient gesture of protection and patronage for one seeking sanctuary.

For months, Debora's *Mi Madre de Los Angeles* was my computer's desktop image. Sometimes, if I regarded it for long enough, I even prayed with it. The image would take on a dynamic quality: I could almost see Mary's mantle falling open to cover the young man's painted shoulders, or her hands unfolding to caress the scars on the back of his head. What is more, I found myself wanting Mary to do the same for me in my own moments of difficulty, however little they seemed when compared with the deep struggles of the tattooed supplicant kneeling before her in the image.

We all share a fundamental experience of filiation, of having belonged to a nurturing presence that we call "Mother." Perhaps this is what allows those who, like me, share little of Debora's particular story to enter into the images he produces. But Debora's art does more than merely beckon to our common biological history. As rooted as Debora is in his surroundings, his art makes it clear that he sees his "today" as being surrounded by and grounded in a higher, eternal reality. It challenges a popular worldview that casts times and peoples as disjointed, free-floating units that, like Kipling's east and west, shall never meet. Debora instead sees his world as porous, and as trafficked by figures from ages past who reveal themselves in contemporary guise. And one of the greatest of these figures exemplifies the character of the eternity that surrounds us. This personage, when she appears, presents this eternity as enveloping, nurturing, abiding. Even motherly.

For many of us, this is not at all easy to believe. But Debora's art may be less of a creedal statement than it is a challenge to reconsider our presumptions about our rapport with eternity. Are his works, like the traditional icons of the Near East, a window through which eternity gazes upon us? Or are they merely graphic representations that we, as the sole rational species in the cosmos, appreciate, digest, and then leave behind? I could only decide after having spent time contemplating works like *Tonantzín* and *Mi Madre de Los Angeles*. It is for each of us, I suppose, to find our own answer. Either way, Debora's work succeeds in broadcasting one message quite clearly. It is the same message of the defiant half-man, half-skull who seized my gaze from among a mass of images, saying simply and urgently: *Look.*

9. The Faces We Seek

Paul Lickteig, S.J.

"Who am I?" If we had to pick just one question that dogs our cultural consciousness, this would be it. It's a terribly open-ended query, perhaps a grown-up version of the "how I spent my summer" essays we did in elementary school. Maybe part of the issue is that it sometimes seems like we are still waiting to be rewarded with a gold star for our answers. I mean, in both cases I can remember feeling obliged to respond with something that sounded really awesome, even when the answer was not entirely true. Still, the main problem is not that we spit-shine our lives so that people will be dazzled by their brilliance (and consequently think we are great). It is that, when it comes to naming "who we are," I am not sure that any of us is qualified to answer the question in the first place. At some level, we are always left with a hollow, almost haunting, response: "I don't know."

Acknowledging who we are is obviously more complicated than registering for Facebook. Describing likes and dislikes, influences, hobbies, and whatnot is the easy part. But how do we begin to relate the various impulses and complexes at play in our lives, some of which remain mysterious even to us? How do we explain personal successes and failures at bringing our actions and beliefs into continuity? Even more, what do we do if other people do not agree with our description of who we are?

I know, I know: That sort of thing is not supposed to matter. But it does. We base our self-opinions on what other people say. As this happens, we will often take on various roles, various ways of thinking and acting that we believe will gain us acceptance. In this case, saying "who we are" becomes a matter of saying who *others* think we are. Meanwhile, we may become so busy trying to make sense of where we have been and where we are going that it becomes unclear exactly what we can say about ourselves with any confidence or integrity.

#

T.S. Eliot wrote a poem called "The Love Song of J. Alfred Prufrock." I love this poem. One line in particular wrecks me every time: "There will be time, there will be time / To prepare a face to meet the faces that you meet." Prufrock knows the expectations of others, and he knows his own abilities. He longs for something other than what he sees, even while realizing that his choices have brought obligation, and even though it feels like time is moving him along a winding path toward an inevitable destination.

I love this because it is the song I have heard myself and so many others singing. This is as we are: We sometimes feel locked within the confines of our own lives, always wishing for something more, but obliged to live by the roles we have found ourselves inhabiting. We make choices, and we move along. It can seem that our only option is to live the life that has been assigned to us, while all along we are secretly hoping for something else. The lives we live do not always match the people we think we have become, and we are not sure what we should do.

So, we dress accordingly. We act accordingly. We live, laugh, and love accordingly—all within boundaries fixed by the sources that shape our imaginations (families, social circles, movies, music, etc.). We hope that the communities we find ourselves in will allow us to live well. Some of us, if we find the right path, will be recognized for some form of excellence or another. Others, if we get off on the wrong road, will be branded as failures or deviants. The majority of us will collect bits of happiness strewn along the more modest path of meeting basic needs (food, shelter, etc.) and seeing that our desires are moderately fulfilled (a little love, a little extra money, a little vacation with people we enjoy now and again). Even among this majority, many will feel like they are just scraping by.

In the process, we are graded and appraised, deemed worthy or unfit, and we struggle to find personal value and merit. We will perform acts of selfless love, but we will also make mistakes that hurt others, sometimes deeply. We will work hard and find ways to make ourselves "better," however understood: taking classes, running marathons, trying to set a good example for our kids. When the project of self-improvement fails, as it sometimes does, we will find ways to make ourselves *feel* better (or maybe different-er), perhaps finding momentary escapes in small distractions or, if that does not work, losing ourselves in bigger compulsions. How we do these things will decide who it is that we think we are. We will know because people will tell us, and we will feel like we are either somebody, or nobody, or maybe both ... on the same day.

By the end of Eliot's poem, Prufrock is an old, searching man. He has seen his chance for greatness come and go. He listens to the ocean, that unfathomable abyss. His trousers, once the costume of a more robust figure, are now cuffed to fit his shrunken frame. He ponders the song of mermaids, and he wishes they would sing to him. He longs to immerse himself in that dream of life beneath the waves, rather than drowning in the reality of his own life.

We, in turn, hope that we will find ourselves at the end of life with more gratitude than regret. But in our final moments, the dreams we learned to let swim in our souls will be calling to us. Was it kindness and care or the regret of unfulfilled self-seeking that colors the iconic moments of our lives? Was it love or fear that won the day? Will we long for an escape, or will we long for more life?

How do we even begin to answer that one?

#

This makes me think of a line from another sort of poem, one that is a bit more modern and also set to music. I'm talking about the song "Mofo" by the band U2, especially the line, "Still looking for the face I had before the world was made." "Mofo" is a very different type of song than "Prufrock." It opens with a Ritalin-esque beat from some industrial nightmare, before plunging the listener into a soundscape etched with the peals and groans of highway traffic and subway trains. The lyrics follow like a web-work of neurons racing through the human mind, words that illuminate the confusion and longing of a soul in the sleepless midnight of its discontent. It is the voice of one searching: for a savior, for a father, a brother, a sister and a mother. But it is this image of mother that is evoked again and again.

Truth is, most of us have spent years trying to figure out how to make this life work. We may not think of what will come at the end of our days, but there will often be an experience of living life at the edge of our understanding. Sometimes seeking and sometimes scavenging, we will try to find the thing that would save us amid the dross of our existence. Whether a golden piece of wisdom, a spiritual talisman, a slice of material wealth, we look for something to which we can cling. The longer we live, the greater the likelihood that we will have to enter into moments of total uncertainty. There will be times when we stand at the end of our known worlds, fearing that we might fail, fall off the edge if we continue forward. We will find ourselves in places where there is no map to follow and in situations where no simple maxim will tell us how to continue on.

Words and images will help us understand the person whom we have become then, one who is at the mercy of a cosmos that we did not create. In the flow of life, there are moments of solace, isolated islands of clarity that create a single continuity in our personal narratives. Or, we reach peaks of awareness where we look down upon the tangled roads below, see how we arrived, and get a sense of where we are heading. Still, the land around rivers will change with the seasons. When we ascend the mountain, we always have to come down. With each choice made in life, we may feel like we are moving either closer to or farther from the truth. Still, we can hold on to a memory of the person that we once were and hope in the voice that once guided us.

For we who pray, it is a mother that we often find ourselves seeking. As we meditate on the beads of memories strung together into the continuous narrative we call "our lives," we can find grace threaded through and through. We can cultivate awareness of One who loves us deeply and dearly, who knew us even as we were being knit. As "what ifs" become "what is," we can sometimes get hurt and need to search out a place where our souls can mend. Crawling within, we can be held again by the warmth of the One and feel the simplicity of our being protected from the complexity of a tumultuous universe. In these moments of distress, we find memories of a time before everything happened, where we were nothing but beings of pure potential. From here we begin to learn how we might continue on as ones created by God, seeking to embody the love we have been shown in our relationships with others.

#

We continue to seek a way of life that we can recognize. We look for a vision that will show us not only how to continue living, but who it is that we are called to become. The thing is, we don't really know who we are becoming. Even when we think we do, we are not getting the whole picture.

We might catch glimpses of ourselves in the words and images provided by various media, but that is always a bit like catching sight of oneself in a store window. We might see our faces, but we only catch the image as filtered through the shining things on display behind the glass. We see ourselves reflected in the words of others, but there are always stray bits and pieces in our line of sight that do not seem to fit into the picture. Ultimately, we are looking to catch sight of a face, reflected back to us from the outside, that we can somehow recognize as our own. We long for a face that reveals the goodness of who we wish we were, of the one whom we think we are called to be. We rarely get a clear glimpse.

I like to think that there will come a time when we will be able to see others as they are, neither according to their own opinion nor even according to ours. To see them with God's eyes, in other words. And we will see them as a revelation of God.

In Revelation 22:2-4, there is a line about the coming time when we will meet Christ face to face, and his name will be on our foreheads. Strangely, I am not sure we will ever see the name written upon our own faces. We will only suspect what is there when we turn to others and see their eyes reading

Christ in our face, watching as their lips mouth the word. Then—maybe only then—we will come to understand who we are.

We will see those who had lives spent searching and scraping, innovating and assuming, being beaten by challenges too great for them, and finding strength to triumph. Each one will bear a name—the Name—and it will look and sound different for each of us. In each one of us made perfect in Christ, that perfection will be worked out in a different way. Yet, it will be the same name—a name that reveals the ultimate truth of God's own perfection, made flesh in each of us. We will see people who knew in their lives a hundred visions and revisions. We will see in the eyes of others that the struggle to find who they were has been transformed by the presence of God. We will see ourselves reflected back to us, and finally know who we are.

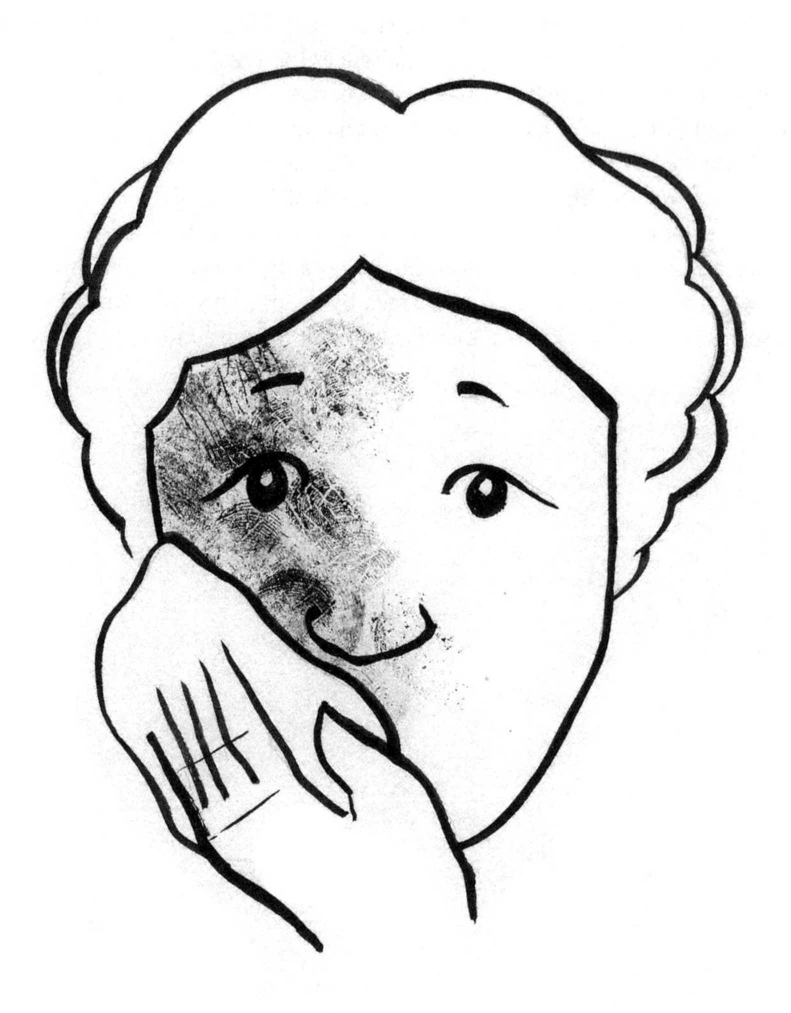

10. A Dirty Little Secret

Joe Simmons, S.J.

The novitiate chapel smelled stony and sweet, the result of years of incense baked into its brick walls. Alone in my pew, I watched the lights above cast strange shadows on the kneeler and floor below. I moved my head back and forth, entertained by my silhouette coming in and out of focus. I held the sheet of paper in clammy hands, excited and anxious. I wondered what this new life would mean for me as my eyes landed on clumps of words on the page. There I found a short passage from Paul's letter to the Ephesians:

> You were taught to put away your former way of life, your old self, corrupt and deluded by its lusts, and to be renewed in the spirit of your minds, and to clothe yourselves with the new self, created according to the likeness of God in true righteousness and holiness. (Eph. 4:22-24)

Here I sat on day two of religious life, having just bid my parents a safe trip home to Milwaukee. Home? Yes, Milwaukee was still home. But was it their home? My home? Stay focused, Joe.

put away your former way of life
    your old self
renewed in the spirit
    clothe yourselves with the new self

Hmm. Who will this new self be? When do I get to meet him? And do I have to?

#

The summer before a person enters religious life has a last-chance urgency to it—at least it did for this young man. Not sure whether he'll get a chance to visit Budapest or Prague or Cinque Terre as a priest, he is scrupulous not to squander his remaining days of freedom. This he accomplishes by squandering his modest savings. Soon he has to—no, wants to—move to the novitiate and "put on" the new self. *Arrivederci, Roma.* Hello, daily Mass.

The novitiate is the first stage of Jesuit formation, often described as a two-year school of prayer. Memories of my European bucket list faded quickly as I scanned the Introduction Sheet in the Jesuit Novitiate of the North American Martyrs. The second-year novices had just graduated from being freshmen, and they were primed to impart their wisdom to us newbies. This they did with the postured gravitas that earns sophomores their universal reputation. To my mind, their quoting from Paul drew a line in the sand: Your life up to now is over. Here's where you put on the new you.

With both wings clipped, the wanderlust of June and July turned to August introspection. I was uncertain who this "new me" would be, and just what parts of my "old me" had worn out their welcome. As I pondered all this, at least one thing was clear: I had some serious "spiritual cleaning" to do. My scalp grew taut over my skull as the austerity of novice life sank in.

#

This all came flooding back recently as I read an article by Michael Pollan in the *New York Times Magazine*.[1] At first blush "Some of My Best Friends Are Germs" has little to do with a life of poverty, chastity, and obedience. Pollan looks at germs and how we in the United States deal with them. The wisdom of most of Western medicine runs like this: The human body, complex and fragile, is at bacterial war with the world. *Homo medicus contra mundum.* Diseases—those ungodly masses of microbes that are ever poised to attack us—must be isolated and eradicated to preserve humanity as we know it. Kill, or be killed.

But now the age-old wisdom that germs and bacteria are bad for us is being reconsidered. Our bodies play host to billions of squiggly little bacteria, good and bad, that feast on us—and this is a good thing. Kids who wrestle puppies and play in the dirt develop fewer allergies, to give just one example.

It also turns out that much of our immunological protection from disease and the world at large comes from being washed in our parents' bacteria. Infants are born with sterile intestines, patches of soil untainted by either seeds or weeds. The intestinal lining is a neutral, fertile bed. It can host good or bad growth. Once an infant is born, she is vulnerable to the world outside. The "miracle of birth" is a messy but necessary first step in equipping her immune system.[2] That natural passage through messiness into the world—

1. Michael Pollan, "Some of My Best Friends Are Germs," *New York Times Magazine* (May 15, 2013).

2. Most males are loathe to recall—let alone write about—those dread videos on birthing

which makes most of us cringe or swoon—is crucial for a baby's health. By age three, we are eating foods that our parents and siblings eat. We encounter the same bacteria, germs, and allergens in the environment. Our intestinal gut bugs have flourished and now closely resemble those of our parents; all the more so if we have pets like dogs that lick us and help to pass the microbiotic love around the house.

Pollan's essay is troubling news for those of us who pride ourselves on cleanliness. My mother paid her way through college by cleaning hotel rooms. She has spent most of her post-collegiate life as a nurse working in emergency rooms and intensive care units. She brooks no germs or dirt. I've lost count of how many sink-side chats we had about washing our hands after playing outside, or touching doorknobs, or feathers, or coins. "Can I play in the ball pit at Chuck E. Cheese?" Forget about it. "What about pets in the house?" Gross. When anti-bacterial soap arrived in clear pump bottles, I was taking antiseptic hits of clean a dozen times a day. Bacteria and germs needed to be destroyed, simple as that. Sure, my hands grew dry and cracked, but one could never be too clean.

#

A Jesuit novice, in undertaking this exciting new thing called religious life, goes about trying to purge himself of his demons. He'll try new prayer practices. He'll entertain new understandings of the church, of prayer, of his awkwardly fitting new identity as a religious. And a young man—at least this young man—will start to get down on himself when he's told to put on the new self while the old self's gut reactions seem so well ingrained.

I assumed that sober self-assessment would cleanse me of all those habits, attitudes, and desires that kept me stuck in the old pre-novice self. (The keen observer will take note, as I did, of the onerous solitude of such a task.) A little self-awareness goes a long way, and my demons were pretty clear to me. I could assess all my faults with clarity, and—hey why not?—others' shortcomings as well. "Judge not, lest ye be judged," Jesus warns. "Remove the beam from your own eye, before removing the mote from your brother's." At the time, judging myself felt like my job, so the path to the new man seemed clear:

> Step One: Remove beam from own eye. Behold reality perfectly.
> Step Two: Assist others with the mote in their own eye. Attain spiritual perfection for all parties. Be revered as guru, hero, or both.

---

from high school health class, what with amniotic fluids, dilations, and emerging slimy newborns. I cringe to write about it even now, which seems a good inhibition to have in most polite conversation. But we are spiritual beings who inhabit real human bodies, which are routinely messy.

> Step Three: Die a spotless death with fellow Jesuits rushing to submit miracle stories and anecdotes for my saintly biography.

Throughout my novitiate, sincerely desiring to grow into this new man, I confused praying with taking spiritual antiobiotics. I'd say to myself, "I wish I were more patient," and wait for God to flush my system of impatience. Frustrated by uncharitable or judgmental thoughts about other novices, I'd try to stifle them by biting my tongue or avoiding the people I didn't like. My old self laughed too much and didn't take things seriously enough; it was time to get serious about life.

Here was the rub: The time I spent "praying" was spent trying to slough off the old self like a clingy younger sibling. I presumed that God would appreciate my candor so much that he'd magically swoop in to remove these faults and replace them with a spotless, loving heart. So I "prayed."

And waited.

And was left wondering why my prayer—and even my God—seemed so singularly unhelpful. Grasping at different postures and attitudes in search of a remedy to my grave self-diagnosis left me loathing the prospect of prayer. I had hoped that God would create in me a clean heart—the kind I read about in Psalm 51. Instead I was left with a heart that felt dried out and cracked, like hands that (sorry, Mom) had been washed too often.

#

In light of my grave self-diagnosis as a novice, I squirmed while reading Pollan's essay—and not just because of the scientific jargon. He explained that sanitizing away our internal messiness may *seem* good for us, but if we try to wipe out all the bacteria, we're actually wiping out ourselves:

> Our resident microbes also appear to play a critical role in training and modulating our immune system.. . . Some researchers believe that the alarming increase in autoimmune diseases in the West may owe to a disruption in the ancient relationship between our bodies and their old friends the microbial symbionts with whom we coevolved.[3]

old self
    new self
old friends . . .
    new friends?

3. Pollan, "Some of My Best Friends Are Germs."

My mind fluttered back to a novitiate visitor who made exactly the same point. Larry Gillick is a Jesuit priest and a renowned spiritual director. He travels the country giving retreats that help reconcile people to the reality of God—and the reality of themselves. He lost his eyesight early in life, yet his spiritual vision is crystal clear. He visited us in the novitiate after our thirty-day retreat to help us debrief from the intense month of prayer.

And he shared with us a dirty little secret.

Father Larry suggested that we *make friends* with our weaknesses, because they were going to be with us, in one form or another, for the rest of our lives. In the moment, I found this idea repugnant. Make peace with everything I hated about my old self? Maybe for the lazy and resigned, I thought, but I'm here to put on the new man. Old me was impatient and critical. New me would shine whiter than wool. Then he said something that will forever stick with me: "Be patient with yourselves. It takes a long time to make a Jesuit." He offered it with unhurried ease; an ease that no sophomore's gravitas could imitate.

#

Surviving in the world means leaving behind the relative sterility of the womb. Surviving beyond the novitiate means accepting the reality that God works in spite of—and in light of—our imperfections. It's taken years for me to recognize that some of those things I wanted to rid myself of as a novice—being critical, impatient, glib—were deeply ingrained in my personality. Trying to scour away those old habits left me feeling raw and alien to myself. If this was the new me, I thought, I'm not sure I like me very much.

But reconciliation happens. Sure, I can be critical; but this same critical mind can be harnessed to discover what-might-be. Impatience, turned on its head, becomes the zeal necessary to turn what could be into reality. As for laughing a bit too much . . . it turns out that a lot of people enjoy Christians who carry themselves lightly. Aristotle wrote somewhere that wit is insolence that has been educated.[4] Is there anything more pitiable than a young man who cannot laugh at himself or the incongruities of the cosmos? Humor defuses tension and when properly deployed can de-fang the unsavory truths that poison our Christian hope. Laughter is the echo of a heart that loves, pulsing through our defenses to reveal that we can still be surprised with delight.

#

4. Aristotle also allegedly wrote that it is unseemly for the young to quote elders, so I'll resort to apocryphal paraphrases.

Jesuits lay no unique claim to the slow process of becoming fully who God intends us to be. It takes a long time to recognize our truest selves in light of God, no matter who we are. Anyone willing to plumb the spiritual depths learns quickly that we are complex creatures, and that growth in life with God entails tumbling into intellectual rabbit holes and spiritual dead ends. We can try to scrub our souls clean, as though God won't allow us a seat at the feast unless a spotless new person shows up.

But here's what I've learned, from Pollan and Gillick alike: Prayer is not an antibiotic, and it's not spiritual steel wool. The great preacher Walter Burghardt wrote that real contemplative prayer is "a long, loving look at the real." For one searching for the new self, contemplation involves a long, *loving* look at the reality of the old self. We must entertain the possibility that, in God's estimation, perhaps we are more than the sum of our faults and limitations. That, in the words of the psalmist, we truly are "fearfully and wonderfully made" by a God who stitched us—old and new alike—together in our mother's womb. If this is true, then praying means welcoming a second opinion on our grave self-diagnoses. This makes prayer less a time of self-recrimination and navel gazing, and more an experience of seeing every aspect of ourselves—our relationships, faults, desires; everything—as God sees us.

It took years after the novitiate for me to let go of the notion that this "new man" in Christ was someone wholly alien to the "old man" who—for the love of God!—was attracted to this unusual mode we call "religious life." The new man doesn't kill or cloak the old one, but grows *within* him, slowly and imperceptibly. Old habits, those friends we can't quite shake, can mature if we let them. The new self emerges through every interaction with a world that is messy, imperfect; a world that looks a whole lot like us.

#

I finished Pollan's essay, and sat thinking back on this young man, twenty-four years young, fresh to religious life. Part of him was mourning the old memories and adventures he had left behind; part of him was afraid of what new things were to come. He sat hunched over in his pew, watching shadows play like demons on the floor below. Over the next two years, he will confuse solitary soul-scouring with prayer and get pulled down by the unreality of his expectations. He will not recognize himself for a while and wonder what he's doing wrong. Even now he looks back and is tempted to be frustrated with this younger self. Part of him would still love to take some purgative medicine, to tidy up the narrative of the first seven years of religious life, resulting in a spotless, beautiful story.

But I catch myself from this harsh reproach; instead, I choose to look with love at that young man who sat in anxious fear of what the new man would look like. Because we are wonderfully, fearfully made. Because it takes a long time to make a Jesuit.

Because scouring away at life's imperfections is a fool's errand, an old way of life that has given way to new.

11. Public Humility, or Talking with One Another Again

Nathaniel Romano, S.J.

"Do you see Jesus in me?! Do you?!!" The shout echoed in the bare room, less a question than an accusation. His eyes opened wide, nostrils flared, the pane of bulletproof glass and the intercom telephone in my hand vibrating with his anger. He was nearly twice my age and had spent most of his life behind glass like that, or bars. I added up the time once—he had spent more time in jail than I had been in school. I'd spent a lot of time in school.

Truth be told, we frustrated each other. When I spoke it was about "the Law" (with a capital letter). In his blunt, obscenity-filled language he spoke about Life. When he talked I would try to filter out the profanity to get to the relevant stuff. He, though, wanted me to see that it was his life that was in the balance, and that his life was important. Mostly I just thought he was trying to be difficult. Undoubtedly he mostly found me condescending.

My mind spun as his question hung in the air, the tension making it hard for me to focus on what I'd come to the prison to talk to him about: his case, what had happened, what sorts of defenses he might have. I'd been doing criminal defense for a little over a year by this point, and I knew the relevant legal issues I needed to map—if he would just focus on what was relevant. He wanted to focus on what was important. "That's really not relevant," I finally responded. It was not the right thing to say.

Encounters like this nagged at me, but it took me a few years (years that saw me move from the practice of law to preparation for priesthood) to understand why. Now I think it's not just that I was wrong, and he was right. I think it's that he and I were speaking different languages, and that this difference reveals a fundamental tension in the law. After all, "the law" is supposed to remain pure, neutral, objective; precise. It never does. How can it when it has to be applied in the chaos of life?

For a long time his question haunted me. On good days, I put it in the back of my mind and just kept going. The other days, well, that's when I prayed.

#

Everyone who's watched *Law and Order* knows what "the Law" is. While being a lawyer or a judge seems to demand ever-increasing technical proficiency, "the Law" is something everyone encounters—if in no other way than through the dramas that litter basic cable. Short, sweet, and direct, "the Law" conjures for us a fixed set of ideas and principles. We know what law is and what it should do. It should promote fairness and create justice. It should preserve equality and encourage ethical behavior. It should vindicate the moral person.

And while this isn't untrue, the Law is more than that, and less. I think that very often people like myself become lawyers and judges because we are mesmerized by the vision of a just world that the Law can represent. We study and think and write because of this beautiful vision we've glimpsed. But the more I practiced law, the more I looked at it day after day, the more ambiguous it became.

This is a common experience for lawyers, judges, clerks—all those professions that demand immersion in the clarity and neutrality of expression that define our sense of law. What many realize—what I realized—is that beneath the meticulous and exact surface of the Law lie sharp disagreements over what it means to be just or what fairness actually looks like. Even more, I realized that the law itself is ill equipped to resolve these disagreements.

#

Debate over the law has a tendency to become abstract. Very often when we speak of policy and politics, ideologies and ideals, we will quickly turn to broad terms like "freedom" or "fairness" or "justice" in order to understand better what is at stake. The thing is, most of the time we really don't know what we mean when we say these words. Or, more accurately, even when we ourselves know precisely what we mean when we say, for example, "justice," there are other members of our same society who mean something quite different by that word. The connotations with which we fill these words are sometimes so different, in fact, as to be almost perfectly opposed to one another.

This complicates things, to say the least, particularly when we want to reform the law or our legal institutions. We rely upon our society having a shared understanding of our ideals, and the words with which we describe them to one another, if for no other reason than because it's these ideals by which we measure our laws. If it's true that our society doesn't seem to have a common sense of what "freedom" or "justice" means, then we have uncovered an enormous problem.

I don't want to pretend to be the first to notice this problem. In fact it was Professor Steven D. Smith of the University of San Diego School of Law who first clarified this for me. Professor Smith has begun to call our inability to agree on the meaning of such words the "disenchantment" of our public discourse.[1] Disenchantment is a great word for what's happening, but not for the reasons we might expect. The term works well to describe the differences in the meaning of the words we use not because it meshes nicely with my own increasing disenchantment with the ability of law to create the just world it envisions. Neither is disenchantment accurate because of some growing cynicism in our society. And it works not because our language can suddenly only speak of mundane, technical things, or because our social and political conversation has the erudition of a fifth grader. Though all of that happens at times, of course.[2]

No, Smith calls the kind of public discussion we have in society today "disenchanted" because it is *necessarily shallow*. That is, the words we use to describe our social values are empty—my client and I could understand "fairness" to mean such conflicting things—precisely because this is the only way for a society as divided as ours to conduct a reasoned and reasonable discourse.

"It is hardly an exaggeration to say that the very point of 'public reason' is to keep public discourse shallow—to keep it from drowning in the perilous depths of questions about 'the nature of the universe,' or the 'the end of the project of life,' or other tenets of our comprehensive doctrines,"[3] Smith writes. In other words, he thinks that "value words" have become little more than shells, hollow vessels that can hold whatever conflicting assumptions we want to fill them with. Even more, he thinks that we Americans lack the confidence to admit this, and that it's this very refusal to see how deeply we disagree that prevents us from coming to any kind of consensus on how the law ought to help us live together.[4]

So, by disenchantment, Smith is not claiming that Americans no longer tell fairy tales. In fact, in some way he's saying that we do nothing but—especially when we think we're talking about the most important things. For Smith, the deep problem is that we use the exact same words to describe competing visions of what a just world is and how ours might become one, and that we are refusing to admit this.

#

1. See, Steven D. Smith, *The Disenchantment of Secular Discourse* (Cambridge, MA: Harvard University Press, 2010).

2. See ibid., 6-11.

3. Ibid., 17.

4. Ibid.

My relationship with this client, it did not end well. Sitting in that cold and sterile cell, we glowered and we glared. We yelled and we shouted. And we parted on bad terms.

It left a sour taste in my mouth. I was not the person I wanted to be. Maybe I could blame him—he provoked me, he was difficult. But there was something else. That sour taste, it highlighted for me my discomfort with the practice of law and how we lawyers often approach our work. This discomfort spurred me into what I now would call discernment. Eventually, this and other discomforts would lead me to a deeper sense of my vocation, and to the Society of Jesus.

It was only after I'd been a Jesuit for some months—in the midst of making the *Spiritual Exercises*, the retreat that forms the heart of Ignatian spirituality and the Jesuit worldview—that I finally understood why it was that my client and I had parted so badly. Saint Ignatius begins the book of the *Exercises* with a small section of notes that precede the prayers themselves. These annotations describe the way St. Ignatius understood God to work with human beings and, in light of that, how we ought to relate to one another during and after making the *Exercises*. It was the twenty-second of these notes that opened my eyes. It reads,

> For a good relationship to develop . . . a mutual respect is very necessary. . . . Every good Christian adopts a more positive acceptance of someone's statement rather than a rejection of it out of hand. And so a favorable interpretation . . . should always be given to the other's statement, and confusions should be cleared up with Christian understanding.[5]

For me, this simple invitation was transformative. It helped me to understand that what was lacking in me was a sense of humility in the face of other people. That, on a deep level, my experience of an event, an idea, a concept does not exhaust its fullness. And that when other persons share their different experiences, they are not wrong. It offered me a new way to approach the world. Disagreements and disputes could be places of growth only if I allowed myself to engage different ideas instead of simply seeking to win an argument. Not that there suddenly wasn't a right and a wrong, but that who's right and who's wrong didn't have to be my first question. Annotation 22 helped me to see that, before asking questions of right and wrong, I first had to ask another question: What do you mean by that?

This is what was going on between me and my combative client. We were saying the same words—"fairness," "justice," "law"—but we weren't

5. David L. Fleming, S.J., *Draw Me into Your Friendship: The Spiritual Exercises. A Literal Translation and a Contemporary Reading* (St. Louis, MO: Institute of Jesuit Sources, 1996), 23.

meaning the same things by them. And neither of us had ever stopped to ask. I remember all this dawning on me while I was making the *Exercises* and suddenly wishing I could do it all over again. Instead of hectoring him to focus on what was relevant, we could begin with mutual respect. I now wanted to give his statements favorable interpretations. Instead of presuming that I had the only right conception of what we meant when we said "justice" or "fairness," I now wanted to bring my experience into an engagement with his. It was as if in my heart there was a clear ground for a moment, a clear point of mediation where our two experiences could be joined. I felt then that I could be an aid in that joining, help both of us see the import of the other.

And perhaps this sort of humility is what we, as a culture, need as well. A public humility. If Smith is right, it is clear that we simply don't understand differing experiences of the same realities. "Freedom." "Justice." "Law." We have become a people separated by a shared language. By the same words, even. One need only skim commentaries on law or politics to understand how this works.

What would happen, though, if we started by acknowledging this separation and then, rather than throwing up our hands at the emptiness of our language or digging even more deeply into our tired trenches, we put Annotation 22 into effect in our public discussions? What if we proceeded with a kind of public humility, by first trying to understand what it is that makes these words mean something different to so many of us? Could we talk to one another again then?

This does not require us to give up on our deeply held beliefs or our moral commitments. Rather, it requires us to recognize that, when we use words like "freedom" or "law," we are using placeholders. That these are shorthand references to our experiences of these concepts. Already, we've filled them, consciously or not, with particular beliefs and commitments. Other people might fill them differently. We are invited, then, to engage, understand, and respect those differences, even while we might in the end disagree with them. We are invited, as Smith puts it, to a "conscientious engagement"[6] arising out of a practiced public humility.

There are no guarantees as to the outcomes. We might not be able to reconcile our disagreements. Life is difficult and not everything will end well. But, like both my client's life and my own, our story is not yet done. It took a personal humility for me to begin to imagine that my client and I were meaning different things, to wonder what experiences were filling the shells of the words we used, to even want to understand. Perhaps a public humility can allow us to rebuild our shared discourse on a larger level, to talk with one another again.

6. Smith, *Disenchantment of Secular Discourse,* 224-25.

12. The Redemption of Superficiality

Michael Rossmann, S.J.

The unexamined life is not worth living.

It's time with God, family, and friends that brings true joy.

Great art reveals the human potential.

And yet we spend our time watching cat videos on the Internet. Clearly, something is not quite right here.

It's not that the Internet hasn't done amazing things. It has. It's opened up new ways to connect with friends, old and new, all around the world, and the wonders of Wikipedia have allowed us to instantly end dinner-table debates.[1] But it's also expanded the (already myriad) ways I have of wasting time . . . greatly. There are more important things in life than listening to my favorite pop song on repeat or laughing at the Overly Attached Girlfriend meme. A life consumed by constantly checking my Facebook feed and tweeting selfies turns pathetic pretty fast.

Fair. But we all know this dichotomy already. Yes, the Internet can easily bring near those who are distant and make distant those who are near. It can connect the whole world but often does so with fluff. I'm just not sure it's that simple, though, which is why I've been asking myself: Are all those seemingly superficial activities, like watching epic fail videos of the cinnamon challenge (so funny!), as shallow as they seem? Are they entirely irredeemable? Or might all this actually be a part of something deeper, part of life in abundance?

Look, I'm an ignorant boob with unrefined taste. Unlike my father, who collected art, or my mother, who is a leader of something called the Raphael Club, I mainly know Raphael as the red ninja turtle. I get inspired to listen to Beethoven every few months and spend the other 98 percent of my days listening to catchy, vapid pop music (so there's a fair chance that I'm humming the above questions to the tune of My Girl B—known by those outside my head as Beyoncé). But despite the rhythm with which I'm asking them, these questions aren't coming out of nowhere.

1. Granted, I kind of miss that.

In fact, a number of them relate to a talk given just a few years ago by the superior general of the Society of Jesus, Adolfo Nicolás. Entitled "Depth, Universality, and Learned Ministry: Challenges to Jesuit Higher Education Today," this address, like many of Nicolás's, was supposedly addressed to a large audience but actually seemed to be directed precisely at me. Personally, I call this one the "Michael, stop wasting so much time online" address.

This now oft-quoted talk is most well known for Fr. Nicolás's discussion of something he pithily calls the "globalization of superficiality."[2] For Nicolás, the globalization of superficiality is his description of the way "critical thinking often gets short-circuited" in our digital age. When one can "friend" or "unfriend" another so quickly, he says, "then relationships can also become superficial." Ultimately, he worries, the globalization of superficiality can cause people to "lose the ability to engage with reality." Given the reality of a world in need, this is anything but a superficial critique of the way the Internet is shaping persons and personalities.

But is all lost for us hopeless pop addicts? Or, is pop culture itself completely hopeless? Are things like Facebook, Twitter, and YouTube just huge distractions that prevent us from seeing well and deeply the world around us? Maybe—but I'm honestly not so sure, and for one reason: While I agree that Internet-mediated relationships can distort how we view ourselves and our world, this *is* still our reality and these *are* still relationships. What I mean is that the Internet itself is now a part of the reality of our world, and depth will be found wherever reality dwells. So, we can criticize pop culture and hide in our bunkers with the Facebook-free remnant, or we can engage the world in which many of us really live.

While Fr. Nicolás's analysis is prescient, I'm convinced that a key way to redeem superficiality is to use the power of these supposedly superficial forms of communication to criticize just such shallowness. For those with eyes to see, there is depth in the seemingly frivolous.

#

But there's one other key before we can even arrive at depth, and that is attention. In our day and age, we live in a world where attention itself has become something of a commodity for advertisers and influencers.[3] The problem is that—for me at least—as illuminating as Nicolás's Mexico City

2. Adolfo Nicolás, S.J., "Depth, Universality, and Learned Ministry: Challenges to Jesuit Higher Education Today," *Networking Jesuit Higher Education: Shaping the Future for a Humane, Just, Sustainable Globe,* April 23, 2010.

3. If you want to read more about the attention economy, I suggest starting with the good *Wired* article "Attention Shoppers." You can find it at http://www.wired.com.

address was, I did not actually remember any of it other than the phrase "globalization of superficiality." I also did not send a copy of it to non-Jesuit friends or bring it up at dinner. Other than that one phrase, it hadn't grabbed my attention.

In contrast, I present to you BuzzFeed, a Website that hilariously captures the latest viral content on the Web. Admittedly, I'm in a love–hate relationship with BuzzFeed; I have wasted time on it by looking at items like "The 19 Stages of Drunk Eating" and thought, "Rossmann, what are you doing with your life?" At the same time, under the façade of lists and funny pictures, BuzzFeed can convey a surprising amount of depth. It can convey a message similar to Fr. Nicolás's but in a way that is far more likely to be understood, remembered, and shared by people like yours truly.

So let me throw out the window the dictum that you ruin a joke by explaining it, because I want to talk for a second about the BuzzFeed list "23 Pictures That Prove Society Is Doomed." In it one sees picture after picture of people sharing the same space, but who are so glued to their phones that they're not able even to acknowledge anyone around them. Each of the twenty-three pictures is accompanied by a tongue-in-cheek description such as "a wonderful family giving thanks for all their blessings at Thanksgiving dinner."[4] Sadly, this dinnertime image in which people cannot look up from their hand-held screens to see their food, let alone each other, looks all too much like some of my Jesuit community meals.

Unlike Nicolás's talk, I shared "23 Pictures" with friends because I found it to be both hilarious and apt social commentary. These silly images communicated perhaps more effectively (not to say better) than his words the mixed effects of modern technology. While BuzzFeed is itself a carrier of much superficiality, it shows we can turn these same modern means of communication back on themselves, ultimately using them to poke holes through our own temptations to superficiality.

#

After attention comes depth. To wit: I present to you the "Harlem Shake" craze of 2013. This viral phenomenon started with five teenagers in the decidedly un-Harlem locale of Australia. In case you missed it, these videos often begin with a roomful of people sitting quietly or holding perfectly still while one person, always wearing a helmet or a mask, dances in their midst. When the first bass beat of the "Harlem Shake" drops, the room explodes into motion, all the people suddenly doing ridiculous dances that include

4. Dave Stopera, "23 Pictures That Prove Society Is Doomed," *BuzzFeed,* June 19, 2013, http://www.buzzfeed.com.

waving their arms like the appendages of a jellyfish. That first video eventually triggered thousands of Harlem Shake videos—videos that were collectively viewed over a billion times around the world. These are videos about nothing, really; they're just fun. And this whole phenomenon happened over the course of about two weeks. And then people got distracted by the next viral sensation.

All of these videos, though, from the original[5] to (one of my personal favorites) the Skydive edition,[6] fit Fr. Nicolás's description of the globalization of superficiality almost perfectly. What depth is there to be found in watching dozens of thirty-second movies of kids in outrageous costumes doing ridiculous pelvic thrusts?

My answer starts when I can realize that the necessary condition for each of these videos is a preexisting community. And not just a community of any kind, a community already willing to get together and do something fun just because it's fun. A community willing to celebrate life together. From this way of looking at them, all these videos are just venues for making visible the creativity that was already present in a community. In other words, the trope of the Harlem Shake became something around which a damp creativity could become combustible. And more: as bizarre as it may have seemed, this video craze actually did unite people from Australia to Harlem (even though it might have united them in a form of particularly ridiculous dancing). This joy of being together and the catholicity of connections are evidence of the glory of God.

I realize some may think, "OK, Rossmann, we realize that Jesuits are supposed to 'find God in all things,' but you're honestly trying to tell us that God is in the Harlem Shake?" Yes. Yes, I am.

While I did not participate in a Harlem Shake knockoff video myself (largely because I now live in Tanzania where the craze never really reached . . . and, OK, because I didn't exactly want this to be the entire legacy of my time in East Africa),[7] I did participate in a previous viral sensation that is ostensibly another example of the globalization of superficiality.

In the spring of 2012, I was sent by my Jesuit superiors to work at Creighton University. Several of the students in the office where I worked listened almost incessantly to Carly Rae Jepson's then-ubiquitous pop anthem "Call Me Maybe." To be honest, I didn't like the song . . . at first. But after a week or so the catchiness of the hook had wrapped itself firmly around my neurons.

5. Pull out your phone and watch the original at http://www.youtube.com/watch?v=384IUU43bfQ.

6. How could I not provide you with a link? Check the video out at http://www.youtube.com/watch?v=RT_4NIPsMCY.

7. Not that I am opposed to leaving a "video trail" of my time here: http://www.youtube.com/watch?v=uKexIwhQRVU.

Soon I found myself singing along with the best thing from Canada since maple syrup.[8]

I wasn't the only one. As happened with the Harlem Shake, "Call Me Maybe" became a commonly parodied (homage-ed?) video. So, in the preparation for our office's end-of-the-year celebration, I half-jokingly proposed that we should make our own parody of the "Call Me Maybe" video. Immediately, one student responded, "Yes! And you'll be The Guy!" (as in The Guy that Carly Rae is asking to call her, maybe, in the video). I was pretty sure that this is not what my superiors had in mind when they sent me to work at Creighton's Center for Service and Justice.

While the finished video[9] probably raised more than a few eyebrows for those who knew that The Guy was actually studying to be a priest, it mostly caused a lot of laughter. In the days following our music video, I could not walk around campus without people staring at me or telling me that they loved it. Many conversations stopped there, but others continued. I developed relationships with students that would not have happened if I were not "that guy in the Call Me Maybe video."

Our staff had created the video as a way to memorialize our shared experiences, and we initially shared it with our friends and family, laughed and talked, and moved on. It was only later that we thought we might as well share it with the world to see. Much to our surprise, thousands of people from around the world actually watched Carly and The Guy, S.J. I'm sure there were any number of people who found themselves, shall we say, "perplexed," after watching the video, but maybe it made a few others think about a vocation to the priesthood. (Check out the video to understand why.)

When I watch the video again now, I can step outside of my experience just enough to know that it looks superficial. But that's really not how I—or the others involved—remember it.[10] For me, the video and the song have become a living artifact of all those friendships—and not just Facebook friendships—I developed at Creighton.[11] Not to be saccharine, but Carly Rae's song isn't superficial at all to me anymore; it's a joyful experience of community, a taste of the Kingdom of God.

I know that most of the people who watch videos of the "Harlem Shake"

---

8. That's right, Bieber, Celine, and Steve Nash, you read that correctly.

9. No, I'm not going to tell you whether this video can still be found on YouTube or that you should search "Call Me Maybe" and then add either "Creighton" or "Rossmann" if you want to see it.

10. I remember it as the start of something that united people and facilitated relationships that then went beyond the surface. When we start with the reality of how people communicate today, connecting through seemingly superficial pop culture might be the portal to something deeper. Maybe Jesus would have used YouTube videos rather than parables if he were here today.

11. And yes, I *still* hear that song, even living halfway around the world.

or "Call Me Maybe" don't see them as living symbols of the glory of God found in community. But a living symbol is not a stop sign; it can't force its meaning upon everyone who sees it.[12] The depth in a living symbol can be seen only if we first learn how to look at it. Ever since my friends and I made our own "Call Me Maybe" video, I've been trying to watch all those other videos, made by all those other living communities of friends, with those same eyes.

#

In the same address in which he describes the "globalization of superficiality," Nicolás describes how, for St. Ignatius, the starting point of spirituality is always what is real. We start with the real and then plumb the depths of that reality "to see the hidden presence and action of God in what is seen, touched, smelt, felt."

Rather than simply bemoaning pop culture and the modern methods of sharing that form such a significant part of our lives, let's help one another see that which is seemingly shallow through the eyes of Ignatius. If we can do that, we'll see that that which looks most superficial might be both the result of, and the key for, opening relationships that are much deeper—relationships that reveal the presence of a God who labors in every culture, even pop culture.

12. See Paul Ricoeur's great book *Symbolism of Evil* (Boston: Beacon Press, 1967), or Sr. Sandra Schneiders's application of Ricoeur's theory to biblical interpretation, *The Revelatory Text* (Collegeville, MN: Liturgical Press, 1999), to read more about the philosophy of symbolism.

13. Dispatches from the Control-F Culture

Ryan Duns, S.J.

Exasperated, the student rolled his eyes and groaned. "Duns, what are you looking for? What's the *answer?"* A smile crept across my face. I was delighted he was having to wrestle with my ambiguous question. It was that time of year again, time for me to teach the Irish poet Seamus Heaney's poem "Mid-Term Break" to my high school seniors.

The poem begins with the line, "I sat all morning in the college sick bay," and, by the time it reaches its conclusion, invites the reader to fathom the depths of the word "morning." I grinned back at my frustrated student. I wanted more from him, wanted him to see more than just the quick answer. I wanted him to see how "morning" refers not only to the length of time the narrator sat waiting but also to his experience of all-consuming grief at the tragic loss of his younger brother. I wanted him to see the bivalence and gravity of "morning" as it was unwrapped, layer by layer, until it lay open, revealed, at the poem's end. I wanted it, but—as all teachers know—my wanting did not make it so.

He wasn't alone, my frustrated eye-roller. The students had all grasped the *facts* of the poem. They knew that the boy was four, that he had been hit by a car, yet they struggled when I asked, "How does the word 'morning' function throughout the poem?" The only thing stronger in the room than their silence was my smile. It was to his credit that my eye-roller was bold enough to tell me one key thing: that he could not find the answer anywhere in the poem itself. I agreed. I then asked again: "How does 'morning' function in the poem? Look beneath the surface, dig into its marrow." They frowned at my encouragement. I smiled.

That evening, his groaning desire for an answer, for clarity, for *the facts Duns!* haunted me. As I thought about his frustration, I looked around my room and noticed the number of devices I owned. The tablet and the laptop for travel. The desktop I use to Skype my niece and nephew, the microphone and camera for the Irish tin whistle videos I make. And then Facebook and Twitter to keep me connected with friends, family, colleagues (and to access

the depthless portal of work and play that is the Internet). My room was full of these devices and portals. And they've enriched my life without question, given me—given all of us—access to resources unimaginable even twenty years past.

Suddenly, it occurred to me that my students' reactions, their groans and eye-rolls, might be more than just an indicator of laziness. Given how hyperconnected we are, given all of our devices, I began to wonder if this reaction might not somehow be indicative of a larger cultural shift, one that's swallowed up both him and me as it has muscled its way into the present.

#

I bought my first cell phone in 2002. It looked like a phaser lifted from George Takei's private stash, and I was embarrassed to be seen with it in public. Now, my phone feels more like another hand than a stun gun. When I'm on the train it lets me play Candy Crush and check the news. While waiting for friends I scour restaurant reviews and send texts. (I've become especially insufferable when a question about an actor, or date, or event is raised. Rather than noodling it out with friends, I reach for my phone and look up the answer, announcing it with aplomb and ending the conversation.) I can hardly bring myself to try a new bottle of wine or watch a movie on Netflix without using my phone to consult the reviews first. And despite my best intentions to use my laptop solely for taking notes, I admit to ordering books and clothing, checking Facebook and G-chatting, reading blogs, and sending tweets during class. Jesus got it right: "The spirit is willing, but the flesh is weak."

All of this—from my students' groans to my inability to stop tweeting—poses a question: How has all this instantaneous communication, and the readily accessible information it brings, changed us? How has it reshaped our cultural context? It makes me wonder why I feel that sudden surge of impatience when I can't get a signal strong enough to check my email, and whether all this access to information has made us not deeper thinkers but more superficial. Are we being swayed away from the difficult, deep down things by the ease with which precision comes in our digital age? Like my students, sometimes I find myself wishing that I could just search out answers with the exactness a search bar allows, hit Control-F on the keyboard of life.

Which is why I want to spend some time describing the traits I see in myself and all around me, traits of what I have dubbed a "Control-F culture." Drawing especially from my experiences teaching high school students, I hope to describe some features of our cultural milieu and to indicate various shadows resulting from an uncritical adoption of technological innovations. As I've admitted, I am in no way anti-technology. Still, I find myself giving my own eye rolls at our society's rush to acquire the latest gadgets without reflecting sufficiently on just how these might be affecting us.

#

The Control-F function is a handy keyboard shortcut that allows a computer user to find exactly what one is looking for and ignore everything else. We are a technologically literate people, capable of splitting our attention between tasks and comfortable being bombarded by our many devices. Faced with such a vast amount of data, I see our Control-F culture placing a high priority on finding the right answers quickly and efficiently. These answers must be accurate, sorting precisely the massive amount of information thrown at us.

Entire industries cater to this culture. SparkNotes relieves students of having to read novels. Google Books lets you search droves of texts as you look for the perfect citation (and is in the process of rendering library visits obsolete). Cramster provides solutions to problems from over 2,500 textbooks. Having to wrestle with a difficult problem, a tricky translation, or a challenging book seems to be an issue of the past. We have come to expect speed, ease, and convenience. Why talk when we can text? Why text when we can tweet? Why go to the store when we can shop online and get overnight delivery? Why pay for, let alone read, an entire novel when I can read a summary for free?

But there are costs that accompany such ease and convenience, and one of the greatest of these is the Control-F function's need for absolute specificity. One's search must be for something in particular, an exact word or phrase. What my eye-rolling student so astutely pointed out about the poem—that the answer toward which I was prodding him was simply not to be found in the text—is true for more that just the play on the word "morning," lovely as that might be. It's true for our lives. And as my own life outside the searchability of the Internet begins to be influenced by the conveniences within it, the frustration I sometimes feel at the world's inscrutability, its inefficiency, starts to make more sense.

But even staying focused on the goodness of what our digital age offers—its connectivity, the instant availability of vast amounts of data—it takes a discerning thinker to sift through the material. Even the most exact and precisely formulated question is insufficient if one wishes to attain both depth and breadth. Why insufficient? Because sound bites and keywords seldom express the context or capture the nuances of an issue. Mastery of an issue transcends knowledge of it in data points.

Indeed, mastery requires understanding something within a larger narrative context, situating those data points on a graph. The Control-F function may give me points, but it can connect neither them nor me to any larger story.

I may be able to regurgitate ideas about the conflict between Israel and Palestine or about debates over healthcare and immigration reform without taking the time to understand why those ideas are put together in the order they are.

Let's return to my story of teaching the poem. What took me some time to realize was that what frustrated my student most was that I'd asked for more than superficial information. I'd asked him to draw inferences from the text, to make non-explicit connections. In so doing I'd pushed him away from the safe mooring of readily available data and encouraged him to plunge into the murky waters of interpretation. It took me some time to see it, but, for a student trained in an educational system where the right answer is prized above all else, what my goading elicited didn't make him smile; it made him anxious. And when I could see that in him it took only a small shift of attention to see it in myself as well.

Without a doubt, right answers matter; knowledge is necessary. I want a doctor who scored well on her boards, and I expect my attorney to have done well on the bar. So it's not that right answers don't matter; it's that they only tell part of the story. It's that when they are absolutized, when all areas of life are believed to be as scrutable as a .pdf, something has been lost. It would hit my students each October, when, one afternoon, the counselors delivered their standardized test scores. The halls would fill with, "Wow! He's a 236??" or "Gee, I thought he was smart, but he's just a 152." If their cultural milieu values solely the correct answer, if they buy into the motto "I am what I score," we should hardly be surprised when, in late October, teachers and counselors find a steady stream of students expressing fear that their test scores mean that they are failures.

No wonder my own students felt anxious, rolled their eyes, when I asked them for more than a correct answer. Because what if they couldn't give it? How would they know they were worthwhile? How would they know if they were right?

#

An assertion: People are not shallow. It's just that most of us don't know that we're deep yet. By no means do I believe that we're a culture fated to superficiality. Nor do I want to suggest that we should unwire ourselves. I do think, however, that there are certain strategies we might employ to help cultivate increasing breadth and depth through technology. It's depth we want—how do we get there?

First, we need to make a concerted effort to cultivate both depth and breadth. As we sort through the information thrust upon us I think that we ought never lose sight of the larger narrative in which these data points make sense. Consider it like this. Many of us know how frustrating it is to ask someone, "How was your day?" and get the response, "Fine." (My brother was a specialist at this. He used to madden my parents when asked, "What did you do at school today?" with his standard, "Nothing." I cackled—and sometimes rolled my eyes.) When trying to pry open the minds and hearts of students I learned to ask open-ended questions such as, "Have you ever considered . . . ?" or, "How would you respond to . . . ?" because they invite greater participation. When I would teach sophomore boys how to read and interpret artistic works, I could hardly say something as banal as, "Do you like it?" Instead, I'd take various depictions of the same scene, the more gruesome the better (versions of "Judith Beheading Holofernes" were fan favorites), and use those specific images to solicit from them their insights into the theology and history reflected in the art. In a single class session, we could cover several artistic masterpieces, discuss a multitude of important theological themes; and the whole time, they were engaged as co-discoverers. Students with tablets could pull up the individual works and examine them up close, zooming in on certain parts or looking at each portrait from various angles. We were not looking for explicit answers but, in raising and thinking through questions, coming to appreciate our shared cultural heritage.

Second, we have to remember our dreams and practice becoming unafraid of our deepest desires. How do we name and claim them, these desires? Here is something that worked well for me: Once a year, I'd ask my students, "How many of you have heard the question, 'What do you want to be when you grow up?'" Nearly everyone in the class would raise his hand. I could then go around and ask each one what he wanted to be, and I would hear a host of different answers: doctor, lawyer, professional athlete, musician, teacher, whatever. That finished, though, I'd pose a second question. "How many of you have ever been asked, 'Who do you want to be when you grow up?' " Not one of my students ever lifted a hand. And, when we went around the room again, they would struggle to say who it was they wanted to be. Are we a culture of "Whats" or can we acknowledge our authentic desires and allow them to guide us into "Who" we desire to be?

Finally, we must embrace the risk and the joy of discovery. Whether through reading poetry, having deep discussions of life's meaning, or engaging in the discernment of a vocation, how can we rekindle a sense of joy as we plunge into new endeavors? Playing on St. Paul's observation that "God loves a cheerful giver," we might consider a theme common to Pope Francis: The world needs, and loves, joyful people. The vast array of technologies available to our generation give us access to vast resources for us to develop our passions, but, and just as important, they permit us to share our joy with others. We're not all going to create a trendy app or Website, but we can all recover a sense of joy found in the pursuit not of right answers but of stimulating questions that open us up to new horizons.

#

Pejoratively, the appellation "Control-F culture" expresses the observable traits of a culture immersed in technology: rapid searches, preference for data points and facts over narrative and context, a lust for simple and convenient answers. It must not be forgotten, however, that at least we are a culture willing to ask questions. In this impulse, I believe, there is great promise: The very technology that can encourage superficiality can be harnessed for depth; the isolation it can create can be inverted and used to show how interconnected we all are. By encouraging breadth and depth, by fostering true desires, and by encouraging joyful discovery, we can cultivate and contribute to a generation of seekers, native users of the Control-F function, valued for who, and not what, we are.

Every light casts a shadow: Just think of the shadow cast on that annoying patron's face when, in a movie theater, he checks his text messages! Our devices and technologies invariably influence our culture, the way we see, live, and respond to the world around us. We do not need to be afraid of technology or cultivate Luddite dispositions, but we do need to look critically and realistically at how our devices influence us. We must cultivate discerning minds and hearts as we venture into the digital frontier as a generation driven by desire and imagination, committed to joyful discovery. Will the light cast from our devices cause a shadow to fall upon us or will their light be revelatory? It will be our decision whether to allow ourselves to be defined by a search function or to find our identities in the freedom made possible by having the world, quite literally, at our fingertips.

14. A Jesuit Who Doubts

Chris Schroeder, S.J.

There are bright secrets and there are dark secrets. Who doesn't relish a bright secret? Coordinating a surprise birthday party. . . . Waiting for your wedding proposal to appear on the Jumbotron. . . . Conspiring to get your community Secret Santa to pick his own perfect Christmas gift while leaving him none the wiser.[1] While we wait for these bright secrets to be revealed, we feel a delicious anticipation and a mounting excitement. When their time comes, such secrets arrive to a joyous welcome. Bright secrets are welcome company, good news that has yet to reach its destination.

But not all secrets give life. Some cause dread. Or shame. Or anxiety. Rather than a temporarily delayed message, these are the secrets we hope to take to the grave. Every moment we carry them, they weigh us down and isolate us from those we love. If someone threatens to expose these secrets, we lash out: We must not be discovered. These are the secrets that kill our spontaneity and sap our joy. After all, who can celebrate while waiting to see which hand will hold the knife that will cut us open?

This is not the story of a bright secret. It is the tale of a dark secret.

This dark secret: I have been a Jesuit for more than ten years, and for long stretches of that time I have doubted that God exists.

It's strange to say it so plainly. I've guarded this secret so long that it's strange to read it on the screen, much less to publish it for all the world to see. It leaves me with a back-of-the-mind tingling that I can't quite shake, like I'm leaving home with the stove still on. I wonder whether I ought not just delete the scandalous words, turn back before I've gone too far.

My hesitancy is not without reason. After all, I am a Jesuit, and people have certain well-founded expectations of what a Jesuit should be. They (we) are men of the church: men living according to vows of chastity, poverty, and obedience, and (at the very least!) men who believe in God. Else why would

1. One of my finest gift-giving moments: I brought my Secret Santa to the store with me under the pretense that the gift we were picking out would be a gag-gift for our friend. At the store, I told him he should pick out the shirt he would want himself. When he finally opened it, he argued with me for a minute under the idea that he had received the wrong gift. I finally convinced him that this was the plan all along. Fun was had.

they go on yapping about the difference God's love makes? And who would listen to them if they did? With that unspoken idea in my mind, it seemed safer, more helpful even, to continue going through the motions even though my insides refused to line up with what I was doing on the outside.[2]

#

Perhaps I shouldn't be surprised that I got myself into this kind of situation. As a young man I was an earnest one, in search of great ideals and going all-in when I found something that moved me. So when I went to college at Saint Louis University, I was ripe for life-altering decisions. And, sure enough, I soon fell in love not only with the Catholic faith of my childhood but also with the discipline of philosophy.

I loved both for their attention to the biggest questions of our human life. I loved them for their all-encompassing explanations. In the process of becoming an adult, it's no surprise that they attracted me. I wanted to know my place, where I should stand in this world. I wanted to know who I should become, and they gave me answers that made sense. Philosophy sought to establish the essence of each thing, animal, vegetable or mineral, and Christian theology pointed out that fully understanding those essences requires one to recognize that they are also gifts of a loving God. As a student, I pursued both with a passion, plumbed their depths for answers and sought to live by what I found there.

And after my sophomore year, with the combination of wisdom and foolishness that only a twenty-year-old semi-adult can summon, I decided to commit myself to the Catholic side of that equation in a way that would determine the course of the rest of my life. I entered the Jesuits. It was an exciting time, but interrupting my schooling had one important, unforeseen, consequence: A little philosophy can be a dangerous thing. To this day I love philosophy, and think it is an important, useful, and (for me at least) enjoyable discipline. Two years of collegiate philosophy studies, however, was just enough to get me asking tough questions but not enough to allow me to come up with mature answers.[3]

---

2. It should be noted here that the problem is not with these expectations themselves. Unlike when a Disney princess faces down the whole world's misguided expectation that she marry some lout just to keep up appearances, standing for things like faith and chastity is a much more reasonable expectation. Whenever I am approached about being a Jesuit, the first question is always some version of, "How do you know?" That is, how do you know that this Christian thing is worth it, and how do you know that God is calling you to stake your life on it? If such honest and well-meaning inquirers can't assume a Jesuit to be relevantly secure in his faith, it would simply make no sense to ask a question like this.

3. A foreshadowing via a lovely Sam Rayburn quote: "Any jackass can kick a barn down, but it takes a carpenter to build one." Discovery of this quote has helped me in sorting through the various degrees of B.S. attendant upon philosophy—including my own. If people spend all

When I first started out thinking big thoughts as an adolescent, it was easy to dive into a worldview as beautiful and coherent as the Catholic one. But that last semester in school, before packing my bags and heading off to Jesuitland, I had that one ornery class on German philosophy. We read Nietzsche (just over-excitable), Marx (can anything good come of materialism?), and Heidegger (I'll be honest, I've yet to understand a thing that guy wrote).

When I read these new, decidedly non-Catholic authors, my first reaction was to fight back, offer counterarguments, claim superiority. My second was to ask if they might be right. What if the things I see every day in this world are not God's long-delayed bright secrets but simply heaps of microscopic atoms? After all, these were smart people, and they had a point: Modern experience has taught us that we don't need to talk about God to fly a plane, govern ourselves, or describe how human beings got such a big brain box. What if I am wrong and my faith is nothing more than literary novelties and false superstitions?

I am aware that a certain stripe of believer will stop me right here. Hold up a hand and say that the moral of this story is: Don't do all of that philosophy stuff. Or claim that faith requires you to put away your doubt and to stop thinking about things that might cause you to doubt. I suppose one way of dealing with a childhood bully is to run away, cede the playground to them, and unearth some sour-grapes reason why I didn't want to play there in the first place; but precisely what had attracted me to Catholicism was its vision, its confident expansiveness. And, even to this day, I think that, if Catholic intellectual life can't trade proverbial blows with the best that atheism has to offer, I am not interested. Running away from doubts was no solution for me.[4]

#

Which brings me back to going through the motions. As the worm of doubt grew, wriggling around in my mind, I had already set myself on a life trajectory that made me—in the minds of many—Mr. Religion. Expectations, good and ill, reasonable and not, accompany the public wearing of a white collar and black shirt.[5] And while I have tried never to lie about the degree of cer-

---

their time as a thinker knocking down the barns of others, it reflects poorly on their ability to build anything comparable themselves.

4. Six points: 1. This is not to say that the best strategy is *always* engagement. There is such a thing as an unfair intellectual playing field, and that can make discretion a better choice than discussion. 2. There is the risk that repeated often enough, the most disturbing and false ideas can become plausible. 3. I don't recommend that just anybody rise up to take on the local New Atheist "bully" . . . unless they are willing to do some intellectual pushups first. 4. Catholicism's best, truest strains have always valued just those intellectual pushups, and we have always been as willing as anybody to engage with whatever idea might pop up as a challenge. 5. And we do this while still admitting that not everybody needs to become a philosophical theologian to be a good Catholic. 6. Six notes in one footnote? Self high-five!

5. I've found this true for both non-Catholics and non-believers as well. In fact, many times

tainty I did or did not feel, the pressure to self-censor was significant. Which means that my problem wasn't just that I had philosophical doubts about God's existence; it means I had a lifestyle problem. Private doubts aren't just private for a person with a public faith commitment. So I often felt like a fraud, well-meaning fraud though I might be.

At first I tried to ignore the doubts. When that didn't work, I cast about for a counterargument to excise them completely. No luck. After several years of this back and forth, desperation began to set in, and I tried labeling the teeming mental cauldron of these thoughts "diabolical temptations," thinking that corralling them in this way might also help me turn my back on them.[6] None of these strategies worked. In fact, the more I thought about them, the more I tried, the more deeply rooted the doubts became.

Invariably, it felt worst in moments of quiet. The bustle of teaching Sunday School to a small pack of urchins made it easy to distance myself from the doubt, but there was always later. There would be a voice—sometimes during prayer, sometimes as I was writing in my journal—"It's not real," it would say, "You're just talking to yourself." Or I would be kneeling at Mass, and precisely at the moment when the priest would elevate the host I would feel that chasm open up between my outside and my inside. While my body kept on praying, a cavity in my chest would open and expand, and I would feel a dark and ravenous tumult inside. "That is a wheat wafer. It is obviously a wheat wafer. It is nothing but a wheat wafer. No amount of words can ever change that." And at night, praying over the events of the day: "I should walk away, but I don't think I could let everybody down. Maybe I should arrange an accident, find an easier way to end this charade."

It's that last thought process that, to me, will always remain the definition of the dark secret—an inner awareness of a pressure, a weight on the windpipe so heavy that death itself seems preferable to facing the true shape of reality. Even if, as it did for me, this awareness lasts only for a moment.

#

If studying philosophy as a college student had led me into doubt, continuing to study it as a Jesuit played a key part in leading me back out. More important than doing more philosophy, though, was learning the limits of philosophy.

---

it is the conscious atheists who are most willing to engage me and inquire as to what it was that led me to do what I do.

6. Strangely, I don't have much trouble believing in the devil (sometimes his handiwork seems a lot more obvious than God's). While I do believe that the devil played his role in what was going on inside me, delighting at every deception and goading every moment of despair, it's clear to me now that there was nothing demonic about the origin of these doubts. It was *my* brain and *my* thoughts that set up the dilemma . . . and there is no exorcism for thinking.

After all, sometimes our best, surest knowledge does not come from logical proofs. Imagine, for example, someone who set out to prove that they were seeing "blue" when they look at the sky. By asking the question, they call their perceptions into question. And ultimately, they cannot close the argument with finality. Someone could always propose some unnoticeable deception, some fault of the mind, or—a favorite of the philosophical crowd—Descartes' show-stopping "brain in a vat" argument.[7] Marshaling logical arguments to prove that one sees the color blue is the worst possible way to be certain about blue. It is best just to see blue.

For me that transition from *proving* to *seeing* took place slowly, although not without pivotal moments along the way. Just as an ornery philosophy class had contributed to my dilemma, another hard-nosed course that I took during my first few years as a Jesuit helped me ease out of it. It was a course on contemporary social philosophy, and in it I had to re-engage all those same doubts and arguments. But there was a difference this time; this time the stakes were slowly changing.[8]

After a couple of months of poring over arguments, back and forth, I began to recognize that what I was doing—spinning faster and faster on the relentless hamster wheel of mental debate—would never go away *so long as I kept doing it.* And more: The joy I had once felt in a philosophy and faith that helped give "answers that made sense" had been subtly transformed into a need for "proofs that were certain." What I sought had slowly changed, and I wanted to change it back. And out of that desire to return I realized something else: Even if I renounced my faith and left the Jesuits, the obsession with certainty wouldn't all of a sudden leave me alone. I would just suddenly be a non-Jesuit stuck wondering if there really was no God instead of a Jesuit doing the same. Either way, the hamster wheel would just keep spinning fruitlessly.

A path began to open, slowly though it came. To be released from the inner torment, I realized, I only had to stop tormenting myself. I had to stop searching for an elusive (and illusive) logical certainty that no philosophy

---

7. It runs a little like this: You think that what you're experiencing is actually happening to you. Your eyes are reading these words, you are holding a book, sitting in chair. But what if we are all just brains in a vat whose senses and ideas are being stimulated by electrodes plugged into our neurons? Well, there is no disproof of that argument that couldn't also be the stimulation of a vat brain, so it is pretty much impossible to get around. Keanu Reeves dealt with this problem in *The Matrix*. I think he solved it by diving inside the guy wearing sunglasses and exploding him.

8. I'll skip over the content of these arguments here since they could fill the space of a whole different essay (and they are not likely to be of great interest to someone who doesn't have the same doubts as I did). Those looking to spar with a rigorous contemporary atheist of the sort that I engaged in that class could do worse than Richard Rorty; we read *Contingency, Irony, and Solidarity* in the class, but he has many quality works. Those looking for the best, most comprehensive Catholic response to those types of objections (and many others) should check out John Henry Newman, especially his "University Sermons."

could ever offer. So slowly I worked to change my expectations. One day at a time, each time the voice of terror suggested that my beliefs were uncertain, I would pause and quietly agree with it on that point. Then I would remind myself that that fact was OK. I was no longer looking for "certain."[9]

Ironically, giving up the need for certainty paved the way for greater personal conviction about my own experiences of the reality of God. Before, my doubts had crowded in on all my encounters with God—whether in prayer, at Mass, or in nature. By paying less attention to the doubts, all of a sudden, I was "seeing" God again in these moments. It was like encountering an old friend I had grown too busy to attend to. Instead of listening to my insecurities, I began to trust that God was there, and did care for me—enough to be present in the small, still voice I still sometimes heard. I could again allow myself to feel the beautiful rightness that the Eucharist occasioned—surrounded by friends, with God at the center, offering life to us all through the bread in the priest's hands . . . the insubstantial, almost-nothing of the bread . . . now become. . . . Everything. And instead of fantasies about escaping it all, I found that, on a hike, I could come upon a panoramic vista, stop stock-still, review my life in an instant, and become amazed at God's goodness to me in all things.

Of course, God had been there all along. But I'd been so worried to prove God, it had become hard to see God, to feel God, or, even more important, to know and love God. Just like a blue sky, God is better experienced than argued about.[10] Peace came when I finally understood that.

#

So, if I had the opportunity to take my younger self aside, that newly minted Jesuit who had just started to feel the wriggling worm of doubt, I would talk to him, help him. I would not recommend that he leave philosophy or earnest thinking behind.[11] If anything, I would encourage him to dive in deep and to wrestle with the great doubts and convictions of the human mind until he had had enough.

But I would not expect these arguments to make him a believer. Ideas can clear the ground for faith, but they are no substitute for a living relationship

9. Which didn't mean not doing philosophy; it just meant realizing that while philosophy could not offer me certainty, it could (and did) offer confidence that my beliefs are reasonable and that my experiences were not deceptive.

10. Just so, we would arch our eyebrows if someone's relationship to his mother consisted entirely of attempts to irrefutably establish that it was indeed she who gave birth to him in that hospital room all those years ago.

11. Indulge me in one final plea: Seeing rather than proving God doesn't mean that faith requires us to tuck our thinking minds away in a drawer. If I hadn't returned to philosophy studies, I wonder if I'd ever have assuaged my doubts.

with God. To truly help that young man I would ask him to trust again the experiences of God he'd already had.

It's in that sense that I had never been far from God. And the same goes for each of us. We each have those moments—impossible to doubt if we only trust them—when we have been overwhelmed by the sight of the Milky Way or by the tangle of our beloved's hair. We have each lost ourselves in the poignant chords of an acoustic guitar and delighted in the untaught generosity of a child sharing her ice cream cone with her inquisitive golden retriever. We have each had experiences of that something *more*, that great secret all the universe holds until such time comes as to reveal it.

So, yes, I'd tell him, think hard. Put yourself through the philosophical wringer. But do not forget where you came from: a world of bright secrets that sing God's praises whether you attend to them or not. It will go better for you if you do.

#

I began this essay by promising to tell you a dark secret, and indeed I have. Not many knew the details of what I've written here. I wonder, though, how dark my secret really is. After all, I am hardly the only person—in the Jesuits or out—who has held such feelings.

In fact, it is because I think that these types of doubts are . . . not uncommon, shall we say, that I share mine now. In a modern, secular world, doubt *will* occur, and that does not mean that a person does not have faith—even deep faith. This will not be the faith of certainty but the faith of plain sight. A sight that may be deceived but without which we may truly be said to have seen nothing at all.

Join me then—whether you began this essay counting yourself among the faithful or the faithless—and turn to our secretive God and pray:

May darkness not overcome but invite us.

May isolation not torture another soul.

May we all understand that when we suffer, we do not do so alone, but with one another.

May we ourselves become a community of the earnest, a communal vessel of shared doubt—believers and half-believers, committed Catholics and honest agnostics, eager seekers and half-baked philosophers.

And may we hold in faith to that promise that "there is nothing hidden, except to be disclosed; nor is anything secret, except to come to light." Amen.

15. The Wander Years

Jeffrey Johnson, S.J.

> My wife and I both love the show and can't wait for the next ones. I am 63 and my wife is 52. I can't help but think how we would have done were we in our early 20's now. Truthfully, it wasn't much different. Similar mistakes and missteps but without "e" gadgets.
>
> —Patrick C.562 from the *Girls* homepage on HBO.com

As a man about to hold forth on HBO's new show *Girls*, I feel as if I'm fifteen years old again and about to pick the lock on my sister's Hello Kitty diary. To read the diary might be exhilarating—and would be a gross violation of her privacy—but odds are I just won't get it. Moreover, as a priest of the Roman Catholic sort, I am associated with a group that has recently been taken to the woodshed for its treatment of women. Any negative criticism on my part might be seen as another attempt to stifle the feminine spirit. So with a judicious portion of caution, I offer a few thoughts on the show that has lit up the blogosphere.

First, it's tough to determine what sort of show we have on our hands. I would prefer *Girls* to be a satire pointing out the common foibles of humanity. It would make me feel better about liking it and about the state of the world depicted in it. But I'm afraid *Girls* is not a satire. It takes itself much too seriously for satire. Although it's full of broad and course humor, it's not quite the same thing as *Bridesmaids* or *The Hangover* in anything but the raunchy humor. In purpose and in spirit, *Girls* is more akin to the late '80s classic *The Wonder Years. Girls* is nearly pure nostalgia and reverie. If *The Wonder Years* allowed Baby Boomers a chance to re-feel their adolescent years, then *Girls* takes the Bobo back in time for a dreamlike trip to her early twenties.

In *Bobos in Paradise*, the *New York Times* columnist David Brooks describes two privileged twenty-somethings; they are lost and confused, and yet boldly striking out on a great adventure. Shortly after setting out, Brooks writes,

---

A version of this essay was published in *The Jesuit Post* on June 4, 2012.

"they look elated, but then they become more and more sober, and finally they look a little terrified. They've emancipated themselves from a certain sort of WASP success, but it dawns on them that they haven't figured out what sort of successful life they would like to lead instead." What they are headed toward is not nearly as clear as what it is they are running from: their parents, the pressures of privilege, the burden of their own potential, and annoyances of received wisdom and ethics.

Brook's analysis makes for an accurate summary of the central dramatic dynamic of *Girls.* He might well be describing the four girls, Hannah, Marnie, Jessa, and Shoshanna, who, according to the show's tag line, are living the dream one mistake at a time. With each mistake comes a few moments of stupefying, cringingly painful sobriety. As when, for example, Jessa's boyfriend reads Hannah's diary and uses the contents for a song performed in some trendy pub in front of both women. The show depicts this triangular moment of betrayal with all the nerves laid bare. It was hard to watch. I cringed for them in my living room. Yet this is one of the show's strongest elements: accurate and evocative depictions of the actual emotional damage caused when late-late-adolescents wield weapons best used by fully grown adults. The show captures the sobering moments mentioned above by Brooks in his description of a couple on the run.

Although he might have been, in the above quotation Brooks is not describing Hannah and her gang of girls, but Benjamin Braddock and Elaine Robinson as they ride off into the sunset at the end of the 1967 film *The Graduate*. And this is the key to understanding *Girls*. As much as *Girls* wants to capture the contemporary escapades of thoroughly early-twenty-first-century wanderers, it is really a piece of nostalgia, a projection of self-expression on behalf of people who are well beyond their early twenties and all of the drama of finding themselves. *Girls*, I'm sad to say, is just a bit of Bobo reverie. If you doubt it's a dreamscape, then look at that tag line again: Living the Dream One Mistake at a Time. We aren't watching the dreams of twenty-somethings in 2012; who in their right mind would want to go through all that? We are watching the fantasies of their parents, men and women in their sixties.

Girls tickles the fancies of men and women of a certain age. Notice Patrick C.562's comment from HBO.com's fanpage quoted above. Patrick is sixty-three. He and his wife love the show, but not because it humorously depicts the struggles and concerns of the working girls of Brooklyn. He and Mrs. C.562 like the show because it reminds them of their own early adulthood. The show reminds and perhaps reinforces the C.562s' own memories of their own lives. Actually, "reinforce" and "memories" are probably not the right words here. *Girls* does not reinforce Patrick C.562's "memories" and self-image so much as it creates new ones. Then Patrick is able to project these new memories and a newly created self-image back onto his own twenties. Thus it's a dream, not a reality, that Patrick C.562 celebrates.

At this point you may be wondering: What on earth is a Bobo? To understand why Patrick C.562 might want to project this dream back onto his own early adulthood and thus edit his self-image for himself and Mrs. C.562, we'd better explore what Brooks is getting at with this neologism. Bobo is the combination of two words (bourgeois and bohemian) and is the product of Brook's "comic sociology." A Bobo is a paradoxical combination of some of the values of the 1960s' bohemian and some of the values of the 1950s' WASPish bourgeoisie. Bobos embody a free-spirited sense of self-discovery with an equally passionate drive for success, and they are the new elite, replacing the old elite, which was based on family connections (think Rockefellers and Vanderbilts). They manage to wed a healthy dose of anti-authoritarianism to a strong sense of personal identity and personal success (think Steve Jobs and Mark Zuckerberg). In short, writes Brooks, "dumb good-looking people with great parents have been displaced by smart, ambitious, educated, and anti-establishment people with scuffed shoes." Bobos are wildly successful, and with success come the rewards of money and power. And happiness, if only their bohemian side would leave them alone.

However, the bohemian part of the Bobo's split personality causes deep anxieties within the hearts of these new elites over their material success. In other words, "The sociologists they read in college taught that consumerism is a disease, and yet now they find themselves shopping for $3,000 refrigerators. They laughed at the plastics scene in *The Graduate,* but now they work for a company that manufactures . . . plastic." They must somehow "confront the anxieties of abundance" through strategies that give them a whiff of the bohemian patchouli. So instead of denying themselves their newfound elitism or shrugging off their anti-establishment leanings, they reconcile the differences (think Ben & Jerry's or Facebook offering an IPO!).

To understand Bobos and their anxieties, Brooks suggests looking at their relationship with money. It's complicated. In the Bobo world, not all wealth is valued equally. According to Brooks, "in the 1950s the best kind of money to have was inherited money. Today in the Bobo establishment the best kind of money is incidental money. It's the kind of money you just happen to earn while you are pursuing your creative vision." The $500,000 dollars earned by a novelist of globally sensitive fiction is worth far more than the $15 million made by a real estate tycoon. They want to give the appearance that money doesn't really matter; in fact, it's a burden. If they happen to make a zillion dollars selling subversive pints of ice-cream, then so be it, at least they have stuck to their bohemian roots. Of course, to maintain the illusion that money really is not important requires quite a bit of cash. To maintain the balance of clashing value systems means that you buy a $900 hat that looks like it was worn by a struggling artist in 1920s' Paris. It means you go ahead and purchase the $3000 refrigerator, but you put it in a newly remodeled kitchen with wood floors salvaged from a nineteenth-century French monastery.

Lena Dunham, the twenty-five-year-old creator of *Girls,* has clearly drunk the Bobo latte. *Girls* is the wooden floor from the monastery, a tool used to soothe the restless bohemian spirit and reconcile the many facets of the Bobo persona. The show celebrates an atmosphere of bohemian caprice while shooing the bourgeois elements under the hand-knitted rug purchased from a recent immigrant in Union Square.

Take Hannah, the character loosely based on Dunham's own life and played by Dunham. She's a writer, but not a writer of novels or journalism, or even of poetry. Hannah is a writer of memoirs, and, of course, we are supposed to laugh at this. She has a very free relationship with money—she walks away from one job and will only take Bobo-appropriate work. McDonald's, as suggested by a friend, will not do. She needs money for rent and a phone, but not that badly. The show desperately wants to create tension around the question, How will Hannah pay her rent?, but this is the least successful element of the drama. It's a comedy, after all; does anyone doubt that the money will appear? And this is the Bobo mythology: We slacked our way through our twenties, and then just woke up one morning in our thirties as president of HBO Entertainment. It was magic.

The truth is that Lena Dunham is a very talented writer and director of a well-put-together series on a network known for giving us high-quality entertainment. The sort of hard work and drive that goes into producing a show of such quality cannot be found among the characters in *Girls.* But to portray holistically women like Dunham would be to show too much of the bourgeois side of the Bobo. The Bobo agenda is better served by depicting girls in their wandering twenties, still lost in the years just before their passionate and quirky individualism pays off. However, it strains credulity to think that characters such as these will end up with a hit TV show by the time they are twenty-five.

In spite of pointing out all of the Bobo's inconsistencies and silliness, Brooks is generally positive about the Bobo ethos and mission. So long as the Bobos can balance their two drives, he thinks that they have quite a bit to offer American society. The danger comes when that balance is lost, and this is the problem with *Girls* and the slacker myth it adores. By hiding the bourgeois drive and determinism that balances the Bobo teeter-totter, the show's creators suggest that through amoral, unprincipled wanderings one finds success, happiness, and, strangely, principles.

16. How Vocations Happen (It Could Happen to You)

Paul Lickteig, S.J.

I was just ordained a Jesuit priest.
The process took (about) eleven years.
Discerning a *vocation*, though . . . that is something else.
It's what I have been doing all along.

We all have stories that describe who we are.
For me . . . becoming a priest was not the tale I wanted to tell.
Of course, we often don't understand *vocations*
until they are already upon us.

So, sometimes I tell the story like I am revealing the life of a minor prophet:
I was just a humble lifter of furniture in the city of *Minneapolis*
stumble-bumming through a fantastic early-twenties existence
with my car and my motorcycle . . . yeah.

It was the early mid-nineties and I was listening to Revolution Radio and spoken word,
drinking coffee and spouting fantastic poems into the night sky.
I could be found in smoke-lit warehouses speaking "my truth," under a pseudonym,
or appearing on a stage called "Balls," at midnight, in the seven corners.

My friends were ex-junkies, street kids, skate-punks, wanna-bes and future felons.
We used to sneak into old buildings to throw up . . . art.
Genius dreams from spray cans spread out
on walls that no one would ever see.

This poem was originally published in *The Jesuit Post* on September 27, 2012.

And then it happened . . .
It's almost fourteen years since I heard "the call."
I can only tell you where I was because it was so completely unexpected,
and I was not all that inclined to listen.

But I did.
After spending years skipping Mass I had finally returned to church.
I felt like I needed to re-examine it . . .
faith . . .

I wanted to dig my fingers into the questions of existence,
to peel the rind off those slices of belief from my youth
and taste something real,
something that named what I felt in my core.

The being of God . . .
I knew there must be something more,
something so big that every word we pinned on it was just an entrée
into another way of seeing its presence.

So there I was on a "priest-drive" Sunday
listening to a gaunt, bespectacled face in the pulpit talk vocations.
"Have you or anyone you know ever thought of being a priest?
Well, call the number on this bulletin and we'll put you in touch with our trained staff . . ."

One minute everything was fine.
I was sitting in the back of church next to my older (much cooler) brother,
thinking about whether or not I was hungry.
The next thing I knew I was crying.

I could feel his eyes from the pulpit,
a guy in a collar I neither liked nor disliked (man or collar) asking me a question.
I put my head down and rubbed the outside of my eye, hiding my face,
trying not to sniffle in a way that my brother would notice.

Whiskey
Tango
Foxtrot
That was the beginning . . .

Like that.
A thunderbolt . . . of the softest kind.
"Oh God.
You duped me, and I let myself be duped."

Despite my best attempts,
I had become a believer.
And ever since
my *vocation* has been one long response.

Thirteen years gone since I met her,
"The one"
a proverbial "Brick House"
(according to the prophets "Commodore" in the book of Motown).

I realized only after some months
while I could not imagine wanting more
in my relationship with her
I could not ignore the feeling that something else was calling me.

Twelve years since I sat waiting in prayer
at some stupid retreat I could not even believe I was going on,
only to hear the words "Oh shit, I think I am going to be a Jesuit"
emerge so crisply and distinctly that my stomach turned in
excitement and fear.

Eleven years since I walked up the gray Novitiate steps
with a backpack and two large Tupperware tubs,
my entire life packed into twelve square feet,
and left my family and friends for reasons I could never quite name.

Ten years since I cried during Eucharist
in front of people that I loved,
for the second time,
and realized for the first time that the blood is real.

It is the blood of Christ mingled with every person,
man or woman,

who has ever tried to live for something more
than their own ends and desires.

Nine years since I lay in my bed at a Jesuit house in the Bronx
thinking of everything that I left behind
and I heard myself say
"I have made the biggest mistake of my life."

Eight years since I told my provincial that I was on the verge of leaving
and he said, "It sounds like you need to imagine
how your life needs to look for you to live it."
As one friend said, "If you are not free to go, you are not free to stay."

Seven years since I realized that my deepest desire was something I had known all along.
I wanted to be a preacher and confessor:
speaking words that few people would listen to,
ministering a sacrament most do not think they need.

Six years since I stood as a first-year teacher
in my poorly decorated classroom
filled with twenty fifteen-year-olds
realizing that *they* would teach *me* forgiveness and generosity.

Five years since I learned
how my greatest failures in keeping the vows
were not physical, but relational.
Vows not lived with patience and compassion are vows not lived at all.

Four years since I accepted
that my desire to live as a celibate
would require me to let go of my desire
to live with a woman.

Three years since I listened
to the critique of the most critical people I knew
and heard them tell me,
"We want you to be our priest."

Two years since I began again
to find life in places that I had thought were taboo:

laughing with renegade seekers,
those who had denied faith in anything at all.

One year since I felt agape:
a friendship so profound that I found myself
rearranging what I believed
a relationship based on vows could be.

One month since the oil bathed my palms,
and three hundred Jesuits placed their hands on my head.
I stood to a thunderous embrace,
as people who had loved me for years erupted in spontaneous
applause.

It was an affirmation of the church:
the people of God,
living out their faith in a time of pain, division, and uncertainty
but filled with hope.

I could hear them say,
"We Love You!" (sigh).
"So don't screw this up" (sigh).
Which Jesus knows is part of why I avoided taking this role
for years.

I never thought I would be vowed,
or learn to navigate the distance between liberals and conservatives,
but looking back, it could not have happened any other way.
See, the story was being told whether I was ready or not.

Our *vocations* are found in stories telling themselves all around us
in the voices of millions of seekers
naming the Truth that will define our lives.
The Truth we name is the Christ, the suffering redeemer.

I now listen to the narrative in millions of voices around me
and know that I am bound through an ancient faith
to a communal hope that transcends my personal narrative.
The story of *vocation* was never my own.

It mercifully unfolds and meshes with the stories of countless others
somehow naming a mystery
we will come to believe . . .

17. At the Corner of St. Peter's Square and Wall Street

Quentin Dupont, S.J.

When I tell people that I am a Jesuit with a background in business, the usual response is, "Oh, so you left stock prices and cash flows behind to be closer to God, right?" Ah . . . well, no. I'm actually interested in bringing business and God closer together. The standard response to this is a confused face—which is, not coincidentally, the same face I made as an undergrad when I discovered that there was a Jesuit on the business faculty.

I remember my first thought being "that's weird," quickly followed by "and that's really cool." To me, and to the church, the financial world is exactly where we ought to be; it's mission territory. While this might sound strange given how rarely we associate the Vatican with Wall Street, it's true. It's also intriguing, because at first it can be hard to see what a conversation between a CEO and a bishop would be like. But that doesn't mean it ought not happen.

#The Finance–Church Puzzle: Standing on Street Corners

There's a long history of Jesuits standing on street corners in the great cities of Europe, preaching the Good News to the world from the pulpit of the curb.[1] Standing at the corner of the church and the world of finance fits squarely in that tradition. The whole idea is based on a simple belief that the church and finance can learn from each other.

Assuredly, the world of finance is in need of some learning. Since the crash of 2008, the financial landscape has shown its "Wild West" side, and the six years since then have revealed some very real and very dangerous difficulties within the global financial system: financial crises, plummeting housing prices, surging unemployment, banking scandals small and large. When I

1. See John W. O'Malley: *The First Jesuits* (Cambridge, MA: Harvard University Press, 1993).

ANC PETRAM
IAM MEAM. T
ES PETRVS
ZED9.5
CLAVES REGNI
ANG8.5

talk about finance with the less-business-minded, usually they are more likely to bring up rogue trading scandals, financial mismanagement, and organized cheating than the church. They're not wrong to do so, either. In fact sometimes the financial news has been so dark lately that even someone as finance-philic as myself ends up wondering what else could possibly go wrong. How am I to react as a man trying to see the Good News in the financial news? Is there any Good News to be heard?

Oddly (or maybe not), it's the church that has affirmed that there is. Two church documents in particular have developed this affirmation. The first is Benedict XVI's 2009 encyclical *Caritas in Veritate*,[2] which has reminded me what business fundamentally is, namely, a particular relationship still rooted in love for the world and one another. The second came from a less-well-known source, the Pontifical Council for Justice and Peace, and is called *Vocation of the Business Leader: A Reflection.*[3] It was impactful because of its reminder that being a businessperson involves a personal calling to improve society. Reading these documents in recent years has helped keep me from two extremes: turning a blind eye to the problems we're facing, and condemning without offering any positive insights. The church is not saying that mistakes haven't been made—surely they have. Instead, though, it's taking the opportunity to offer a reminder that it isn't economic structures themselves that are bad (although a particular structure might be). It's a reminder for which yours truly is grateful.

On the other side of the ball, finance professionals are trying hard to understand how and why our financial system went bad. For an interested party there are a couple of particularly helpful places to look. The first is the many "financial crisis" reports coming into and out of the halls of Congress.[4] And the second are the analyses being performed by various academic communities (including those those that were discussed at conferences[5] and those written for a larger public[6]).

So, the finance community is in search of deeper answers.[7] And the church is looking to talk. How about that for an intriguing street-corner conversation?

---

2. Benedict XVI, *Caritas in Veritate*. Online at http://www.vatican.va.

3. Pontifical Council for Justice and Peace, *The Vocation of the Business Leader: A Reflection*, published in 2012. Online at http://www.stthomas.edu.

4. Financial Crisis Inquiry Commission (and dissenting views), http://fcic.law.stanford.edu/report. Many other reports and accounts exist, some more journalistic, some more academic.

5. For example, Alan Blinder, Andrew Lo, and Robert Solow, eds., *Rethinking the Financial Crisis* (New York: Russell Sage Foundation, 2013).

6. Robert J. Schiller, *Finance and the Good Society* (Princeton, NJ: Princeton University Press, 2012).

7. For example, see Kenneth R. French, et al., *The Squam Lake Report: Fixing the Financial System* (Princeton, NJ: Princeton University Press, 2010).

#Why the Church Cares about Finance

The church's involvement in economic issues is not a recent fad—it's even older than the Jesuit economics teacher I had when I was an undergrad. Truth is, the church has walked with the ups and downs of economic innovation for much of its history. And over the last hundred or so years it's put together a body of literature called "Catholic social teaching," or CST, for short. CST was given birth to in 1891 by Pope Leo XIII, when he wrote an encyclical (basically a papal open letter) titled *Rerum Novarum*. This first encyclical coincided with the burst of industrialization. *Quadragesimo Anno*, written by Pope Pius XI in the middle of the Great Depression (1931 to be exact), addressed the economic crises of those decades. Much nearer our own, more prosperous, economic era, Pope John XXIII wrote his own encyclicals: *Mater et Magistra* in 1961 and *Pacem in Terris* in 1963. The list goes on, each letter (and the theological and economic thinking it sparked) contributing to a now-century-long dialogue. Over these years the church has continued to discuss economic change and innovation and to embrace free markets—all while emphasizing that care for the common good and the dignity of the human person must be an essential part of a functioning economic marketplace.

In light of all we've heard in the past six years about financial bubbles, judicial troubles, trading fumbles, and employment tumbles, the church has not backed down from this long-standing tradition. Benedict XVI's own 2009 encyclical, *Caritas in Veritate*, was published right at the heart of the financial hangover that followed the collapse of the subprime mortgage market.[8] Those were head-splitting times for me.

As a Jesuit, I didn't have to worry about my house being worth half of what it had been a month before, but my friends in L.A., Silicon Valley, and New York certainly did. I remember the pain and uncertainty I heard in their voices when a few called to tell me about having to "short sell" their homes, some after losing jobs or being cut from full to part time. Some called just in hope of a word of support; others wanting to understand exactly what had happened to them—why houses that had looked like such good investments had turned into money pits. And though I listened and did my best both to care for them and to answer, as a student of finance I found my explanations lacking. And I wasn't alone. Even the best economists have found it difficult to understand precisely why the bursting of the "subprime mortgage bubble" coated the rest of our economy with a film of recession during those years.

8. It's also part of a trilogy of encyclicals written or co-written by Pope Emeritus Benedict XVI on the theological virtues of hope (*Spe Salvi*), love (*Caritas in Veritate*), and faith (*Lumen Fidei*).

With even the best of economists in disagreement about how the mortgage crisis triggered a major global economic slowdown, it might seem like hubris for an eighty-plus-year-old theologian to weigh in. But weigh in Pope Benedict did, and, if I might say so, quite effectively. This efficaciousness was precisely because Pope Benedict's response was steeped in CST and in the vision of what it means to be human that it contains.

As such, *Caritas in Veritate* presents the economy in a quite Catholic way. For Benedict, the economy isn't primarily a profit machine; it's a mechanism for right relationship—including solidarity with and care for the poor. Benedict was asking different questions than were economists, valuable questions about how the economy could learn from CST; how it could be more just. From the church's perspective, it's these things that give economic activity a purpose at all. For the church, economics is a means to a better world, not an end in itself.[9] In his own suave style, the pope offered a critique of a system that had become too detached from these principles, too anchored in self-gain, and too uprooted from the love that shapes our lives and directs us to care for one another.[10] But while Benedict was preaching the Good News on the corner of Wall Street, others did not see a fundamentally good structure that had been ill tended.

#99 Percent v. 1 Percent?

In the midst of these economic earthquakes, the Occupy movement gave voice to a critique of the economic system as a whole and the financial realm in particular. And the "99 percent versus the 1 percent" slogan was more that just snappy rhetoric; it was an insightful call for a more just society. Like Occupy, the church is strongly in favor of building a more just society. It generally does not, however, think that the entire financial system has been corrupted and needs to be replaced.

To be sure, the economic system isn't perfect. There is information that should be shared but is not; there are thieves and rogue traders; there is even organized cheating—not that any of this is new under the sun. But just remembering that this has all happened before doesn't answer the question of whether the financial system has been fractured. It doesn't much help my friends who had to short-sell their houses after years of hard work. So what's going on? I think there are three things at play: First, financial markets are much bigger than they've ever been before. Second, they're more complex and

9. If you want to read more about this, you can read some of the so-called social papal encyclicals, or check out Pontifical Council for Justice and Peace, *Compendium of the Social Doctrine of the Church* (Washington D.C.: US Council of Catholic Bishops, 2005).

10. See in particular *Caritas in Veritate,* nos. 35-37 and 45-47.

competitive than ever before. Third, we all just know more about what's going on in the twenty-first century than we have in the past, more about the good and certainly more about the bad.

Let me start with that last point, that we know more today. For everyone involved in trading in financial markets, information has become currency.[11] These days it's easy for someone in New York to see that another someone in Paris is taking enormous positions on, say, market index futures.[12] And since we have journalists who specialize in just such financial information, not just other traders, you and I can know about this too. Which means that a couple of days later we all know that some trader from Société Générale in Paris lost some 2 . . . no, it's 4 . . . no, now it's 6 billion dollars because of some trade. As any journalist will tell you, this kind of transparency is by and large a great thing (especially since financial companies now have to disclose the identity of the rogue traders who were the cause of such enormous losses, hopefully preventing them from doing so again). And today there is arguably more transparency in the system than ever. So we hear about more scandals, not necessarily because there are more scandals than before, but because they are easier to uncover and often must be reported. Not coincidentally, Pope Benedict, in *Caritas in Veritate*, argued for still greater transparency. And he's right: There is hope that more information flow allows us to sort the wheat from the chaff more easily.

At the same time, though, more information available means that the competition for information has greatly increased while the ability to take advantage of it has decreased. I'm not talking about Martha Stewart getting prosecuted for insider trading here. At the level of the finance industry, traders and bankers are under enormous pressure to act quickly because squeezing profit out of information everyone has is harder. Since decision makers have less time to act, they are going to make riskier decisions because . . . who knows when they'll get the next chance? Just like in Vegas, less time to think and more doubling down means more bad bets.

And it's undeniable that the size of financial markets, and the influence of finance over the economy, have both increased tremendously over the years. Not only individuals but entire firms are under greater pressure to perform as the number and kinds of financial actors and financial instruments have

11. I'm thinking of something a bit more advanced than Yahoo! Finance here. Information service subscriptions (Bloomberg, Thompson-Reuters) allow finance pros and journalists to have access to real-time, or quasi-real-time, information on financial transactions, especially their size and nature (e.g., that 10,000 shares of GM at $30.24 were exchanged on Friday at 10:22AM).

12. That amounts to taking a bet that, say, the S&P 500 benchmark index—or its equivalent on a foreign market—will go up, or down, depending on the direction of the trade.

multiplied by the dozens, if not the hundreds.[13] I cannot think of any industry—not even the aeronautic or the tech industry—that has complexified as rapidly as the finance industry. And this isn't just the increased complexity of the same kind of instruments we used thirty years ago, it's new ways of practicing finance that hadn't been thought of in 1980, which means there are also more ways of being at risk than there were when Ronald Reagan took office.[14]

So, markets are bigger, more complex, more loaded with information and rules, and more cutthroat. It's after recognizing this that critics of the current financial system ask a pointed question: How is all this systematic change not a systemic problem?

Given those factors, you could argue that it is. But what we'd be saying then is not that the systematic structure is flawed, it's that we human beings are operating it at too high a speed. These new factors we just discussed aren't bad in and of themselves; they are just products of creativity and greater efficiency. And creativity and efficiency are both good things—as long as they are properly thought out. That's the key here. We may have super-fast trading computers, but they still need to be programmed adequately. We have more information, yet it still needs to be read well and interpreted carefully. The "weak link" and the rich soil of financial markets are not techniques or instruments so much as they are human beings that form the system and give it direction. That's why the church is so insistent on taking seriously the intentions and motivations of the human beings involved in the markets.

And that's why the *Vocation of the Business Leader* document is such an important part of the conversation between the church and finance. This document takes the "bottom-up" view, starting with the people who live and work within the financial system, and aims at explaining why doing good can also mean doing well financially. The *Vocation* document shows how the principles of Catholic social teaching apply to actual business practices, and explains why the church speaks to business in the way it does. While it stops just short of offering a step-by-step implementation plan, it's a practical document written in direct language. It's so clear that I've had former colleagues from my

---

13. Back in the day there were regional banks and maybe some investment funds. Now we have national banks, international banks, money market funds, index funds, hedge funds, holding companies, private equity firms, venture capitalists, etc. In terms of financial products, the old cash/stock/bonds combo has exploded into thousands of products that offer greater flexibility but also more room for error.

14. Planes are pretty much the same thing they were thirty years ago, and the room for change is quite finite (even though a new way to make a plane can be incredibly damaging: look at Boeing's Dreamliner). Computers are much faster and more able than they ever have been. But the kind of computer or operating software we use has not grown as wildly as financial instruments have. There are desktops, laptops, tablets, and smartphones. Each on three or four platforms. In financial derivatives alone, there are dozens of types of structured notes; in mutual funds, dozens of possibilities and mixes of assets. The list goes on.

business school teaching days telling me of their plans to write about *Vocation* for business journals. Now that's the start of an interesting conversation on a Wall Street corner.

Deep down, the message of *Vocation* is the same as it has been in the tradition of CST documents: Human dignity and care for the common good ought to be made the center of our financial fabric. And lest I give the impression that this completely flies in the face of all of business theory, I ought to note that, as finance professionals move away from the obvious inadequacy of the perpetually self-interested and always-optimizing "homo economicus," other models of motivation and decision making will be needed.[15]

From where I stand, it certainly looks like the worlds of church and finance are ready for a street-corner conversation like the one I had with a colleague on my way to class one day about the role of the church in the financial world. As we bantered arguments back and forth, our voices rising and falling as we spoke and listened, students began to gather around us. They were fascinated, puzzled, intrigued, interested. It was seeing their interest that filled me with hope. "This is possible," I thought to myself later that night, "they actually were wondering what the church had to do with the markets."

Still, triggering such interest will happen only if we remember that dialogue involves both speaking and listening. Let's have a look at what the church has to say on a couple of particular points.

#CST-Based Reforms

So where is this conversation going? Well, the church has recently waded into the shark-infested waters of concrete economic plans by proposing specific reforms for the global financial system. In particular, it has recently argued for the creation of an international financial "watchdog."[16] The church uses the CST principle of subsidiarity (that problems should be solved at the lowest possible level) as the hinge of its argument for the implementation of such an international financial authority. This watchdog would be a sort of combination of the United Nations and the Security and Exchange Commission.[17]

While it might sound outlandish or out-of-reach, this is a practical suggestion, one that squares directly with the current "do we need more regulation?"

15. The field of behavioral economics, and in particular behavioral finance, which aims at studying psychological bias in economic/financial decision making, continues to develop. A very readable introduction to behavioral finance is Hersh Shefrin, *Beyond Greed and Fear: Understanding Behavioral Finance and the Psychology of Investing* (London: Oxford University Press, 2007).

16. Pontifical Council for Justice and Peace, *Towards Reforming the International Financial and Monetary Systems in the Context of Global Public Authority*. Online at http://www.vatican.va.

17. The S.E.C. regulates financial markets here in the United States.

debate. It also benefits from one of the church's unquestioned strengths, which is this: The principles of CST aren't steeped in the ideological divides that so often dominate our current imagination. That is, it is able to avoid a portion of the current "I hate regulation" vs. "We always need more rules" impasse by putting the principle of subsidiarity into practice. In this case, subsidiarity holds that, since problems should be solved at the lowest organizational levels possible and at the highest level necessary, and since we have a global financial crisis, we need a global body to address the problems facing us. In other words, for the church this proposal is not about reining people in or keeping them free. It's about creatively solving a problem where it can best be solved by human beings in possession of inalienable dignity.

It's this kind of priority given to the dignity of human beings that Pope Benedict also echoed in a beautiful passage of *Caritas in Veritate*. He writes,

> Finance, therefore—through the renewed structures and operating methods that have to be designed after its misuse, which wreaked such havoc on the real economy—now needs to go back to being an instrument directed towards improved wealth creation and development. . . . Financiers must rediscover the genuinely ethical foundation of their activity, so as not to abuse the sophisticated instruments which can serve to betray the interests of savers. Right intention, transparency, and the search for positive results are mutually compatible and must never be detached from one another. If love is wise, it can find ways of working in accordance with provident and just expediency.[18]

As I read this one thing in particular stood out: This is a vision of finance based on love. Of course, the question of how to implement such a call must also include finance experts—all dialogues must include two partners. But the surprising thing is that such experts are already engaging in a very similar conversation. Finance academics such as Robert Schiller and Alan Blinder are presenting their views in the pages of the *New York Times* and the *Wall Street Journal*. These are two smart guys who care about the common good as well as the good of the financial system, and who express their concerns and ideas in a simplified vocabulary and through an accessible medium. The stage is set for a discussion between CST-professionals and finance experts such as these.

Both parties can benefit from this conversation and its outcomes, if for no other reason than that the church's social doctrine can help the financial world articulate one of its fundamental assumptions: that trust between people

18. *Caritas in Veritate,* no. 65.

possessing dignity is inherent to any business relationship; that fairness builds the common good; that justice is implicit in any kind of contract enforcement.

Financial and economic structures can provide the means to the church's goal of realizing greater human dignity throughout the world, decreasing and eventually eradicating poverty, and sharing resources and wealth more equitably. This wealth, as recent popes have emphasized, is not simply made of dollars. It is primarily the wealth of personhood, the joy of being, of forming community; dollars facilitate this, certainly, but they can't replace it.

There is a space for Wall Street pinstripes to meet Vatican church types. There is a community to be formed and deepened at the corner of Wall Street and St. Peter's Square.

18. The Guinea Worm, or In Defense of a Fiery Serpent

John Shea, S.J.

Let me begin, if I may, with the story of a fiery serpent. Well, OK, it's also a story of the Exodus and of whining and punishment and healing, too, but mostly it's about fiery serpents. It goes like this:

> From Mount Hor they set out by the way to the Red Sea, to go around the land of Edom; but the people became impatient on the way. The people spoke against God and against Moses, "Why have you brought us up out of Egypt to die in the wilderness? For there is no food and no water, and we detest this miserable food." Then the Lord sent fiery serpents among the people, and they bit the people, so that many Israelites died. The people came to Moses and said, "We have sinned by speaking against the Lord and against you; pray to the Lord to take away the serpents from us." So Moses prayed for the people. And the Lord said to Moses, "Make a fiery serpent, and set it on a pole; and everyone who is bitten shall look at it and live." So Moses made a serpent of bronze, and put it upon a pole; and whenever a serpent bit someone, that person would look at the serpent of bronze and live. (Numbers 21:4-9)

It's a good story, and not only because of the homiletic wisdom that, no doubt, has been wrung from it over many years by many preachers. Aside from being the occasion of some inflammatory rhetorical brilliance, this little passage has long been the subject of curiosity by scientists and biologists and parasitologists—such as myself. Because, while we'll probably never be sure, there are some scientists who think that they have identified the ancient scourge mentioned in the book of Numbers. They think that the fiery serpents might actually be the parasitic nematode *Dracunculus medinensis*, that is, the Guinea worm.

"Wait, the what?" I can hear you asking. Yeah, fair. And it's a fair question, because while cases of Guinea worm disease were once common in rural parts of Asia, Africa, and the Middle East, only about five hundred such cases remain in the entire world. Thanks mainly to the efforts of the Carter Foundation, this painful disease "is poised to be the next human disease after smallpox to be eradicated."[1] Yep, modern medicine and the Carter foundation are poised to wipe the fiery serpent from the face of the earth. Take that bronze serpent on a pole.

But hold the party just a second. Before we celebrate too much, we ought to think about just what it is we're celebrating. Namely, the intentional—and eternal—extinction of a living being.

Now, I'm not saying that those who suffer from this disease don't deserve to be healed—not at all. What I am saying is that, as a Christian, I believe that God created the world and "found it was very good" (Gen. 1:30). I also believe that, unless Genesis has a long lost, secret "exemption" clause, this *good* creation includes parasites such as mosquitoes, malaria, hookworms, and, yes, even the Guinea worm. I agree with writer Evelyn Underhill, who once wrote, "All things are perceived in the light of charity, and hence under the aspect of beauty; for beauty is simply reality seen with the eyes of love."[2]

Beauty is reality seen with eyes of love. But how can we learn to look lovingly at something like a parasite? I'll admit that, for many, it's not easy. But that doesn't mean it's impossible, or not worth our time. After many years of studying and teaching about parasites, I've come to realize that it was learning the stories of parasites that allowed me to see lovingly, and so better appreciate their goodness and beauty.

I'm going to come out and say it: By virtue of being created by God, these parasites must, in and of themselves, be *good.* And it's their stories that so often help us to see them as they truly are—as God sees them. So, despite the suffering and death parasites cause (which admittedly can be catastrophic) can we find some good and beauty in the Guinea worm? Can we look at it lovingly? Let's start with what we know.

#

Humans become infected with *D. medinensis* by drinking water contaminated with infected copepods (which are basically tiny swimming crustaceans). These parasites then mature in the abdominal cavity of their human hosts, growing up to three feet long before mating. (Yeah, sometimes even I need to

1. http://www.cartercenter.org.

2. Evelyn Underhill, *Mysticism* (Santa Cruz, CA: Evinity Publishing, 2009), Kindle Electronic Edition, Location 4859.

pause for a second when it dawns on me that there can be three-foot worms mating in our bellies. OK, on with it.)

About one year after infection, fertilized females migrate to the skin surface, where a burning blister forms. Then, when the human host seeks a water source to alleviate the burning, the blister bursts open and the female releases her larvae into the water supply where a copepod can consume them, thereby continuing the life cycle. Now I know this sounds kind of gross, but in all honesty it's pretty amazing. I mean, other than Sigourney Weaver in *Alien*, it's pretty rare to see a "lowly" parasite manipulate the behavior of its human hosts to facilitate its life cycle.[3] No, think about it—*D. medinensis* has actually dictated human behavior. How did it come to do this? We don't know.

And this is only one of a whole set of questions *D. medinensis* raises that we haven't answered yet. We still don't know how this manipulation occurs, or how the parasite avoids the human immune system. And we still don't know whether infection by the Guinea worm confers any benefit to the host. We don't even know how this parasite shaped our own evolutionary history. Relatively few research papers have been published on these questions in the scholarly community, and the opportunity to answer these questions seems to be fading fast. (Of course, there is at least one good reason for this dearth of studies: Rearing *D. medinensis* requires a human host.)

Wiping this parasite from the face of the earth means not only eliminating a created being, it means that humanity will forever lose the answers to these important biological questions. But biological unknowns are only part of the story that might help us learn to love the Guinea worm. History is another, and if the Guinea worm is eradicated, we will lose an important player in both biblical and medical history.

#

Scientists and biblical historians have come up with three reasons for believing that the "fiery serpents" (also called "seraphs") of Numbers actually refer to *Dracunculus* (from the Latin for "little dragon"—also the name I want to give my dog if my Jesuit superiors ever let me get one).

First, consider the symptoms. In the second century BCE, the Greek historian Agatharchidas of Cnidus[4] describes the disease caused by the Guinea worm: "The people who live near the Red Sea are tormented by an extraordinary and hitherto-unheard-of disease. Small worms issue from their bodies in the form of serpents which gnaw their arms and legs; when these creatures are touched they withdraw themselves and insinuating themselves between the

3. Yes, I suppose the *Body Snatcher* movies qualify too. Good work, *Body Snatcher* fans.

4. Now that, my friends, is a name.

muscles give rise to horrible sufferings."[5] Thus, we actually have pretty solid ancient evidence that the Israelites could have been exposed to the Guinea worm, and that the burning felt by Israelites "bitten" by the snake may actually refer to the blisters created by the parasite.

Second, we have an epidemiological reason for suspecting the Guinea worm. Not to dismiss Robert Frost, but sometimes I think that other famous poet, Jerry Seinfeld, was right when he said that the road less traveled is less traveled for a reason. In the book of Numbers, we read that the Israelites detoured around Edom, taking the Red Sea route. Perhaps they didn't know the locations of safe drinking water along this different route. Desperate for water in the desert, they may have exposed themselves to contaminated water supplies and thereby been introduced to our endangered friend *Dracunculus*.[6]

Finally, the ancient cure for the Guinea worm, still preferred today where surgery is not possible,[7] actually resembles the biblical description of the bronze serpent on a pole. The ancients would remove the parasite with a small stick, around which they would wind one end of the worm. Over the course of a few days,[8] the stick is slowly wound up, pulling out more of the worm and preventing it from retreating back into the blister. If, however, the procedure goes awry and the worm breaks and dies under the skin, the result is an intense burning sensation (and an increased risk of secondary infection). This suggests that Moses' staff, wrapped in a bronze serpent, may well have modeled the worm removal procedure.[9] If the historical roots of this passage lie in parasitic worms, then the text may make more literal sense with those who "looked at the bronze serpent" representing those who underwent the treatment of winding the worm around a stick and being healed.

This has relevance beyond biblical history as well. If this "parasite hypothesis" is correct, then it may also explain the origins of the Rod of Asclepius, which depicts a single "snake" intertwined around a pole (see the drawing on p. 125). Asclepius was the Greek god of medicine and healing, which is why his rod symbolizes professional medical associations. Most theories that try to explain the origins of this symbol assume that a snake is wrapped around the rod. A more likely explanation is that it's not a snake, but our friend the Guinea worm who is wrapped there. This means that it's the Guinea worm that lies at the origin of this ancient symbol for the treatment of disease.

As provocative, even as *possible*, as this idea is, I don't want to pretend

5. L. S. Roberts and J. Janovy, citing Agatharchidas of Cnidus, in *Foundations of Parasitology* (7th ed.; New York: McGraw-Hill, 2005), 479.

6. Ibid., 482.

7. Ibid., 481.

8. !!!!!!! Days!

9. Maurice B. Gordon, "Medicine among the Ancient Hebrews," *Isis* 33.4 (1941): 475.

it's foolproof either. One of the more serious problems with our fiery serpent hypothesis is that it does not explain why the author of Numbers didn't simply use the word "worm" to describe this typically small (40–800 millimeters,[10] or about half the size of most cell phone charging cords) nematode. Another problem with this parasite hypothesis is that the Israelites describe people dying after being bitten by the fiery serpent. *D. medinensis* on the other hand, although very painful, is rarely fatal. But let's recall simple human psychology. People who complain—like, say, the Israelites wandering in the desert—tend to exaggerate to justify their complaints. In the same way a small garden spider becomes a huge, cat-eating tarantula, a small worm can quickly become a fatal serpent, especially if the burning infection occurs in an, ahem, sensitive area of the male anatomy.

#

Even with such an illustrious history and with important scientific questions still unanswered, the Guinea worm has few defenders. Still, the imminent demise of this parasite has inspired the Save the Guinea Worm Foundation. Their Website has existed for at least the past five years, but is almost certainly a hoax. Still, the site correctly points out that the Guinea worm faces extinction and claims to defend the world's most endangered species. The site contrasts the eradication of Guinea worms with smallpox, noting, "the Guinea Worm is not a disease microbe, but a living animal. It has a nervous system. Its hearts pump blood through its small body. It experiences pain."[11] Despite its satirical tone, the site does raise an important ethical issue:

> The Guinea Worm has few defenders. Guinea Worms are neither cute nor fluffy. An animated Guinea Worm with a humorous voice has never appeared in a Disney movie. Yet the Guinea Worm is as endangered as any species today. When the last one has been killed, the earth's biodiversity will have been irrevocably harmed.[12]

They are right. It will have been. Though it is one of Earth's many endangered species, why should we care about the Guinea worm? Why bother saving a parasite most consider disgusting and which has been the cause of so much suffering over humanity's evolutionary history? Can protecting the health and well-being of our fellow humans justify the extinction of God's creatures through disease eradication programs? Could the same justification

10. Roberts and Janovy, *Foundations of Parasitology*, 479.
11. http://www.deadlysins.com/guineaworm/crisis.htm.
12. http://deadlysins.com/guineaworm/foundation.htm.

apply to hunting, overfishing, and habitat destruction? To avoid this we need to discern carefully how and when we justify the intentional extinction of a species.

Failure to do so risks the permanent loss of amazing creatures—including the Guinea worm. Despite the suffering it causes, this little worm, with its remarkably complex life cycle, offers a wealth of scientific information and plays an important role in humanity's religious, medical, and evolutionary history.

While few will mourn the Guinea worm's extinction, I hope this tribute will help us all remember this astonishing parasite's story. And remembering its story will help us appreciate its value and goodness in the eyes of God. And this can help us discern our relationships with creation and with one another.

Not that the fight to save the Guinea worm is quite over yet. In fact, if you feel called to act on behalf of the Guinea worm, you can always sign up at the Save the Guinea Worm Foundation to be a Preserver, offering your body to host a few parasites. I tried, but every time I log onto to their website they claim to have received an overwhelming response and will not consider any new applications.

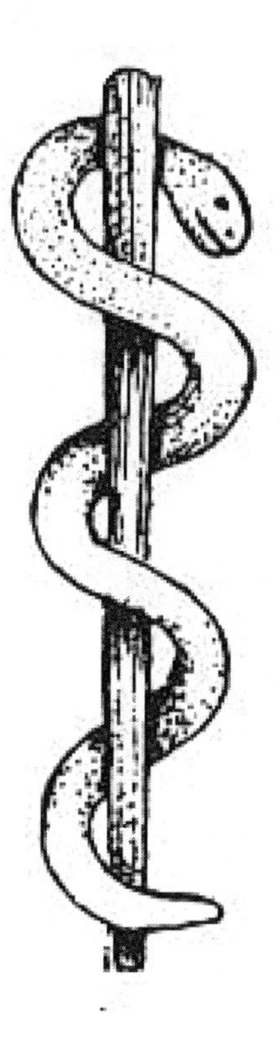

The Rod of Asclepius, symbolizing healing and medicine, may depict the ancient treatment for Guinea worms.

19. The Tyranny of Possibility and the One Thing Wanted: Freedom, Commitment, and the Duty of Love

Brendan Busse, S.J.

> Happy is the man who no longer thinks all possibilities are open to him.
>
> —Søren Kierkegaard

What do you want to be when you grow up? This used to be a question for children. More and more we find ourselves answering it into our third or fourth decade of life. I've heard it said that the thirties are the new twenties. I wonder what that even means, especially if, as I've also heard, the forties are the new thirties and the fifties are the new forties. Apart from the implications of this game for the first ten years of our lives, all of this seems a bit ridiculous. We can slide these scales all we want, and this may make us feel better for a while. But the question's still there. We ought to figure out what it is we want in this life while we still can.

When we are young, our desires are fickle, rooted perhaps in some fundamental interest or passion but generally applicable in a thousand ways. Kids are adaptable by design; their minds malleable, creative, open. They are flooded with options and teeming with potential. What did I want to be when I grew up? It's hard to say because there were a lot of answers. I would often say that I wanted to be an architect, mostly because I liked watching *This Old House* and because there were some changes I wanted to make to my own. When I broke my arm in the third grade I said that I wanted to be a scientist. This was so I could invent a more comfortable cast for people with broken arms. Mostly I just wanted there to be less suffering in the world. I wanted people to treat one another differently, and better. But what did I know? I was just a kid.

Our desires alone don't change the world. But there is creative interplay between our desires, the actions that flow from them, and our lived experience. This is important to know about us. What we want runs into what we're offered, and in that great encounter is the stuff of life, the art of discernment and, I think, the secret to real freedom. Gandhi suggested that "we become the change we want to see in the world." This means that it's not just what we want but who we become that matters. We don't create the world we live in, but we must live creatively within the world that we're given.

As a child, I never claimed writing as a passion, and Jesuit life wasn't even imaginable, but the seed of those desires, the urge to creativity, finds its expression in my life now in words more than biomedical engineering or suburban remodeling projects. The latter options would have paid better I suppose, but I'm happy enough. To listen to people and their lives as a Jesuit, and to write about joys and sorrows as a fellow human being, is not the only thing I could have done with myself, but it's the one thing that I have. The one thing I have. Isn't that something?

#

We live in a culture that says we can have it all, that we are able to possess whatever we want. I don't think this is true. The truth is more conditional at least, more smudged with possibility. You *might* have it all. You *could* have it all, but you probably won't. You can't, actually. Unless, of course, by "all" you mean simply having what's yours to have. But in this sense it's not so much having it all as becoming wholly who you are; that is to say, being one who has it all together. This is different from saying you can have it all. One has something to do with the number of toys accumulated, and the other has something to do with maturity.

Søren Kierkegaard prayed once for the grace to "will one thing." Like most students of Kierkegaard, I'm not entirely sure what he meant by that, but I like the sound of it. I'd like to have the courage to will one thing. I'm not sure that I do, so I often wonder what the one thing I want might be so that I can ask for it. It's a clarifying exercise. In the middle of a busy day, taking a few deep breaths and meditating on the one thing wanted brings a purity of purpose to an otherwise distracted existence. It may change from day to day or hour to hour, but I find the asking and answering to be helpful. *Right now, in this moment, what is "the one thing wanted"?*

It could be anything. But, I assure you, it's probably not everything.

Having it all together—self-possession, that is—is a paradoxical thing. True self-possession requires that we give ourselves to something. There's the trick. Ignazio Silone writes, "In every period and in whatever society the supreme act is to give oneself, to lose oneself to find oneself. You have only what you give." Kierkegaard would say that we give our all when we find the grace to will one thing. He thinks it has something to do with the duty of love; it's about purity of heart, and the gift given and received is our self. In any case, you have to choose something. And choice means . . . well, it means you can't have it all. This is our predicament. You can only have it all when you give your all.

Perhaps our clichés about having it all are simply an indication that we've not yet chosen anything. We say things like this all the time: I like my life, my independence, and my freedom. But autonomy can be isolating. This generation, perhaps the freest of all, is also among the loneliest. It's the desolation of finding solitude at the cash bar of someone else's wedding, one you never really wanted to attend. The creeping pressure of adulthood pushes options (and responsibilities) at us. They emerge in the nasally voices of concerned relatives—"Aren't you getting married soon?" It's not that we have only one option that bothers us as much as our fear of what might happen when we actually choose one.

It sucks being a single young adult at endless weddings and baby showers answering (or not answering) that childish "what do you want to be when you grow up" question because most people only want an answer that involves your being someone other than who you already are. For many years the response buried deep inside of me was, "F--k off. Let me drink in peace." The most helpful answer? Not quite. Immature? Absolutely. Honest? That too.

T.S. Eliot puts it a bit more, well, poetically than I did at the time in his poem "East Coker": "Do not let me hear/ Of the wisdom of old men, but rather of their folly, / Their fear of fear and frenzy, their fear of possession, / Of belonging to another, or to others, or to God." Eventually our childish desire needs to choose something, to commit to something, or, even more frightening, to someone. This is hard to do. We're afraid of doing it because, as Eliot notes, it reminds us of finality, and finality reminds us of death. To choose one thing seemingly issues a death sentence to every other thing. And then there's the mire of second guessing. If I marry this person, what if . . . ? If I have this child, what if . . . ? If I promise poverty, chastity, and obedience, what if . . .

We feel trapped between the tyranny of possibility and the slavery of commitment.

It seems counterintuitive, but we begin to feel like our choice limits our freedom. It does so only in commitment. Endless choice is a thin kind of liberty. Real freedom is experienced in becoming who you're meant to be, who you most deeply want to be. Real freedom consists in becoming who you are.

What is hard to see, if not impossible, is the freedom that lives on the other side of commitment. To choose to love someone, and to commit yourself to act upon that love, frees you from all paths that distract from becoming a lover. Of course, I'm free to stop loving this person, but only if I'm really free to continue loving them as well.

Here it is: Choice is made constantly in commitment. Freedom is exercised, and strengthened, as we affirm our choice in a thousand different ways as our lives progress and circumstances change. Freedom is claimed as our desires encounter our lives, which we cannot create but are given to us. To possess we must be possessed, to love we must be loved, and to live in freedom we must make a choice.

#

As a young adult I was really just waking up to my own desires. The vague and passive wants of my childhood became less appealing than the persistent and deeply rooted passions of late adolescence. I wanted to live simply and justly with others; I wanted community; I wanted to belong somewhere. These were deeper than my desires to be an architect or a scientist, and they endured long after I realized that math made my brain hurt.

Struggling to find a place to put them, I tried to put them every place. I tried putting them into my work, into my relationships. The fit was never quite right. Really, I failed to let them put *me* into any particular place. I failed to commit to anything, to really be present to anyone or any place. I was too concerned about the future, about where my choices would lead me. Mostly, I worried: about the possible consequences of any commitment, about which choice to make, about what I wanted to have. Rarely did I wonder about what I could actually do, what I had to offer, what I could give myself to.

Dag Hammarskjöld famously said that he didn't know where or when, but at some point in life he said yes to something. I found it practical, necessary, to start saying yes to things; and in each of my yeses I began making a life. Slowly. I made little commitments and received great gifts in return. What can I give myself to? Can I give two years to the Jesuit Volunteer Corps? Yes. Can I give myself to my work in campus ministry for a few years? Yes. Can I give myself to a three-day retreat to feel out whether I actually want to be married? Yes. Can I give myself two years as a Jesuit novice? OK, God, you are clearly insane. But yes, I suppose I can.

When I began to give myself to all of these commitments they returned the gifts, they gave me other options, other ways of knowing myself and the world around me. They opened up new possibilities, possibilities I could only know by having first committed myself.

Not everyone vows poverty, chastity, and obedience; you realize this the minute you do. But my vows, likc those of my married friends, have freed me from the tyranny of possibility to receive the grace of a loving reality. I live now in the freedom that comes on the other side of commitment—the very commitment to which we are often so highly allergic.

People I love sometimes grieve my perceived lack of freedom. Some days I join them; most days I don't. They ask me: *Wouldn't you like to have a wife and kids? Isn't the poverty thing a little restricting? How can you possibly tolerate obedience to this church or, for that matter, to anyone other than yourself?* Of course I can't live a life without love, a life of deprivation for its own sake, or submit to an abstract obedience that exists outside of real relationships of mutuality and trust.

But the truth is that my vows haven't asked me to do any of these things. My love is for real people; my poverty is a joyful simplicity; my obedience is to a particular person, a religious superior, not a faceless committee or an institution, but a real human being with his own gifts and weaknesses. My lived reality feels a lot more like freedom now that I've chosen a life and a way of loving that seem to be my own. In this commitment I find little to grieve.

#

Choice is a risky proposition. We may wander sometimes in the desert of our freedom. Like the Hebrew slaves liberated from Egypt, we may even wonder whether we were better off before our wild choice to flee—before we decided to trust that stuttering orphan Moses, before we saw the pillar of fire and the walls of water and all those drowned charioteers, before our living in the midst of those cruel plagues in which we found strange comfort. This is just to say that we may forget the hunger we knew before because of the thirst we carry with us.

But it's only the dead who live without hunger or thirst. To desire is to live. To choose is to become. To commit is to love. Egypt, like Sinai, was a desert, too. In one we were slaves and in the other we suffered for the love of our choosing. We failed a hell of a lot, but we practiced. We're still practicing.

On the other side of the dangerous desert of commitment lies the promised land, the only thing that really matters: the life you're given to live, the one that's yours. To avoid choice and commitment is to pretend to be something, anything, everything other than who you are. But to find your way toward that other side is to become more and more yourself and less and less the swirl of possibilities from which you arose. You came out of the mud of potential but to become the one you are, to do the thing you want, to will the one thing; you must become what this world needs in order to continue. You must become loving.

On a recent flight, I found myself gazing out of the window of the plane. Between one experience and another I found myself at peace in that particular place. A stillness filled me as I sailed hundreds of miles an hour through the blue sky. I asked myself that question: What's the one thing wanted? I could hear something deep inside of me express the desire for nothing more than what I had, to be nowhere other than where I was. My dry eyes thirsted for only that moment: for the clouds and those farms, for the mountain peaks and that distant horizon.

Like the Hebrews wandering in the desert I looked down upon that place; it could have been any place. I saw the promised land. I knew one thing: The land has been promised to us but we must choose to live there. Otherwise we're just pillaging wanderers, never responsible, never at home, forever enslaved. We must want to live in that land. The one thing wanted must be our God. The will to one thing ought only to be our duty to love.

20. Ministry on Death Row

George Williams, S.J.

For this is my body, which will be given up for you.

Saying these words, I lift up the host for the men inside the cage to see.

The "chapel" in San Quentin State Prison's Death Row is a windowless old shower room encased in a heavy metal cage. Inside it there are six wooden benches bolted to the floor, on which the members of my congregation sit. I stand, wearing both priestly vestments and a black stab-proof vest, inside my own cage, which is about twice the size of an old phone booth. As required by the department, I have padlocked myself inside. All this makes me, to my knowledge, the only Jesuit in my community who regularly celebrates Mass in a Kevlar vest.

There is a harsh florescent light overhead, and as I raise the consecrated host the light illuminates it. I look past the host to the men in the cage. They are quiet and focused. It's at this point of the Mass that I often imagine, as I am standing there facing them, separated by the steel mesh, that the light of Christ is streaming forth from that host, dispelling the dark shadows of "East Block"—San Quentin's Death Row for men.

There are 725 men currently condemned to death in the state of California—all of them housed at San Quentin.[1] I work as the Catholic chaplain on the largest Death Row in the United States,[2] possibly the Western Hemisphere. Some of these men have called Death Row home for over thirty years, ever since the death penalty was reinstated in California in 1972. Executions were resumed that year by Proposition 17, a voter initiative that amended the state's constitution, overturning previous court decisions that had found capital punishment unconstitutional. In the past thirty years far more men have died of old age (or from suicide) on San Quentin's Death Row than

A version of the essay was originally published in *The Jesuit Post* on July 23, 2012.

1. There are nineteen women condemned to death as well, but they are housed in another prison.

2. According to the Death Penalty Information Centers, accessed at http://www.deathpenaltyinfo.org.

the thirteen who have been put to death by the state. Their hopelessness and despair linger in the shadows, long after the bodies are wheeled out.

#

It is a building of many, many shadows. Visitors invariably comment on how eerie and dark the place looks and feels. The twelve-foot-high black doors at the entrance of the building, above which the word "CONDEMNED" is written in calligraphic lettering, don't help. Inside those doors, an almost palpable air of oppression broods over the place. There are plenty of ghosts too.

Walking onto Death Row, one is at first taken aback by the size of the place. As long as a city block, five floors (or tiers) high, the place looks like some kind of huge warehouse. There are windows that are so dirty that they are practically opaque. They let in a yellow light that does nothing to brighten the cavernous and lifeless space. There are fifty cells to each tier, so, standing at the bottom, you ought to be able to see 250 prison cells spread out in front of you. But you cannot; the cells of the top two tiers can't be seen from the ground level because the view is blocked by a wall of gray and black metal.

Death Row, perhaps surprisingly, is not very noisy. The loudest (and most annoying) noise is the incessant intercom at the guard's station, calling the Tier Officers to bring inmates to and from visits, medical appointments, or the shower. The concrete and metal walls trap the intercom's sound, echoing it back and forth. The cold space smells like a locker room mixed with a cafeteria mixed with an outhouse. As you walk past the cells, the smell of a recent bowel movement blends nauseatingly with the smell of a neighbor cooking rice and beans in a hot pot.

Each man has his own cell. Windowless, fronted by a heavy metal mesh, a barred door and a food slot with a cover that is padlocked shut most of the time, each cell measures five feet wide by about ten feet deep. The cells are dark and cramped. At the back of the cell, at about eye level, there is a shelf, and below it a stainless steel toilet with a stainless steel sink built into the top. A small, round metal stool is attached to one wall, and in front of the stool is a bed. Most of the men take the thin, one-inch thick cotton mattress and put it on the floor to sleep. They use the flat metal platform of the bed as a desk instead. All the men have small televisions, which are always on, and which provide them their only view of the outside world.

One set of cell fronts face east, toward the Bay that cannot be seen through the dirty windows. The other 250 cells face "the Yard"—a World War II-era, rusting, corrugated-metal-roof structure housing a dozen large, free-standing cages that look like kennels. It is inside these cages that the men on "walk-alone" status go to "recreate" for a few hours each week. These men are on "walk alone" status because they have shown themselves too dangerous to mix with other prisoners. It is these who are, in the main, responsible for the frequent stabbings and assaults that occur within a group of men who have nothing else to lose and who live in a tiny world of petty gossip and verbal abuse. Every man there has told me, at one point or another, that the worst part of his life on Death Row is loneliness. I have been surprised, during these same conversations, to learn that not all of the men on Death Row are against the death penalty. Some would welcome it.

#

This is my body which will be given up for you.

These words were spoken at the last meal of a man about to be condemned by the state and executed. It's strange how the words of the Gospel take on a different resonance on Death Row. Jesus, the executed prisoner, reflected in the eyes of men also sentenced to die. I know Jesus was innocent, and I know what these men have done to earn their cells and sentences. It took some doing on their part. It often took horrible, brutal crimes—the stuff of horror movies and nightmares. Over one hundred of these men tortured their victims before killing them. Nearly two hundred molested and killed children.

But as I raise the host, I don't see heinous murderers standing in front of me; I see human beings. And if his body were not given up for them too, then what difference would our religion make? The fact that his love reaches down into this pit of hell is what gives my life its meaning and purpose. I am often moved to tears at this part of the Mass, the part where it dawns on me again what a gift I have been given to be able to stand there and bear witness to the mercy of Christ embodied in this sacrament in such a dark place.

At the Sign of Peace we shake hands through our cages. This is the only point of physical contact with these men—they reach their hands through a 4-x12-inch slot in the mesh wall to shake mine. I am often surprised at the way they grasp my hand—there is so little human touch on Death Row. In some ways, it feels to me like they are trying to grab hold of a different reality than the cold and lifeless place they live in. The handshake of a serial killer, a child molester, a torturer, feels the same as any other handshake.

#

There are moments of (admittedly dark) humor too. Recently, one of my serial killer parishioners said to me, "Now Father, don't do anything I wouldn't do!" This is no doubt the best advice I've received from a serial killer to date.

It might seem strange to you, reading this, that I love this work. But I do. I feel it is the best ministry I could ever do; that I wouldn't trade it for tenure at Harvard. Seriously. When I leave the prison, or when I'm driving in to work over the Richmond Bridge with the breathtakingly beautiful Bay to my left, I feel like I must be dreaming to work at a place so charged with the power of the gospel.

But if there is any drawback for me about this work, it is well summed up in the words of Dr. Martin Luther King, Jr., who, in *Stride toward Freedom*, wrote, "He who accepts evil without protesting against it is really cooperating with it." Am I cooperating with evil by working in a system that I believe to be—in a very real sense—demonic? If the California voters act foolishly and fail to abolish the death penalty this November, how will I deal with the prospect of having to accompany some of these men I have come to know to their executions? Is my work on Death Row somehow being complicit in state murder?

Ultimately I don't think so. But, over many years of working in prisons and doing prison ministry, I have come to believe that prisons themselves are a mistake. I believe that they do far more harm to both prisoners and society than any purported good other than incapacitating and warehousing human beings.

The United States of America is now the prison capital of the world. We incarcerate a higher proportion of our population than any other country on earth. (And, yes, that includes China.) Structural and institutionalized racism lies behind the fact that, while blacks and whites commit crimes at an equal rate, one in five black men in America can expect to spend some time in prison in his life, while for white men the ratio is one in thirty-five.

So, no, my work in the prison does not mean I approve of prison. It means that I am going where the church often is absent. *If I don't go, who will?* I ask myself. There are not scores of priests banging on wardens' doors, begging to be hired as chaplains. I wish there were.

In the same way, if I were to choose to fight against prisons instead of going into them to minister to the prisoners (and the guards to some extent), what would I accomplish? Only my own exclusion. And I would never get to hold up the Blessed Sacrament as a sign of light and hope in a human hell. As a priest, I have come to see my work as one of resisting the evil of prison from the inside, where I find Christ living.

21. The Five Best Pieces of Jesuit Wisdom I've Ever Heard

James Martin, S.J.

Unlike most of the guys who write for *The Jesuit Post*, I'm not exactly a "young Jesuit." I'm fifty-one. (On the other hand, these days anyone under ninety could be considered "young" in a religious order.) But even though I may not know as much about the latest music (read: *nothing*) I have a leg up when it comes to experience.

I've been a Jesuit for twenty-three years. I'll spare you the complete description of my training, or "formation," as we say. (Short version: Boston to Jamaica to Chicago to Nairobi to New York to Boston to New York to California to New York.) Instead, I'd like to boil down the most helpful things that I've heard from my elders: those who have trained me, who have been my spiritual directors, who have been my superiors, and who have been my colleagues and friends.

All of these pieces of wisdom stopped me in my tracks and left me speechless; all of them changed the way I look at life, God, and my fellow human beings. And all of them, I hope, will be helpful to you, whether or not you're a Jesuit.

#1. "Allow yourself to be human."

In 1989, as a brand-new twenty-eight-year-old Jesuit novice in Boston, I was told that I would be sent to work for four months in the slums of Kingston, Jamaica. Though work with the poor was part of our life, I was terrified. Never having spent any time in the developing world, I was almost paralyzed with fear. What if I got mugged? What if I got sick? (It didn't help that one of the second-year novices kept telling me how dangerous it was; he was, by the way, exaggerating.)

A version of this essay was published in *The Jesuit Post* on February 8, 2012.

The night before leaving for Kingston I was sitting in the living room staring at (I was too nervous to read) *The Boston Globe*. An elderly Jesuit came in to say hi. Joe McCormick, an experienced spiritual director, was one of the freest people I knew: warm, open, joyful. "Ready for Jamaica?" he said. Out came my worries. Joe patiently listened to them all.

"What's your biggest fear?" he said. I told him that I was worried that I'd get so sick I would have to come home. That would be embarrassing, I thought darkly.

Joe nodded and said, "Can you allow yourself to get sick, Jim? You're a human being with a body, after all, and sometimes bodies get sick. The worst that could happen—coming home—isn't the end of the world. So why not just *allow* yourself to be human?"

A cloud lifted. Yeah, why *not* just relax and be human? Getting sick wouldn't be the end of the world. I went to Jamaica . . . and never once got sick. But I got more human.

#2. "You don't have to be someone else to be holy."

Too much of my time as a novice was spent trying to be like other people. I knew that I wasn't holy myself, and saw other novices who seemed far more holy, so, I figured, I needed to be like them. One guy was soft-spoken and diffident, and he was pretty holy, so I decided to be meek and mild. "What's wrong with *you?*" another novice said after seeing me piously moping around the house. Another novice woke up super-early and prayed before our morning prayers at 7 A.M. He seemed holy, too; so I started to get up super-early. "Wow, you look tired," one guy said. "Aren't you getting any sleep?"

Finally I said to my spiritual director, David Donovan, "I'm not sure how to be holy. Who should I imitate in the novitiate? Who's doing it right?"

"Jim," he said, "you don't have to be someone else to be holy. Just be yourself. *That's* the person God called into the Jesuits, after all." David's advice helped me to relax, and to be appreciated for who I was, not for who I wasn't. Plus I got more sleep.

#3. "You're not married to everyone."

When I was in philosophy studies at Loyola University in Chicago, I lived in a great Jesuit community, where I made tons of friends. But there was a problem: Many of the community members had, not surprisingly, different likes and dislikes. It was the first time I had lived in a large community with so many different ways of looking at life.

For example, one guy got annoyed if you didn't move his wet clothes from the washer to the dryer. ("Why didn't you put them in the dryer? They're all wet!") Another got angry if you *did* put them in the dryer. ("Why did you put my clothes in the dryer? They'll shrink!") Another guy didn't like to talk about his studies at meals: too stressful. Another did: It helped him let off steam. I found it hard to keep track. How could I please everyone? One day I said to my superior, "I feel like I have to remember what everyone wants. And what everyone's little likes and dislikes are. It's driving me nuts."

Dick Vande Velde, the director of the Jesuits in formation in Chicago, smiled and said, "You're not married to everyone, Jim. There's no need to please everyone. Plus, you couldn't if you tried. Just be kind and generous and the rest will take care of itself."

Behind the good desire to please everyone was the not-so-good desire to have everyone like you. Which is impossible. Even Jesus in his earthly life wasn't universally admired. Why should I be?

#4. "Don't let anyone prevent you from becoming the person you want to be."

I'll keep this story vague. At one point in my Jesuit training I lived with a difficult person in community. (Imagine that!) He had many good qualities, but he was also argumentative and combative. (Eventually he would leave the Jesuits.) Since I was always running into him, it seemed that I was slowly changing in response. I was always on guard—combative and argumentative myself—in order to protect myself.

At one point, I told my spiritual director that his personality seemed to be making me into a different person, someone I didn't like. I was becoming someone in *reaction* to him.

"Don't let anyone prevent you from becoming the person you want to be," he counseled. "He has no right to do that, nor does he really have the power. God desires you to become loving and charitable. Don't let him distract you."

It was hard advice to follow. But it was essential. Rather than let someone else's problems mold you, become the person God wants you to become.

#5. "You're not Jesus."

After philosophy studies, I worked with the Jesuit Refugee Service in Nairobi, Kenya. It was fantastic work. (Needless to say, I had gotten over my worries about working in the developing world: I *asked* to go!) But gradually I started to fret about doing all that needed to be done. Our work was helping East African refugees start small businesses, which meant meeting with them on a regular basis, checking on their businesses (tailoring shops, bakeries, restaurants, chicken farms), helping them navigate their way through government agencies, arranging for them to get medical help when they were sick, and just listening to them. How could I do it all?

After a few months, I confessed to my spiritual director, George Drury, a New England Jesuit stationed in Nairobi, how overwhelmed I felt. "Where did you get the idea that you had to do everything all at once?" he said.

What a dumb question, I thought. Well, I said, that's what *Jesus* would do. *He* would visit them. *He* would check on their businesses. *He* would fix their problems. *He* would help to heal them. *He* would listen to them. And George said, "That's true. But I've got news for you: You're not Jesus! No one person can do everything. And even Jesus didn't heal everyone in Palestine." Accepting my limitations and my "poverty of spirit," that is, my own limitations, helped me to do my best and leave the rest up to God.

Later on, another spiritual director put it more succinctly: "There is Good News and there is the Better News. The Good News is that there is a Messiah. The Better News is that it's not you!"

22. Against Complacency: The Lessons of Victor Hugo

Vinny Marchionni, S.J.

As I walked into the local Jimmy John's to meet a friend for lunch, I was expecting a tuna sub and some good conversation. I would ingest much more than tuna during our lunch, though I did not know that then. Over the course of the hour or so we were together, my lunch partner relayed to me an issue with which she was grappling. Raised Catholic, she and her family had faded away from regular Catholic practice over time. When she had begun to notice something missing in her life, in the place previously occupied by religious observance, she filled this void by attending non-denominational Christian churches.

"Do you attend Mass much anymore?" I asked.

"Not really," she sighed, sipping a soda. "I just don't feel that comfortable or welcomed. The Mass is dry and I can't connect to the people there. Like, when I go to this other church, the music is up-tempo, the sermons are really practical, and everyone just seems to want to be there."

I expected a tuna sub. What I encountered was yet another victim of complacent Catholicism.

#

There is a deep desire among those who count themselves as both spiritual and religious for a worshipping community that is vibrant and warm. Some place where we really want to be, surrounded by people seeking a life-giving home. In my own experience of both worship and ministry in the church, I have been a part of congregations that have radiated the light of a happy, spiritually nourished community. In so doing, they radiated the light of God into the world. And the church has made great strides in the last fifty years or so, strides in the direction of openness to the world as it is today, and in the direction of meeting people where they are. As a small example, I think of my friends and I seeking (and finding) a Sunday evening Mass before dinner. As a weightier example, I think of my non-Catholic colleagues at the Jesuit high school where I teach.

But too often I have encountered people like the friend mentioned above. I wish she were alone in her experience, but she's not. It's a familiar story: People have chosen to part ways with Catholicism not because of a crisis of belief or disagreements over the major tenets of the faith, but because their experience of church is airless, lifeless, and brittle. Perhaps you've heard it from a friend or family member, as I have many times. Or maybe it is your story.

That airless, lifeless, and brittle community is what I call "complacent Catholicism." We as a church are complacent when our rituals and our teaching effect no movement, that is, when we do not allow the Spirit to move us to those we are supposed to serve. We are complacent when we erect walls—intentionally or accidentally—around our cozy Catholic clique; others can come to us, but always on our terms. Perhaps I sound presumptuous for speaking this way. Yet my experience tells me that for every positive, welcoming experience that people have in practicing the faith, there are as many negative experiences borne from a lackluster liturgy or pastoral ineptitude that demonstrates such complacency.

This is a big problem, and one that I think about often, because the people who are stepping away from the church are people I care deeply about. They are *good* people who have *good* desires and who seek God. Alienation is not a family value, so when I see people alienated from the community, I know something is amiss. If St. Paul was right in saying that we as church are the "body of Christ" (I think he was), then we may have to begin grappling with the fact that this body might look funny without hands, feet, and eyes.

Moreover, though the church is more than clerics and religious, we need to honestly admit that those of us who are "professionally religious" bear a disproportionate responsibility to challenge our complacency and to model a different way of being church in today's world. As a Jesuit in formation, this is a question that haunts me in the best possible way. It has prompted me continually to ask a number of questions: How am I being prepared for service? How can I help foster communities that radiate God's light into the world, rather than the stale congregations that seem to have "Enter If You Dare" in stained glass over the front doors of the parish? Simply put, am I really the symbol of God that people need me to be?

I've learned many lessons from many people, religious professionals and not, as I've continued asking these questions. But perhaps the most surprising teacher of all has been Victor Hugo.[1] (Yes, that Victor Hugo.) A novelist from the past has taught me how to shift from neutral to overdrive to challenge today's complacent Catholicism. While his popularity has sky-rocketed in

1. For an introduction to Victor Hugo's relationship with the church, see Doris Donnelly, "The Cleric Behind 'Les Mis,'" *The Wall Street Journal*, January 3, 2013, accessed July 15, 2013, http://online.wsj.com.

recent times with new versions of his magnum opus, *Les Misérables*, a broader look at Hugo's work has offered me different sketches of Catholicism and has allowed me to witness Hugo capturing a faith that ranges from awful to awe-inspiring.[2] What Hugo has shown me are the antitype and the archetype of the church minister—and of a Christian generally.

#

> There was no expression in his eyes, no feeling in his voice, no meaning in his gestures. Yet how could it be otherwise? The priest was the official chaplain of the prison.[3]

Written in 1829, *The Last Day of a Condemned Man* is Hugo's earliest novel and one of his lesser-known works. In it Hugo depicts the experience of a man condemned to death. We see the condemned anguishing over his life in his last days, scribbling final thoughts in a journal that no one will ever read. Hugo almost forces the reader to sympathize with a guilty man whose daughter no longer recognizes him and who desperately hopes for a stay of execution.

In *Last Day*, complacency takes the form of shallow routine. Perhaps oddly, considering how moving the storyline is, the one person who does not seem moved is the prison chaplain. He maintains a rigidity borne from rote recitation of rites and right teaching. The excerpt above describes the prisoner's meeting with the chaplain as he arrives to hear the condemned man's final confession. Both Hugo and the prisoner see this priest as a "good and charitable man" with a "kind and gentle face."[4] But that is all. The condemned is flabbergasted that the chaplain's voice does not move him, that the chaplain cannot inflame his heart with love, that the chaplain cannot even stimulate him intellectually. The condemned lukewarmly—but positively—responds to the chaplain's prodding to witness to his belief by reciting the Apostle's Creed. Yet the chaplain maintains a dismissive demeanor and then "talked a long time; he used many words."[5]

After the chaplain's eloquent discourse featuring Augustine and Gregory the Great, the condemned man is left feeling even more listless and despondent than he was at the outset. The prisoner is so despondent that he asks the priest to leave without making a final confession. In other words, he makes a

---

2. For a deep draught of Hugo's anti-clericalism, look no further than *The Hunchback of Notre-Dame*. Though I will not treat it in this essay, *Notre-Dame's* antagonist, Archdeacon Claude Frollo, is not the pastor any of us would want—nor the minister any would aspire to follow.

3. Victor Hugo, *The Last Day of a Condemned Man* (New York: Thomas Crowell, 1887), Kindle Electronic Edition, Chapter 30, Location 1266.

4. Ibid., Location 1252.

5. Ibid., Location 1257.

conscious decision not to receive any sacramental succor in his last hours. The priest only shakes his head in disappointment.

Hugo laments that the chaplain has fallen into a drab routine that fails to capture the Spirit's movement and fails to enkindle the spirit of the condemned. In the story, anonymity is a crucial concept. Hugo leaves both the condemned and his crime anonymous, and when it comes to making space for the reader to feel sympathy for the condemned man it is quite effective: The person and the crime remain separate. But anonymity is precisely the problem when it comes to the chaplain, who issues a numb and numbing exhortation that he has recited dozens of times to dozens of prisoners. He has been chaplain to that prison for years, and his ministry has become one size fits all. The condemned sighs that the chaplain no doubt "has his copybook" and he has rehearsed all his priestly lines.[6] No matter how benevolent, the chaplain lacks depth, prayer, and genuine knowledge of the condemned man. The chaplain is complacent with the thought that he has the answers and that the condemned can meet him where he is—not the other way around.

The condemned man desires exactly what so many seek from those who serve in ministry: an encounter with God. How he longed for a chaplain of deep prayer who brought him a fresh look at God. How he longed for a priest willing to be wrested from his regularly scheduled programming, those routines that carve the ruts of complacency. How he longed for the chaplain to be the symbol of the dynamic God who is all too eager to console the sorrowful and repentant. The condemned neither desired nor needed a prepackaged, moribund God and church. But that is all the chaplain could provide. And that is the real tragedy of *Last Day*.

#

> On the following day, the thirty-six patients were installed in the Bishop's palace, and the Bishop was settled in the hospital.[7]

Over three decades later, Hugo penned another novel that allowed him to express his frustration at a complacent church. Rather than a diatribe, *Les Misérables* tells an authentically Christian story of redemption. Giving us Bishop Bienvenu, Hugo offers the example of a man who shunned complacency by being continually open to the needs of the people. The beloved Bishop did not abide by the standard routine of his office and did not fear to let his interactions with the people change him. Previously known as Charles Myriel, this former nobleman lost everyone and everything in the years

6. Ibid., Location 1275.

7. Victor Hugo, *Les Misérables* (New York: Thomas Crowell, 1887), Kindle Electronic Edition: Volume 1, Book 1, Chapter 2, Location 343.

following the storming of the Bastille in July of 1789. When he resurfaced in France during Napoleon's reign, he did so not as a noble seeking to recover lost privileges but as a priest who avoided the social rank that had been his due. He knew that society had changed and that he too needed to change for the sake of those he served.

It is the movement of the Spirit that literally moves the Bishop from his home. Named bishop of the humble see of Digne, the Bishop's *modus operandi* differed greatly from that of his predecessors. He was to move into the "huge and beautiful" episcopal palace, a "genuine seigniorial residence." Adjoining it was a "low and narrow building of a single story"—the town hospital. On the third day of his service in Digne, the Bishop rose from his palace and toured the hospital with its director. Twenty-six sick persons were "crowded against each other" in the rooms that doubled as the hallway. As the director explained the hospital's plight to the Bishop, including its poor ventilation and frequent epidemics, he sighed, "What would you have, Monseigneur? One must resign one's self."[8]

For his part, the Bishop made it abundantly clear that this resignation was a symptom of the complacency that bogged Digne in a mire of a poor understanding of God. Such a view separated God—symbolized in the ministers—from the people who needed God most of all. Had the Bishop continued a cozy routine of saying a few prayers for the suffering and then enjoying a well-aged wine after supper with his guests, he and the rest of Digne would have accepted it: The poor people simply live in squalor; nothing can be done. Instead, he moves into the tiny hospital space and moves the sick into his own palace. As Hugo depicts it, such symbolic actions cannot but have a ripple effect.

In his actions the Bishop symbolized a God who continually sought to take part in the "gritty reality of the world."[9] And they went beyond a snazzy publicity stunt. He continually went to his people and invited them into a more habitable dwelling in keeping with their innate human dignity. This dwelling could be physical, as in the case of the hospital. It was also spiritual and social. Hugo spends page after page detailing how the Bishop ensured that he visited each of the "thirty-two curacies, forty-one vicarships, and two hundred and eighty-five auxiliary chapels" of his mountainous bishopric. Having sold his carriage for alms, a donkey served as his transport. When he found injustice, immorality, or just plain selfishness, he exhorted without being preachy and gave practical advice where he could.[10]

His movement toward the people moved the people themselves, among

8. Ibid., Location 316-33.

9. See Peter-Hans Kolvenbach, S.J., "Keynote Address at Santa Clara University's Justice Conference, October 6, 2000," http://loyola.edu/Justice/commitment/Kolvenbach.html.

10. Hugo, *Les Misérables*, Kindle Electronic Edition: Volume 1, Book 1, Chapter 2, Location 408, 425.

the most notable of whom was the escaped convict Jean Valjean. Recitations from Church Fathers or dry rites would not have moved Valjean. Such a circumstance would only have further alienated a man who trusted no one. Only living mercy could have softened Valjean's heart, a mercy enacted beautifully by the Bishop. After Valjean's encounter with the Bishop, he reforms his life; the rest is literary history.

#

I'm a daydreamer extraordinaire, and have often caught myself thinking as I read about the Bishop's exploits, "Gosh, you know, what if ... Nah, nevermind. It's impossible." Maybe it is. But although it's easy to brush off these works of fiction as mere fantasy, we do so at our church's peril. When we resign ourselves to thinking that these stories are just nice stories, we exhibit the same hopeless complacency as the director of the hospital in *Les Mis*. People in churches everywhere have met the priest from *Last Day*, ministers whose pastoral practice is so lifeless and rote that it's easy to begin wondering whether even *they* believe the stuff they're spouting. Thank God the opposite is also true. We've also seen what can happen when the gospel becomes more walk than talk.

In all these stories—whether my lunch at Jimmy John's, or Hugo's novels—the common truth is that we hunger for a God who is not complacent or comfortably ensconced in a distant heaven. We strain to know the God who is one of us, who is incarnate. Fortunately, God has a similar hunger: to be with his people, where they are. This is the God in whose name I am being formed to minister as a Jesuit, and the God that the church is called to incarnate in the world. This is the God who moves toward people who seek and hope to find. If we who serve in the church are distant, prepackaged, and complacent, then the people in (and not in) the pews will sense God as such. If we're generous, compassionate, and eager to know and serve them, then the people in (and not in) the pews will sense God as such.

To be sure, all of this is a tall order for the People of God and for their ministers. Complacency in Catholicism is not the type of thing that can be solved in an essay (or, for that matter, over a tuna sub). But the promise that Hugo holds out to all of us is not that the undertaking will be easy or even perfectly successful, but that in breaking out of our complacency—in drawing near to one another—we will also draw near to the God who calls us together in the first place.

23. S--t Christian Poets Say: The Problems of God-Talk, Sentimentality, and Style

Jayme Stayer, S.J.

Most contemporary Christian poetry is revolting. For all I know, there may be piles of finger-lickin'-good poems written for Muslim and Jewish consumption, but I can say with certainty that I would rather be crushed under a load of bricks than read another saccharine poem with the words "precious baby Jesus" in it. And yet, as a teacher and critic of poetry, and as a vowed Jesuit, I can't pretend I don't have an interest in poetic expressions of religiosity. The problem is not one of "taste" (preference or liking)—a narrow category of aesthetics whose primary function is to protect even the most boneheaded ideas from serious inquiry. The problem, in a nutshell, is one of style.

The contemporary problem of style can be summarized by way of contrast: Religious sentiment is all about sincerity, and yet the dominant mode of expression in popular culture is irony. Irony and sincerity need not be mutually exclusive (we can tease the ones we love), but it does rather complicate matters for public venues and religious content. A parody of a song is still a song, but a parody of a prayer is not a prayer. In considering the problem of how a poet achieves a convincing style for religious poetry, we should also recall that just as irony does not preclude sincerity, neither does irony necessarily lend itself to destruction. In an ironic atmosphere, the religious poet will seek indirect, rather than direct modes of expression.

Our contemporary notions of appropriate discourse for religious poetry are shaped by many factors, primary among which are the long history of our religious traditions, our liturgical texts and prayers, and the various translations of the Bible, especially the King James Version, as they affected English-language poetry. Our sense of linguistic decorum is also shaped by our modern secular history as it impinges on poetic creation: the collapse of monarchical and religious authority, the bathos of late nineteenth-century piety, and the march of successive poetic styles, namely, heart-on-sleeve romanticism, followed by earnest Victoriana, followed by the ascetic modernist reaction, followed by the ironic postmodern take. My historical sketch here, while laughably inadequate, is intended to get us away from the hoary bugbear of "secularism" by which angry religionists blame the Enlightenment for everything they despise about modern culture. When Virginia Woolf writes dyspeptically in a letter, "there's something obscene in a living person sitting by the fire and believing in God," her incredulity and the hostility of the age to which she belongs cannot be blamed so conveniently on Descartes or Darwin.[1] And since this brief essay is neither an argument about historical change nor a sociological analysis of discourse usage, we will simply take the problem as a given rather than query how we came to be stuck with this nearly unbridgeable gap: on the one side, a cramped and crusty decorum for religious language (Thees, Thous, and O Most Holys), and on the other side, the romantic-modernist-postmodernist nexus. To fling a lyric poem across such an abyss is surely to watch it crash on the slopes below.

When I say that most contemporary Christian poetry is dreadful, I am not talking about poetry that admits of God. There are scores of fine contemporary poets who flirt with the transcendent in their poems. But trembling with intimations of immortality or positing a generic, deist god are very different projects from translating the work of an incarnational Christian theology into a compelling poetic form. It is why we do not have, in the realm of poetry, a Christian monument equivalent to Dante's *Divine Comedy* for our own age.[2] Nor am I talking about devotional poetry, which is orthodox, inoffensive, and safe for liturgical use. Religious poetry, by contrast, may be deeply unsettling and even blasphemous, as it is concerned not with hewing to the orthodox line, but with articulating the human experience as it opens onto the mystery of God. Maintaining such distinctions between devotional poetry and religious poetry allows for some surprising candidates for "religious poet." T.S. Eliot thought that Charles Baudelaire—that arrogant misanthrope who dallied with Satanism—was a "first-rate blasphem[er]," by which Eliot intended a high compliment. Unlike the petty religious versifiers of his day, Baudelaire—though no believer—showed why Christian salvation was necessary. For Eliot, Baudelaire invented Christianity from the raw material of his own experience. That contemporary scholars do not read Baudelaire in this way is immaterial: Eliot was looking for models of how to write serious religious verse, and in his interpretation of the great French symbolist, Baudelaire had

1. Virginia Woolf, *The Letters of Virginia Woolf.* Volume 3: *1923-1928* (ed. Nigel Nicolson and Joanne Trautmann; New York: Harcourt Brace, 1976), 457-58.

2. Though Geoffrey Hill is not primarily concerned with problems of belief (especially recently), his erudite and allusive work is probably the closest we can get to such an English-language monument, even in spite of its willful obscurity.

recuperated the medieval conception of sin by making salvation and damnation terrifyingly real.[3]

While an uncensored attention to the human experience may lead to blasphemy, by contrast, avoiding the messiness of the human experience results in sentimentality. Sentimentality is the trap religious poets are most likely to fall into, though sentimentality is not unique to devotional or religious literature. In his own definition of sentimentality, James Baldwin argues that the underside of sentimentality is brutality:

> Sentimentality, the ostentatious parading of excessive and spurious emotion, is the mark of dishonesty, the inability to feel; the wet eyes of the sentimentalist betray his aversion to experience, his fear of life, his arid heart; and it is always, therefore, the signal of secret and violent inhumanity, the mask of cruelty.[4]

For an example of how naïve, pious sentimentality can mask a brutal ideology, Ricky Bobby's prayer to the "dear Lord baby Jesus" (in Will Farrell's *Talladega Nights*) is the last word on the matter. But I don't concur with the morally indignant absolutes of Baldwin's thesis. Sentimentality does not "always" mask brutality. More forgivably, sometimes sentimentality covers an unwillingness to plumb the contradictions of human experience. In this gentler view, sentimentality is a desire for a tidier narrative than human experience offers.

Though T.S. Eliot does not explicitly name this phenomenon as sentimentality, he puts his finger on the problem as it relates to religious poetry: "The great danger, for the poet who would write religious verse, is that of setting down what he would like to feel rather than be faithful to the expression of what he really feels."[5] The problem, as Eliot indicates, is that part of the job of religion is to explain the doctrine to which its members communally assent. Religion also sets modes of conduct and feeling that curb some human instincts. But such stances rub against our romantic notion of the poet as a Byronic individualist. By assenting to communal truths and a shared moral vision, the religious poet is therefore in danger of whitewashing human

---

3. T.S. Eliot, "Baudelaire," in *Selected Prose of T.S. Eliot* (New York: Harcourt Brace Jovanovich, 1975). See also Eliot's *After Strange Gods* (London: Faber & Faber, 1934), 52; and Ronald Schuchard's chapter "First-Rate Blasphemy," in his book *Eliot's Dark Angel* (Oxford: Oxford University Press, 1999).

4. This definition of sentimentality is occasioned by Baldwin's belligerent, gratuitous attack on Harriet Beecher Stowe's anti-slavery novel *Uncle Tom's Cabin.* But by misrepresenting the rhetorical means at Stowe's disposal and the intentions directed at her audience, Baldwin comes up with a memorable description of the intentional falsity of sentimentality. See James Baldwin, "Everybody's Protest Novel," in *Notes of a Native Son* (Boston: Beacon, 1984), 14.

5. T.S. Eliot, *George Herbert* (Harlow, UK: Longmans, Green, 1968), 26.

experience. The result can be a hollow reverence that has no connection to the felt experience of being human.

The nauseating horseshit of "Footprints in the Sand" is an obvious example, even though it's not really a poem. It's a parable arbitrarily broken up into lines so that it will look like poetry and thus appear more "artistic."[6] I teach this work in a religious poetry course in order to get students to think hard about the limits of sentimentality. While a few students are fans of the poem (it's always good to have dissenting voices in the classroom), I am mostly intrigued by the majority of students who do not like it. I find it odd that such students—who are comfortable with the raunch and sarcasm of modern media, and thus the most likely candidates to dismiss the pietism of "Footprints"—have a hard time articulating what they instinctively dislike about the poem.

A discussion of style is the most congenial entry point for them: an admission of the sort that expressions such as "my precious child" (a variant reading in the many versions of the poem) are not the kind of discourse they use for love. But this objection resides too close to the realm of taste: "I don't like the poem, because that's not how I speak." Or, "that's not my piety." In a discussion of aesthetics, these are not honest reasons for disliking any poem. Nor is it the poem's theology that these students dislike. It is a theology, I point out to them, that is unobjectionably orthodox: The moral of "Footprints" is that God aids us and comforts us even when we are not conscious of it. So why does this paraphrase of the poem's theological meaning ring true, while the poem annoys?

It is because the rhetoric of the poem makes the reader feel stupid. The poem claims that God has been working like mad, carrying us through our sorrows: "When you saw only one set of footprints, my pwecious, pwecious, smoochy-woochy child, it was then that I carried you." (Warranting assumption: You're a blind dumbass for not noticing. Conclusion: quit complaining.) But the poem gives the readers no clue as to how we are to recognize God's grace *other than in retrospect*. I ask students annoyed by the poem how they would feel if, instead of concluding with God's unarguable truth, the poem continued with the speaker's question: "So why the hell did you wait until now to tell me, *huh?*" Does such a response turn the poem into a parody or a different kind of prayer? I then ask students to posit a zippy or compassionate comeback God might utter to the benighted speaker ("Look, kid, do you want me to *list* the times I tried to get it across to you?" Or, "Since when is that my job?"). In these improvised addenda to the poem, students rehearse their

6. There are at least three identifiable variants of the poem. Some modern adaptations end with the image of dancing rather than being carried by the Lord. All of these versions are equally horrifying. At the *Poetry Foundation* Website, Rachel Aviv has a fine essay on the multiple figures who have claimed authorship of the poem: "Enter Sandman: Who Wrote 'Footprints'?" http://www.poetryfoundation.org.

own spiritual struggles. Their questions are thereby honored, instead of their spiritual ignorance being chastised. The point of the exercise is to show them that such further questioning of assumptions and a fuller acknowledgment of the human condition might be the beginning of an interesting poem, instead of the platitude into which the poem so smugly plunges for its conclusion. It is not the poem's piety that is offensive, but its short-circuiting of the spiritual quest by bullying the reader into submission instead of honoring the complexity of discernment. Perhaps the poem masks some brutality, after all.[7]

On the topic of sensitivity to one's audience, when I teach this poem to illustrate problems of sentiment and form, I strictly forbid my students from going home and ripping the laminated, illustrated copy of "Footsteps" off of grandmother's refrigerator. *Leave Grandma alone.* What is at stake in this discussion is not personal sincerity or private piety, but public rhetoric for serious religious poetry: the ability of a poetic language, steeped in the poetic forms and traditions of its culture, to address adequately its object (God) and its content (the complexities, joys, and contradictions of religious faith).

But subjecting "Footprints" to critique is akin to shooting fish in a barrel. The real test comes when serious poets set themselves the task of writing good religious verse. As a scholar of T.S. Eliot's work, I admire, though do not love unconditionally, his *Four Quartets*, which many critics consider the greatest poetic statement on faith in the twentieth century. I prefer the electrifying poetry Eliot wrote before his conversion to Anglo-Catholicism, poems written from febrile spaces of doubt and fear, such as "The Love Song of J. Alfred Prufrock" and *The Waste Land*, that terrifying record of spiritual drought. Christianity was given a great stroke of fortune when such a respected poet and critic as Eliot became a believer, thence turning his attention to articulating the problems of faith in poetic and dramatic forms. *Ash-Wednesday* is the first major work published after Eliot's conversion in 1927. As an illustration of my thesis, this otherwise poignant poem has some wretched moments in it. The fifth section of the poem does not start promisingly:

> Still is the unspoken word, the Word unheard,
> The Word without a word, the Word within
> The world and for the world [. . .]

And then things go from bad to worse:

---

7. Given the popularity of "Footprints," the reading of the poem I press here raises the question of whether its rhetoric in fact works this way. Does its legion of fans enjoy being bullied? The answer to this question would require an excursus into hermeneutics, rhetorical theory, and reader-response theory. But the prospect of hauling out such artillery for the sake of this poem is so depressing that I here bury the issue in a footnote.

Against the Word the unstilled world still whirled
About the centre of the silent Word.[8]

The paradoxes are struggling to say something Deeply Mysterious about the incarnation but end up sounding facile and pretentious. And the piling up of internal rhymes—heard, word, world, Word, whirled—is the sonic equivalent of beating a dead horse. This stanza and the one that follows it are about as wince-makingly awful as ever penned by a great poet. It might seem unbalanced to single out these weak lines in a poem that in other ways affectingly describes the pain of renouncing a beloved, the poet barely able to believe that a heart-breaking loss might be translated into a spiritual gain. But what is telling is that Eliot's fine musical ear fails him here, in the very spot where he moves away from personal experience and attempts to say something explicitly theological.

Eliot's problem is one of style rather than sentimentality. E.E. Cummings is another twentieth-century poet who occasionally stumbles when he turns to God-talk, though his problem has less to do with style—which is both original and responsive to his aims—than with sentimentality. But because Cummings is willing to risk sentimentality, he also has some of the most exuberant religious poems, satisfyingly direct (emotionally, if not linguistically) and filled with unabashed praise language. With his Unitarian roots and individualist ethos, Cummings is hardly concerned with Christian orthodoxy. But he merits attention here as a religious poet because of the way Cummings shrugged his shoulders at the dominant irony of his day. His poem "i thank You God for most this amazing day" is typical of Cummings's religious praise poems, in that it slops happily through both mawkish tripe and lovely turns of phrase. Any religious poet who wants to write praise poems needs to keep Cummings in mind, both as an example and as a warning.

But Eliot and Cummings are already a century behind us. And so, to see how contemporary poets negotiate this complex landscape, let's consider Mary Karr's recent book *Sinners Welcome* (2006).[9] Karr's volume is the best attempt at serious Christian poetry since Mark Jarman's *Questions for Ecclesiastes* (1997) and *Unholy Sonnets* (2000). Like Eliot, Karr loses her footing when she leaves her personal experience behind and tries to "do theology." A number of her poems are Christological meditations, scattered throughout the volume amid her more confessional poems. In "Descending Theology: The Nativity," Karr struggles to make such familiar terrain come alive:

[. . .] his lolling head lurched, and the sloppy mouth
found that first fullness—her milk

8. T.S. Eliot, *The Complete Poems and Plays, 1909-1950* (New York: Harcourt, 1962).
9. Mary Karr, *Sinners Welcome* (New York: HarperCollins, 2006).

spilled along his throat, while his pure being
flooded her.

We are perilously close to bathos here, and once the speaker strides into "pure being," we know the poet has thrown over the hard work of phrase-making in favor of philosophical clichés. But Karr recovers herself, turning the poem to a more effective ending:

Some animal muzzle
against his swaddling perhaps breathed him warm
till sleep came pouring that first draught
of death, the one he'd wake from
(as we all do) screaming.

In general, this strictly theological stuff is not bad. But it just doesn't quite work either, though cheers to her for trying.

Karr is the author of the best-selling memoir *The Liar's Club* (1995). And so her well-known background of alcoholism, abuse, and betrayal already give her sufficient street cred as a religious poet. Before you open the volume, you already know these poems are not going to be ones that Little Flower would have penned. "Delinquent Missive" tells the story of the speaker's work tutoring at a juvenile detention center. It opens,

Before David Ricardo stabbed his daddy
sixteen times with a fork—*Once*
for every year of my fuckwad life—he'd long
showed signs of being bent.

The danger of sketching such a character is that the speaker will get stuck in the expected narrative: finding something to love in this troubled child. Fortunately, the speaker offers no such comfort: "If radiance shone from those mudhole eyes, / I missed it." Writing this poem years after their teacher–student relationship, she can only presume he has by now found his way to the electric chair; she hopes that before this inevitable end "some organism drew your care—orchid / or cockroach even." The speaker's human experience finds no spark of God in this sociopath, but her theology is the wiser guide to which she accedes. She walks a tight line by relying on her theology without betraying her experience. She avoids the trap Eliot warns of by not pretending to feel other than the way she feels. When the delinquent waves at her at lunch, she flinches. She does not dissolve in tears thinking that she has touched his heart. She concludes by wishing that

[. . .] the unbudgeable stone
that plugged the tomb hole

in your chest could roll back, and in your sad
  slit eyes could blaze
that star adored by its maker.

This leap to the transcendent at the end of a poem is always a temptation for any poet. (It is Mary Oliver's most overused trick, and the Poetry Foundation should fine her for every time she reverts to it.) But here, even though the allusion to the resurrection is handled a little clumsily, the hopeful conclusion is warranted.

Karr's "Waiting for God: Self-Portrait as Skeleton" is another poem that doesn't shy away from the stench of despair and confusion, this time about her mother's piteous alcoholism as it played out in her final years. After the mother's death, the speaker is drowning in her own problems, which involved praying

with my middle finger bone aimed at the light fixture—*Come out,*
You fuck, I'd say, then wait for God to finish me
where I knelt[.]

There's that f-word again, even though there are plenty of poems in Karr's volume that are PG- or G-rated. But I've deliberately chosen these last two poems on the assumption that if we're looking for a barometer of the problem this essay addresses, then cursing in a religious poem is a good indicator of the discursive weather. Looking at how salty language fits into religious poetry illuminates in miniature the larger problem: How do we inject or absorb the varied discourses that surround us into our God-talk? Because of modern censorship issues, cursing in any kind of literature also happens to be a barometer of how secular culture gauges public morality. Allen Ginsberg caught hell from the authorities of his day for using the f-word in *Howl.* But as a matter of poetic usage, it was not problematic: *Howl* is not a religious poem. It has a rambling, narrative style, and a hallucinatory (and hallucinogenic) atmosphere. It would have seemed odd if Ginsberg had *not* used the f-word in such a poem. But in a lyric mode, the word "fuck" has a tendency to take all the air out of a poem, even one that is strictly secular. Whether deployed as a red-blooded curse or a wry exclamation, the f-bomb may have a forceful initial impact in a poem, but on rereadings, it can seem showy: Look at me! I can swear!

In Karr's "Delinquent Missive," the sociopath's expression "*fuckwad life*" is earned, not because it is put in the mouth of someone other than the speaker, but because the poem unsentimentally portrays a troubled teenager. In Karr's "Waiting for God" though, her "*You fuck*" throbs like a bruised elbow, unnecessarily calling attention to itself. That both expressions are in italics doesn't help either. My distaste for the f-word in this poem is not a question of prudishness. (In my personal life, I happen to swear like a sailor.) It's a question of decorum. The appropriateness of words can only be weighed against an audience's needs and expectations, and the reasons a speaker has for pushing those boundaries. I might swear with abandon around friends, but I don't swear from the pulpit when I'm giving a homily. Vulgarity, in other words, resides not in any particular expression, but in a rhetorical situation.[10]

I would encourage anyone who is angry at God to swear as much as they like in their personal prayer. God's a Big Guy. He can take some abuse, especially if it's genuine communication. I'm convinced he'd prefer your skirting blasphemy to pious flattery that hides internal anguish. Karr may have sworn in exactly this manner in her personal prayer. But a poem is a made thing and needn't strictly record facts as if it were a newspaper article. Poems must find traction in a public language and a public forum. The problem of style is not only communal but historically inherited. It is not a private problem, one that Karr can solve on her own, by making better decisions, for example, or banning the f-word from her poems.

A large part of the problem is the medium of poetry itself: The pressure that the lyric mode exerts on language makes the words vibrate with intensity. The problem of style is solved much more easily in prose. The casual, button-down modes of prose—such as narrative, memoir, or personal essay—are roomier places to switch registers of discourse. Karr's own prose, as well as Ann Lamott's, has wedded a refreshingly commonsensical piety to a breezy prose style that would not be out of place in an issue of *The New Yorker*. Their salty language is of a piece with the humorous, reverent, and affecting stories they tell.

I sometimes joke that the last great religious poet was Gerard Manley Hopkins, who died in 1889. And yet even his sonnets, miraculous as they are, do not add up to a coherent vision or statement on Christian faith. If we had more poets like Karr and Jarman, we would have more religious poems in which nothing human is alien: the full range of human expression, which includes cursing, grumbling, singing, shouting—the varied ways in which we express the operatic extremes of loathing, despair, gratitude, reverence, and ecstasy. But while such a bounty would be welcome, it would not keep us from flinching when we read a poem about the baby Jesus. For that to happen—an atmosphere in which grand Christian epics are hewn from the discursive soil around us—we'd need a paradigm shift, some tremendous cultural change, slouching toward Los Angeles to be born.

10. If you're the type of person who does not swear, then my hat is off to you. But here is a very different issue: If you're the type of person who thinks that no one should ever swear, least of all a poet or a Jesuit, and that "gosh" and "darn" are perfectly adequate expressions of human despair and confusion, then . . . well. . . . Then I guess I don't know what to say, except: Gee whiz, how did you make it this far into the essay?

24. Mental Health in America

Jason Welle, S.J.

Adam Lanza's mother apparently once warned a sitter not to leave him alone.[1] James Holmes had previously sought help for mental health issues.[2] Seung-Hui Cho had likewise been diagnosed with mental disorders but discontinued treatment before coming to Virginia Tech.[3] During pre-trial hearings, Jared Loughner was diagnosed with schizophrenia.[4] All of them seemed to be wrestling with mental illness. Or perhaps they weren't wrestling anymore; the illness—at least momentarily—had won. What has happened that these people have fallen through the cracks? How did no one notice the potentially dangerous behavior in some, or not take appropriate action in others?

It isn't surprising that gun control is back on the national agenda. We've been witness to thirty-one mass killings in the United States since Columbine in 1999. We may finally be seeing a paradigm shift when it comes to new gun regulation. But something deeper is happening with these events, contributing to the violence in an important way. A closer look at the string of massacres that have happened just since 1999 should tell us that we need more than gun regulation alone.

#

When I was a Jesuit novice, I spent several mornings a week working at the Downtown Chapel in Portland, Oregon. Our work was simple: to offer

A version of this essay was originally published in *The Jesuit Post* on February 7, 2013.

1. Adam Lanza committed the killings at Sandy Hook elementary school in Newtown, Connecticut, in December 2012. Andrew Solomon's editorial in the *New York Times* is a helpful overview and analysis. It was published on December 22, 2012, and can be accessed at http://www.nytimes.com. The well-known essay "I Am Adam Lanza's Mother," from the mother of a son with a similar mental illness, can be accessed at http://gawker.com.

2. James Holmes is the admitted perpetrator of the Aurora movie theater shooting in July of 2012.

3. Seung-Hui Cho killed thirty-two people and wounded seventeen others in April 2007 at Virginia Polytechnic Institute in Blacksburg, Virginia.

4. In January 2011 Jared Loughner killed six people and injured twelve others, including U.S. Representative Gabrielle Giffords, in a shooting spree in Tucson, Arizona.

hospitality to anyone who came through the doors. We offered a warm, dry place to sit and rest, a hot cup of coffee, a little bit to eat, a few toiletries.

The men and women who came into the Downtown Chapel ended up on the streets for all kinds of reasons, but for many, mental health issues were, as social workers and psychologists might put it, "major contributing factors." Mental illness can make it hard for people to hold down steady employment. Mental illness can make it difficult to stay in stable housing.[5] Mental illness can break family relationships.

Some had disorders such as schizophrenia or bipolar disorder. They held frenzied conversations with invisible counterparts, or sat in silence, disengaged from their surroundings. Sometimes they had fought these same demons since childhood, or these demons appeared later in life, often suddenly, like the grating buzz of an alarm clock in the morning, only instead of waking up they were entering a nightmare. There were a few military vets with PTSD. Some of them fought in the most recent wars in Iraq and Afghanistan; some had been struggling since Vietnam. They seemed constantly angry and agitated, trying to regain the grip on life lost in crossfire on a far-away battlefield.

I remember one man in particular. "Johnny" was about my age. He had fought in Iraq and was discharged honorably. But upon coming home he lost control of his life. Something changed in him overseas. He was angry and prone to uncontrollable outbursts. They were verbal and sometimes physical. He was paranoid about the people around him. He lost his job when he couldn't show up regularly, and without a job he lost his home. His family became afraid of him and cut off contact.

It was years later that I met him at the Downtown Chapel. Praying in the evening after being there I'd wonder: Did his family even recognize the nature of his illness? Did he recognize it himself? Jobless and homeless, drugs like marijuana at least gave him a sense of calm. Experts in the field euphemistically call that "self-medication"; when it leads to addiction the problem is only made worse.

Many of the men and women I met at Downtown Chapel were left in a bleak situation, often separated from family, with few friends and little support, imprisoned in loneliness and isolation, not only physically but psychologically, homeless and lacking basic medical care, much less mental health care. Certainly there are those who question whether mental health is a real cause of gun violence. There are some who say that it's unfair to ask about mental health when it is responsible for such a small percentage of

5. See "Separate and Unequal: The Struggle of Tenants with Mental Illness to Maintain Housing," at http://www.bazelon.org/LinkClick.aspx?fileticket=G6Nv3gIsUX8%3D&tabid=241.

gun violence.[6] But I can't help wondering: Even if there was no connection between mental health and gun massacres in this country, is the neglect of these mentally ill people not utterly inhumane? How do we abandon our sons and daughters and brothers and sisters to such darkness?

And how did we end up here, with people on the street instead of in appropriate care, "self-medicating" instead of receiving proper medicine? "Ronald Reagan shut down all the mental hospitals, and drove all those people onto the streets." That's a trope I've often heard to explain the prevalence of mentally ill people among the homeless population. I heard it from my dad when I was a kid. I heard it when I was in college, in some class on "the causes of homelessness." I've heard it among the volunteers I've met along the way, including at Downtown Chapel. At this point, it's well-ingrained in my own psyche.

#

It's not that simple, of course, and the reality, as always, is more complicated than I'm often willing to allow. What is true is that the care and treatment provided to the mentally ill is entwined with the political history of the last thirty-five years. That takes us all the way back to the presidency of the peanut farmer from Georgia: Jimmy Carter.

President Carter established a Presidential Commission on Mental Health in 1977—the first time a study of mental health care in the United States had been taken at such an authoritative level. By this time, the causes and effects of mental illness in veterans from the major wars of the twentieth century had drawn attention to the issue, and mental health care had shifted away from institutionalized care toward community-based care.[7]

As a result of Carter's mental health commission the Mental Health Systems Act, passed overwhelmingly by Congress, was signed into law in 1980. Beyond drawing national attention to the issue of mental health, the act was intended to strengthen long-term mental health care in the United States by reinvigorating the Community Mental Health Center model.[8]

---

6. See "Focus on Mental Health Laws to Curb Violence Is Unfair, Some Say," at http://www.nytimes.com/2013/02/01/us/focus-on-mental-health-laws-to-curb-violence-is-unfair-some-say.html?_r=0.

7. See Gerald N. Grobb, "Public Policy and Mental Illness: Jimmy Carter's Presidential Commission on Mental Health," in *The Milbank Quarterly* 83.3 (2005). Online via JSTOR at http://www.jstor.org/stable/30045624. The move to community-based mental health care, and more restrictive guidelines for involuntary commitment, was not without criticism.

8. See Alexander Thomas, "Ronald Reagan and the Commitment of the Mentally Ill: Capital, Interest Groups, and the Eclipse of Social Policy," in *Electronic Journal of Sociology* (1998). At http://www.sociology.org/content/vol003.004/thomas.html.

Early in President Reagan's administration, the Mental Health Systems Act was effectively nullified. The new administration oversaw a shift in the political economy away from socially oriented policy decisions to fiscally directed ones. Budgetary bills in the first two years of Reagan's administration repealed the Mental Health Systems Act and cut federal funding for initiatives contained in the law.[9] Trained and qualified mental health professionals soon left when federal funds dried up, and resources for mental health care quickly vanished. Rosalynn Carter, who acted as the honorary chair of the Commission on Mental Health and testified before Congress for the passage of the Mental Health Systems Act, wrote, "Many of our dreams were gone. It was a bitter loss." It turns out my dad and my college professor and fellow volunteers may have had a point after all.[10]

Warp speed to thirty years later. What's happened in the meantime? For starters, psychiatric medicine has become more neuroscientifically oriented.[11] Pharmaceutical advances made the treatment of mental illness available through primary care physicians instead of in hospitals and like institutions. But visits to the doctor and the drugs you get there are expensive, and apparently the people who need that service aren't taking advantage of it.[12] And many people, like Johnny and a lot of the others at Downtown Chapel, are still falling through the cracks in the community-health model, and they're often ending up on the streets, and then sometimes in jail.

#

I'm neither a politician nor a public health professional. I'm just a concerned citizen, sitting alongside many of you in a post-Newtown America. I'm watching gun control move into the overheated debate halls of Congress and the seats of the Sunday talk-show circuit. I'm reading that President Obama has included mental health care in his own proposals[13] to curb gun-related violence. It's from this place that I'm asking: So what's next? Where do we go from here?

---

9. Ibid.

10. E.g., Phyllis Vine, "Ronald Reagan, Mental Health, and Spin" (February 9, 2011), available at: http://www.miwatch.org/2011/02/_ronald_reagan_and_mental.html.

11. E.g., David Mechanic, "Mental Health Services Then and Now," *Health Affairs* 26.6 (2007): 1548-50, available at http://content.healthaffairs.org/content/26/6/1548.full.

12. Sarah Kliff, "Seven Facts about America's Mental Health-Care System." Published in the *Washington Post*'s Wonkblog on December 17, 2012. Available online at http://www.washingtonpost.com/blogs/wonkblog/wp/2012/12/17/seven-facts-about-americas-mental-health-care-system.

13. *New York Times,* "What's in Obama's Gun Control Proposal," published on January 16, 2013. Available at http://www.nytimes.com/interactive/2013/01/16/us/obama-gun-control-proposal.html?_r=0.

What about revisiting the Mental Health Systems Act, for starters? The president's plan calls for another "national conversation" about mental health. Though imperfect by most accounts, the act provided valuable resources at both the local level for treatment options and at the national level for the study of mental health. Are there aspects of that old system that might be brought back online? What loopholes did it leave open that need to be closed?

And let's not forget the Affordable Care Act, our love-it-or-hate-it law of the land, the one where the national conversation feels more like a family feud. The debate over the Affordable Care Act illustrated, I hope, that a sound fiscal policy doesn't have to exclude good social policy; sometimes strong social care—and maybe sound mental health care—can be financially sound in the future.

What a paradox we live in here in the United States: Gun ownership is a right, but health care is an entitlement. Or worse, universal health care is now being painted as a suspension of liberty, even though in our Declaration of Independence we hold that all of us have the right to "life, liberty, and the pursuit of happiness." Life holds prime position in that list, and not by accident. Life comes first because without it, liberty and the pursuit of happiness are moot. Life must be cared for, including the preservation of health—and that includes the preservation and care of mental health. For people who struggle with mental illness, life can seem a prison, and liberty and the pursuit of happiness are fleeting.

We are failing to protect the living in our country, and that is a shame. Gun control alone may not be enough to prevent future massacres; changes in mental health care alone might not either. But in too many of the tragedies we have witnessed since Columbine, someone with a fully apparent and inadequately cared for mental illness has managed to obtain firearms and rapidly murder dozens of people. We need a comprehensive response that truly defends the living. For the sake of our humanity, caring for the mentally ill needs to be part of that.

I
S
IRA
DEI

25. The Rise of Expertise and the Fall of Fr. Athanasius Kircher, S.J.

Matt Spotts, S.J.

The director of the education workshop I was attending concluded the day's presentation by playing a series of TED talks. It was a fine choice, and they were everything I'd come to expect from the franchise. The confident, polished master of ceremonies introduced confident, polished speakers. If the talks had been any more carefully rehearsed, they'd have come across as overscripted, but as usual these seemed smooth, even elegant. And, no doubt as a direct result of the speakers' unparalleled expertise (aided in no small part by inch-perfect posture and hand gestures of which Bob Fosse would have been jealous[1]), the speakers surgically sliced through the Gordian Knot of American education policy, sprinkling the remains with witty aphorisms. The audience laughed along. Then the speakers boldly presented the Great New Vision for American Education. The audience nodded in approval.

All the while, part of me—the part of me that intuitively distrusts easy answers—was howling. There is no way, I thought, that an issue as big and as complicated as education can be explored in any meaningful way in less than half an hour. Despite my discomfiture, however, I kept listening, and for a single reason: These people were experts. And by experts, I mean that they were people I'd never heard of. But still, that polished MC had told me that they were experts. The high production value told me that they were experts. Their poise and preparation all told me that these people are experts. The skeptic in me was momentarily soothed. Instead of scoffing, I found myself listening and listening closely.

#

1. In four years of competitive collegiate debating I witnessed some of the sharpest orators in the world. The best of the best consistently could deliver speeches that sounded like the favored offspring of MLK's "I Have a Dream" speech and the Sermon on the Mount, and they *still* occasionally lapsed into hand motions that resembled a wounded albatross struggling for flight. Score one for TED, I guess.

Days later I was still admiring and remembering those talks. In particular I caught myself noticing the care the entire TED ensemble took to convey to the viewer a single message: These people are experts. Clearly, a tremendous amount of time and care had gone into creating the aesthetic that we, the viewers, expect to accompany expertise. And then a moment later, my mind made one of those strange associative leaps, this time back to another expert, a fascinating figure who stands large in my own ongoing academic life: the renowned seventeenth-century Jesuit, Fr. Athanasius Kircher, S.J.

I'm not alone in my fascination with Kircher. Historians continue to produce a steady stream of works on him, aimed at scholars and a more general audience alike.[2] What's captivating enough about Kircher to make this possible? Most biographies begin (rather unhelpfully) by declaring that Kircher was a "polymath," which is a way of saying that Kircher was interested in, and involved in, everything.[3] Actually, "interested in" fails to capture the stickiness of Kircher's intellectual fingers; the works left behind by the Jesuit boil over with the enthusiasm of an unquenchably curious mind. For Kircher, the whole world was rife with things to be known, and Kircher wanted to know them all. Not surprisingly, the product of his eclectic thinking could be messy. When as lively, imaginative, and untidy a thinker as Kircher tried to distill his thoughts into written form, the result was that Kircher's unbounded infatuation frequently overran his ability to synthesize. To use Kircher scholar Paula Findlen's especially apropos phrase, "Kircher's writing is some of the most rebarbative, unreliable, undigested and polyglot the world has ever known, bursting at the seams with learning, overflowing with ideas and possibilities, and pointing confusingly in many different directions."[4]

For most of us (i.e., those for whom the idea of reading labyrinthine Baroque Latin sounds like one of Dante's circles of hell) Kircher left behind not just his writings but also a treasury of illustrations that alternately awe us with their magnificence and estrange us with their weirdness. It's hard not to be impressed with the jaw-dropping intricacy of the hieroglyphs that decorate the temples and obelisks in Kircher's works on Egyptology. Even stranger are Kircher's imaginations of underground caverns and allegorical depictions of the cosmos. And careening toward the downright bizarre are pictures of some of Kircher's purported inventions, such as the "magic lantern" (a

2. In fact, as recently as 2012, a biography of Kircher, aimed at a general audience and written by John Glassie, was published under the title *A Man of Misconceptions: The Life of an Eccentric in an Age of Change* (New York: Riverhead Books, 2012).

3. Hypothesis: Gratuitous use of "polymath" is clearly a ploy to generate Web traffic for Wikipedia, Dictionary.com, etc.

4. Paula Findlen, "Kircher's Cosmos: On Athanasius Kircher," in *The Nation*, April 22, 2013. Accessed at www.thenation.com.

sort of projector complete with a creepy, dancing genie) and the "cat piano" (Google it yourself—no, really, I highly recommend you do so). Still, the illustrations executed by an army of artists scattered across Europe bring Kircher's enchanted mental universe to life in a way his lumbering prose cannot. Kircher's is a world in which secret knowledge lies hidden just beneath the surface of nature, a world in which all things are a fit subject for study because all knowledge, from languages to zoology to geology to magnetism, are connected through mysterious, even mystical and magical, means.

More than anything, what captivates and confuses about Kircher, what attracts and annoys, is what was, for him, a rather basic intellectual assumption: that there is such a thing as universal knowledge. In our own intellectual climate, writers spend years painstakingly acquiring the expertise and credibility to write an article or deliver a TED talk on a narrow topic or two. Kircher's writings, on the other hand, waltz through topics as varied as magnetism, optics, music, acoustics, epidemiology, and the study of languages obscure, dead, and invented. He drew pictures of deep underground caverns without any obvious experience of spelunking, and wrote a lengthy treatise on microscopic causes of a plague epidemic without previously having studied medicine. While our intellectual climate looks on the amateur dabbler with suspicion or scorn, Kircher's contemporaries thought that the Jesuit was, ahem, kind of a big deal.

One great testimony to Kircher's celebrity was the sheer cultural and physical distance that his ideas managed to travel. In a Europe that was fractured along political and religious lines, writings by Kircher—a Catholic and Jesuit, doubly suspicious!—were read in England by the famous diarist Samuel Pepys and within the confines of that soon-to-be-prestigious scientific organization, the Royal Society of London. In a world where information traveled much more slowly than in our own, a missionary thanked Kircher for a treatise on the plague (*librum de peste*) by sending Kircher two pounds of chocolate and assorted New World peppers.[5] Today, we'd be bewildered or simply dismissive of someone who claims expertise without narrow training, but most of Kircher's contemporaries didn't see him that way. Quite the contrary; for a brief, shining moment in his career, Kircher was a locus of knowledge, a one-stop shop for virtually anything one could wish to know.

#

The problem is that Kircher's career straddled two intellectual worlds, the world of the polymath and a world much more closely resembling our own.

5. John Edward Fletcher, "Medical Men and Medicine in the Correspondence of Athanasius Kircher," in *Janus: Revue internationale de l'histoire des sciences, de la médecine, de la pharmacie, et de la technique* 56 (1969): 265.

And as that intellectual climate began to change, Kircher lived to see his reputation begin to crumble. Early in his career, Kircher had the public intellectual capital to capture no less an intellect than the famed philosopher and mathematician Gottfried Leibniz. As a young man Leibniz had written admiringly to Kircher and studied his works, but as time wore on Leibniz's admiration gave way to skepticism, and not for no reason. Among Kircher's most dubious accomplishments must be ranked his pretension to have translated hieroglyphics, a fact observed by Leibniz who, after poring through Kircher's writings on ancient Egyptian language and translations of hieroglyphics, trenchantly concluded of Kircher, "he understands nothing."[6] Similarly, a 1715 book entitled *The Charlatanry of the Learned* detailed several pranks ostensibly played on Kircher to expose the Jesuit's gullibility. In one, a certain Andreas Müller reportedly sent a specious Egyptian manuscript, which Father Kircher obligingly translated, apparently without realizing that it was a forgery.[7] Placed under the microscope of new research methods and standards, the man behind the curtain was suddenly and dramatically exposed. Kircher ceased to be the savant and started to be silly.

But the increased perception of Kircher as a fraud does not mean he was a fool. Kircher began his career in the waning years of the Renaissance, a period in which the strict divide we maintain between "science" and "superstition" was still largely unformed. For us, it's patently obvious that science and astrology, alchemy and chemistry and magic are dramatically different from one another. Today we hold science to be true and most other claimants false, worthy mainly of dismissal and ridicule. In Kircher's day, however, all of those categories blended together; they could occupy the mental world of a single individual all at once—even when that individual was among history's most celebrated intellects. In fact, in the seventeenth century it wouldn't have been obvious at all that science and alchemy, or astrology and astronomy, were qualitatively different sorts of knowledge, much less that one was Good and the others Bad.

The problem with Kircher's reputation for expertise gets clarified when we look at it through this kind of glass. Through it we can see not that Kircher was a fool but that he lived beyond the twilight of his intellectual milieu. He lived to see the birth of a new mental culture. In fact, by his death in 1680, Kircher had outlived some of those who gave birth to this new culture of Enlightenment, including René Descartes (d. 1650), Galileo Galilei (d. 1642), and Francis Bacon (d. 1626). Kircher began his career in an intellectual world in which nearly mystical knowledge of all things was not only possible but

6. Quoted in Paula Findlen, ed., "The Last Man Who Knew Everything . . . or Did He?" In *Athanasius Kircher: The Last Man Who Knew Everything* (New York: Routledge, 2004), 6.

7. Findlen, "The Last Man Who Knew Everything," 7.

prestigious; he lived to see the all-knowing genius ridiculed and replaced with the particular specialist of the Enlightenment: the empiricist, the experimentalist, the expert.

#

At this point in this essay, the truly bold choice would be to stake my claim on Kircher's mental world of mystically interconnected knowledge. I could decry (not without some justice) the pernicious compartmentalization of contemporary Western academic culture that makes "interdisciplinary" a bullet point on an academic *curriculum vitae* rather than a habit of thought. I could, were I brave, reject the polished expertise of TED presenters in favor of the rambling, eclectic enthusiasm of Kircher's broad genius.

But I'm not going to argue that, and for the simple reason that I don't really believe it. I'm too much a product of my—our—culture to believe that the almost-mystical unity that characterized Kircher's intellectual culture is actually superior to the particularity that allows TED-talk experts to fix education in America in under a half hour. And, in all honesty, I like many of the byproducts of the Enlightenment. I like the idea that hypotheses should be tested using observable evidence. I like the idea that theories about how the world works should be subject to scrutiny, and that the results of these scrutinies can be tested by intellectual communities. And I like our version of expertise. I'm comfortable with the notion that the world is a terribly complicated place, and I'm fully convinced that many fields of knowledge may take a lifetime to master.

Over the years, I've learned a nuanced vocabulary to express my preference for such expertise. Sitting in a classroom, I've learned to call a particular work "academic" and another "popular." I've learned to mean by this what we all mean: that, while the latter is not necessarily bad, the former is certainly more reliable for the simple reason that a group of "experts" has reviewed it and found it satisfactory. It's very nearly circular reasoning, but it's circular reasoning that I've learned to find necessary, even compelling. The term "expert" itself is a powerful statement of preference in our intellectual culture, especially when measured against its opposite. In the right context, "amateur" is either purely descriptive or, just as often, entirely patronizing.[8] While a (very big) part of me has no interest in a TED talk that poses pithy solutions to mammoth problems, I'm willing to listen because the presenters are the opposite of amateurish: poised, prepared, credentialed. And I listen

8. Interestingly there's no such ambiguity in the adjectival form; at this point in history "amateurish" only implies unadulterated contempt.

because, even though in our culture experts can be wrong, they are unarguably the ones who drive our public discourse.

This returns us to the case of Fr. Kircher. Like people in every era, I would wager that the majority of you, like me, have a strong predilection for our own intellectual culture. Most of the time this predilection isn't even a choice; we're most often not aware of when it is that our culture is at work. But it is, and in powerful ways. Given our strong penchant for equating expertise with "worth reading/watching/listening to," what are we supposed to do with Athanasius Kircher? Can he ever again be anything but the debunked crazy uncle on the Jesuit family tree?

My answer is this: Athanasius Kircher matters not *despite* the fact that he strikes us as weird but *precisely because* of it. Allow me a half-step back in order to clarify the gift of Kircher's weirdness. On a very different subject, the historian Robert Darnton tried to make sense of another "weird" historical case. In this instance, Darnton wrestled with a French record that suggested "The funniest thing that ever happened in the printing shop of Jacques Vincent, according to a worker who witnessed it, was a riotous massacre of cats."[9] The fairly disturbing episode is worth evoking merely for Darnton's commentary, which has a lot to say about Kircher. He writes of the massacre of cats:[10]

> Yet it strikes the modern reader as unfunny, if not downright repulsive. Where is the humor in a group of grown men bleating like goats and banging with their tools while an adolescent reenacts the ritual slaughter of a defenseless animal? Our own inability to get the joke is an indication of the distance that separates us from the workers of preindustrial Europe. The perception of that distance may serve as the starting point of an investigation, for anthropologists have found that the best points of entry in an attempt to penetrate an alien culture can be those where it seems to be most opaque. When you realize that you are not getting something—a joke, a proverb, a ceremony—that is particularly meaningful to the natives, you can see where to grasp a system of foreign meaning in order to unravel it.[11]

Kircher's massive and diverse work, a product of prodigious talent and a life's labor, was not a joke, at least not an intentional one. And yet, as with the joke about Darnton's cats, the centuries that separate us from Kircher can

9. Robert Darnton, *The Great Cat Massacre and Other Episodes in French Cultural History* (New York: Basic Books, 1984), 75.

10. Between the "cat piano" and *The Great Cat Massacre*, it's been a rough essay for cats. It's not personal. I like cats. No really, I do.

11. Darnton, *The Great Cat Massacre*, 78.

render his assumptions and objective, his motivations and methods, utterly opaque to us. The fact that Kircher's work strikes us as so utterly bizarre leaves us with a fascinating choice, particularly when coupled with the inconvenient reality that Kircher was not simply respected during much of his own lifetime but rather venerated as an intellectual giant. Seeing this strangeness, it strikes me, presents us with two choices.

The first choice, of course, is to do as Kircher's critics have done since the last years of Kircher's life and dismiss him as a fraud and a quack. The second choice is subtler, more demanding of us. It asks that, instead of treating Kircher as a failed example of our own intellectual culture, we look at him as a somewhat complicated exemplar of another, alien intellectual culture. It asks that we seize onto those moments where Kircher seems most strange not as an obstacle to understanding the Jesuit or his own time, but rather as a window into a mental world where the quest for universal knowledge was lauded and those who attempted it revered as sages. It asks that, instead of dismissing Kircher as a relic discarded en route toward a better, purer knowledge, we learn to see him as a man who, like all of us, used a particular set of cultural, temporal, evidential, and intellectual givens to make sense of the world around him.

This is less than easy. The easiest thing to do with Kircher is to dismiss him. To see him, for all his undeniable brilliance, as an example of a bad way of thinking that had to be discarded on the way to our present, good ways of thinking. The harder work is to allow Kircher's genius to unmask the hidden assumptions of our own intellectual culture. What bewilders us about Kircher is not just the man himself but rather the collective habit of thought he represents. In turn, this raises the possibility that if Athanasius Kircher's intellectual culture is one possible culture among many, then it's more than possible that our own intellectual culture is the same: merely one among many. The idea that our habits of thought, the way we identify experts and evaluate evidence might someday, for another human being, seem equally strange gives me pause. In that pause is revealed an unspoken, deeply held, assumption: that our own mental culture (and the standards of expertise it supports) is the perfect end result of the long chain of intellectual evolution. That it might not be is, for me, a supremely weird thought.

#

But with weirdness comes insight. Such as the recognition that, as I was watching those TED talks, I didn't even have to choose to evaluate the experts' attire to see that it spoke of competence, their style of mental substance. This is obviously my mental culture speaking, and to hear its voice out loud sounds strange. As is being able to notice that, when I describe a speaker as "polished," and make the leap to "credible," that this assessment too is a product of my mental culture. Or that a particular tone of voice, or accent, means "trustworthy." All these are suddenly noticeable.

But the real work of making strange my own hidden assumptions comes in the realization of how deep down my assumptions actually run, that my very conceptions of what credibility itself is, or what it means to be trustworthy, or to possess mental acuity, are themselves bound up in a host of culturally defined rules of evidence, performance, and behavior. Most of these sneaky, hidden assumptions are not even shared across twenty-first-century cultures, much less across the chasm of human cultural history. All of us inhabit an indescribably complex mental cathedral, the construction of which began long before our births and the shaping and reshaping of which we share with a tremendously broad community.

The precipitous topple of Kircher from the very pinnacle of intellectual celebrity suggests that he fell not just because he was a fool or a fraud (although he may have been both at times—that's another matter). The fall of Kircher shows us how fragilely constructed are our own intellectual cultures, that our own intellectual heroes—of the TED variety or otherwise—can and will fall not because they are fools but because what makes for intellectual stardom is itself a fragile construction. As goes the culture itself, so too is likely to go some of the luster of the intellectual culture's spokespeople. More important still, the dissonance caused by the attempt to square the intellectual culture of our own time with that of the polymaths of the high Renaissance, the Kirchers with the Hawkings, say, might just be an opportunity to rattle us loose enough from our own intellectual culture to allow us to peek at the pillars of what we count as knowledge and wonder at how those pillars come to be.

26. Not Even Wrong: Answering the New Atheism with Better Belief, Not Better Arguments

Sam Sawyer, S.J.

"This isn't right. It's not even wrong." That's what Wolfgang Pauli, a pioneer of quantum mechanics, reportedly said after reviewing a particularly bad scientific paper. A writer in *Scientific American* once called it the "ne plus ultra put-down" in science[1] because it manages to convey the intellectual frustration of confronting an idea that is not just incorrect, but so comprehensively misinformed that it makes any further discussion counterproductive. Pauli's quip is what you say when even the exact opposite position is as inaccurate as the original claim. Correcting such not-even-wrong claims is like trying to climb out of a pit of quicksand: you expend monumental effort only to wind up in the same place you started.

Though it may have been coined for a bad physics paper, here I want to adopt Pauli's phrase in connection with a contemporary philosophical and theological problem which often claims scientific warrant: "New Atheism." To be clear at the outset: there is no such thing as a monolithic "New Atheism" with any one set of arguments or claims (something it shares with the "religion" that it seeks to refute—a theism derived from Christianity which itself lacks any single, universal set of beliefs, other than some acknowledgment of God as creator).[2] When I say "New Atheism," I mean the set of aggressive denials of God's existence that have risen to cultural prominence in the last decade or so, which claim that scientific evidence easily and obviously renders God unnecessary, improbable, and unbelievable.[3]

The New Atheism isn't right. It's not even wrong.

1. Michael Shermer, "Wronger Than Wrong," *Scientific American*, October 16, 2006.

2. No doubt the frustration in defining the "opponent" is mutual.

3. Whether or not New Atheism has a coherent intellectual identity is an interesting question, but one for another time. What it certainly does have is a public profile, and my interest here is in what that public profile tells us not about New Atheism itself but about the current situation of religious belief.

#

Because its claims are far from being right, it is tempting for those who know anything at all about theology to dispatch them quickly with corrections, as if swatting away flies ("No, that's not how the argument from design works." "Of course you can be a Christian and still accept evolution." "But who made the laws of physics? Where do they come from?"—you get the picture). However, because New Atheism is not just not right but in fact not even wrong, these attempts have been, and continue to be, doomed to failure. The people who need to hear them aren't listening, and because they tend to interpret even the most careful theological explanations as simply more irrational special pleading for religion, they often *can't* listen.

At the same time, given the vast cultural interest it has generated, we must recognize the attractive power of the New Atheism. By now we can say it is not arguments that make New Atheism alluring—because its arguments are amateurish and unconvincing.[1] Still, significant numbers of people *want* to be convinced by these arguments, and that is a phenomenon that deserves the very best of any believer's attention. It's the desire beneath that attraction that fascinates me.

Put differently, and contrary to the prevailing narrative, this is not primarily a matter of science putting religion on the ropes. Religion is not in trouble because scientific reason has unmasked it as mythology; religion is in trouble because many people want to be able to reject it, and New Atheism gives them a way to do so. It is the *source* of the science/religion tension, rather than its outcome, that is most interesting. This means that the primary challenge facing Christians ought to change with the problem. Today the task is not to answer the arguments of the New Atheism on their own grounds. Rather, we should ask what it is *in Christianity* that does such an effective job of making New Atheism attractive. Moreover, we need to be open to the possibility that this "no" to belief responds to distorted elements of Christian belief, elements that make faith seem ridiculous enough that the New Atheism appears to be the more rational option.

Still, perhaps my summary dismissal of New Atheist arguments is overly quick. In a nutshell, then, here's why the New Atheism is "not even wrong":

1. The philosophical and theological refutation of New Atheism has been, in a word, thorough; it has also been fairly thoroughly ignored by the New Atheists. I certainly do not wish to reproduce the whole sorry mess here. The best (shorter) starting place is probably Terry Eagleton's devastating review of Richard Dawkins's *The God Delusion* in the *London Review of Books* 28.20 (October 19, 2006): 32-34. For a more thorough and systematic discussion, a good starting point is John F. Haught's *God and the New Atheism: A Critical Response to Dawkins, Harris, and Hitchens* (Louisville, KY: Westminster John Knox Press, 2008).

because the God it rejects is not the God that believers actually, well, believe in—either naïvely or even when they think about it carefully. It is a laughably incoherent concept of the Divine that New Atheism argues against, one believers only affirm when the alternative seems to be denying God's existence outright.

Painted into that corner, Christians can end up defending a god who is not God—or more precisely, defending certain claims about God as if they were the ground of faith, rather than its consequents, and the not-even-wrongness of the debate increases exponentially from there. The problem is that these defenses center on definitions of God as "creator," "supreme being," or "first cause," which are abstractions on which most believers do not expend much time, effort, or thought. They pray, worship, and live their religious lives through community, ritual, and relationship.[2] Does this belief in God meet the test of scientific reason, the New Atheists ask? The question is largely meaningless, since the claims made by such belief do not generally infringe upon areas of scientific competence. Do friendships meet the test of scientific reason? Do marriages and love for children? These are category errors, not meaningful questions. Meanwhile, those who have thought through their idea of God in more formal terms have ample resources to parry the objections of these most recent proponents of atheism.

Whatever other claims might be fairly leveled against it, Christian theology has at least avoided a concept of God so flimsy as to be easily disproved by evolutionary theory or the latest discoveries about matter and energy popping into existence out of the quantum vacuum. The God believed in and confessed over the course of theological history is—and has been, for centuries—far beyond these sorts of objections.[3] This is not to say that these sorts of problems are silly or trivial, but rather to point out that they have been successfully understood and integrated into the way theology discusses God.

2. In general, the prominent New Atheist thinkers do not seem to spend much time or effort on "lived religion," with the possible exception of evolutionary-psychology explanations of how a number of behaviors which then give rise to religion as a by-product could have come about as adaptations in response to selection pressure; see, for example, Steven Pinker's 2004 address on receipt of "The Emperor's New Clothes Award" from the Freedom from Religion Foundation, http://pinker.wjh.harvard.edu.

3. The basic reason that God escapes these objections is because God is not one existing thing among others, but the very source and ground of existence. Put another way, Christian theology recognizes that when we ask "why" and "how" questions about the *totality of existence itself*, we are operating on a much different level than when we ask about how stellar fusion works, or why we have opposable thumbs, or even what conditions were like during the Big Bang. When Christian theology asks after a designer, it seeks not the one who scripted the events of evolution but the one who designed existence itself such that evolution could occur; when it reflects on a creator, it seeks not the first thing that popped into existence out of a vacuum but the very reason for the vacuum itself existing at all.

In fact, the development of "scientific reason" itself can be traced in part to advances in philosophy and theology that allowed us to mark off certain sets of questions as amenable to purely empirical investigation.

#

Unfortunately, the proponents of the New Atheism do not seem especially interested in engaging religion in its most rational and well-articulated forms, where it has thought seriously about its relationship with science.[4] Instead, treating all religion monolithically—a set of superstitious, mythical claims to be debunked—they respond to and reinforce a "not even wrong" understanding of theology itself: faith reduced to a set of dogmatic propositions that the believer holds to be true or false.[5] New Atheist polemics are directed largely against a religion for which revelation is principally a source of explanations—the kind of religion described to us when we learned about Greek mythology. You remember: explaining the sound of thunder by reference to Zeus or Mount Etna's eruptions by Typhon being trapped underneath it. A similar approach has appeared in some Christian circles, reading the book of Genesis as a just-so story of what God did while making everything. This model of religion is inadequate for understanding Greek mythology; it is worse than useless as applied to Christianity.

That said, the New Atheists aren't alone in setting poor terms for the debate, as Christianity itself has defenders who seem eager to confirm the worst suspicions of the New Atheists, including those who insist on literal interpretations of scripture that fly in the face of science (and who then try to force those interpretations into school curricula or leverage them into the rejection of other scientific claims for political ends—as with global warming). Of the many things that could be said about this, I will confine myself to

4. Richard Dawkins, for instance, recently commented on Twitter, "I'm told theology is outside my field of expertise. But is theology a 'field' at all? Is there anything in 'theology' to be expert ABOUT?"; http://twitter.com/RichardDawkins/ (April 16, 2013). Lawrence Krauss, author of *A Universe from Nothing: Why There Is Something Rather Than Nothing*, when pushed in an interview to acknowledge that the "nothing" from which he argues the universe arises is in fact not "nothing" in the sense that a philosopher or theologian means it (because it has a "something" consisting of the laws of physics), replied, "But I don't really give a damn about what 'nothing' means to philosophers; I care about the 'nothing' of reality. And if the 'nothing' of reality is full of stuff, then I'll go with that." See Ross Andersen, "Has Physics Made Religion and Philosophy Obsolete?" *The Atlantic,* http://www.theatlantic.com (April 23, 2012). Krauss does at least bother to understand the objection; he just rejects it as uninteresting—which delivers us back to the problem of how to respond to New Atheist claims other than by correcting their mistakes.

5. Another version of this essay is likely possible, in which the blame for starting the "not even wrong" cycle would be laid at Christianity's door for the conditions in which fundamentalism arose.

three. First, this is what happens when arguments over not-even-wrong claims get going—no amount of scientific evidence can convince a scriptural literalist, because the (scientific) method by which the evidence is obtained already belongs to the "enemy."

Second, this is not a new problem. St. Augustine had cause in the fifth century to counsel against allowing an unbeliever "to hear a Christian, presumably giving the meaning of Holy Scripture, talking nonsense" on scientific topics such as the motion of the stars and the kinds and variety of animals.[6] The danger Augustine was concerned with was not that the Christian would look foolish, but that the Christian would cause the Bible to appear foolish by offering an unnecessary and poorly informed interpretation in which scripture contradicted reality.

Third, and perhaps most important, there is an opportunity here for rational, non-fundamentalist Christians to make common cause with the defenders of science. In truth, they have even more reason than the New Atheists to reject such strained readings of scripture, because they not only prevent knowledge of science but also encourage an incoherent and even blasphemous view of God. A God who is so fragile as to require believers to imagine that perhaps fossils were created *in situ*, only appearing to be millions of years old, is scarcely worthy of the name. Worse yet, fear of scientific investigation amounts to a rejection of the gift of human intelligence and thus a disfiguring of the image of God in which human beings are made. Rational Christianity wants to, and does, celebrate science as among the human achievements that give glory to God. However, so long as the authority of science is claimed to require us to judge belief in God irrational in itself, very little progress can be made: We will remain stuck in the loop where one side thinks God is routinely overruling science while the other celebrates ignorance of theology. How can we get off the not-even-wrong merry-go-round?

#

I propose that we start by asking why New Atheism is so attractive and convincing for some people, rather than whether it is correct per se. As a popular phenomenon, New Atheism does not succeed because of the cogency of its arguments, but because it offers an apparently convincing way to resolve a difficult question. The popularity of New Atheism tells us that there is both a fascination and a frustration with the persistent "problem of God." On one hand, the fascination ought to give us hope as an echo of that restlessness that moves our hearts until they rest in God. On the other, the frustration requires

6. Augustine of Hippo, *The Literal Meaning of Genesis*, 1.19.39.

our attention, because it reveals a considerable desire for a way simply to head off the problem by dismissing it at its source.

Most religious belief does not begin with philosophical and theological arguments for God's existence. The broad popularity of New Atheism, *despite* its shoddy arguments, suggests that we can perhaps say much the same about unbelief. Something else is going on. New Atheism offers a rational justification for abandoning religion, which may serve to resolve more basic struggles that people have with religious claims. These must not be dismissed out of hand. They tell us that a significant number of people experience the claims of religion not only as oppressive, arbitrary, and irrational but further as offering no real good in exchange for the sacrifices demanded. It would be hubris to assume that this is principally a failure of understanding on the part of the nonreligious; we may in fact discover that they have a clearer view of some pathologies in lived Christian belief than those of us who are closer to them.

New Atheism succeeds because it tells people that their negative experience of religion and religious believers is exactly as it should be, because religion itself is just a pernicious side effect of the need for social control. Or that religion is a vestige of our tendency to detect agency in the world, or some other evolved capacity. It succeeds because it tells people that a God whose main purpose is to balance the metaphysical ledger and account for the beginning and design of things is scientifically unnecessary and more than a little crazy. Therefore, the argument goes, this God should not get to make demands about what we do with our Sunday mornings, much less what we do with our sexuality. It succeeds because it offers an apparent Ockham's Razor-esque explanation of the hypocrisy of Christian moralizing: There was never anything real there to begin with, just stories to scare us into being good little boys and girls with the threat of hell. It succeeds because in the wake of clergy-abuse scandals and the church's recent interventions in politics, it can seem that more public effort has been devoted to self-protection than to the service of others (which is exactly what one would predict if belief really is just a security blanket). New Atheism has traction because it offers people a way to reject a superficial shadow of Christianity, a self-satisfied, self-assured, and self-indulgent church; a lifeless zombie instead of the living Body of Christ.

And God knows—literally—that such a distortion of faith deserves rejection. We religious types too rarely admit this.

A common rhetorical trope among New Atheists is to claim that everyone living rejects most of the gods humanity has ever believed in, and they just go "one god further." Richard Dawkins, making this point in a 2002 TED talk, defined an atheist as "just somebody who feels about Yahweh the way any decent Christian feels about Thor or Baal or the golden calf." This is much like a religious person, upon hearing a strange conception of God, replying, "I don't believe in that God, either."

But I think Dawkins is on to something even deeper here, because the rejection is not just casual, the way we might dismiss Zeus as merely mythical. Passionate atheism is the rejection of a false God, not just an imaginary one. Perhaps much of contemporary atheism can be explained as the (mistaken) rejection of God as if he were merely an idol, or more bluntly, as the (proper) rejection of the idol called "God" (or "Jesus," or "church," or "Christian values") that far too many Christians worship in place of the Living God.

The arguments of New Atheism may be "not even wrong," but the underlying motive for accepting them—and this should give us pause—might just come from God. After all, idols are not to be tolerated, or even to be dismissed and disbelieved and set off to one side. They need to be unmade.

The true threat of an idol is not what it represents—because what it represents has no independent real existence—but what it obscures. To the degree that religious language, especially our claims about God, are heard merely as assertions of authority, to be believed simply because we say so or even because we say that God says so, they have become idols. They obstruct a deeper authentic relationship because they are limited to addressing God as the mere conclusion of our arguments, or as filtered through the "literal" meaning of scripture. That is the very definition of idolatry: a god we can dominate and deploy for our own purposes. Whether or not such a domesticated deity ought to be dismissed as nonexistent, it certainly ought to be rejected as unworthy of worship.

The challenge then becomes to announce the God who *is* worthy of worship, and careful arguments, while necessary, cannot be sufficient to that task. However grateful we are for those who tirelessly correct the theological ignorance of the New Atheists, however clear and convincing we can make our apologetics, neither of these can be the real solution—at least not if contemporary atheism is actually an allergic response to idolatry instead of the disease itself.

New Atheism is not right—but what is actually wrong is our feeble belief in a god cut down to the size of our own understanding rather than in God, the creator and redeemer of all that is, who is in love with and in search of his people. The answer is not to proclaim more loudly the "God" the New Atheism not-even-wrongly denies, but to confess more humbly and honestly our encounter with God who is greater than we can imagine.

27. My Opium Addiction: God, Religion, and Other Drugs

Timothy O'Brien, S.J.

Times are tough for Karl Marx, and not just because he's been dead for over a hundred and thirty years. As the nations most directly influenced by his thought have foundered (Cuba), collapsed spectacularly (the Soviet Union), or backed slowly away from outright communism (China), a good number of his ideas seem to live only in the tattered copies of *The Marx-Engels Reader* sold in college bookstores. A good number, but not all.

Even if fewer and fewer living souls still think that communism is the destination of our relentless economic march, Marx's most famous dictum—that "Religion is the opium of the people"[1]—is still alive and kicking. Maybe more so today than when he first committed it to paper. In fact, due in no small measure to its delicious pithiness, "religion as opiate" remains one of the handiest definitions of religion around. It's one of those phrases that I've heard so many times that I can't even remember exactly where I first heard it.

Though I can't place my first exposure to the idea, I still remember my initial reaction to it, which remained consistent through my undergraduate career: resistance, of a strongly dismissive type. I've spent a good bit of time trying (without success) to recall exactly what it was that I jotted in the book's margin upon stumbling upon the storied passage. "Ha!" or "Please!" would have been too tame. I'm an active and at times aggressive reader, so it's a fair bet that an expletive may have been involved. You get the picture.

But unlike its companions in the landfill of ideas I've encountered and quickly discarded, Marx's quip has had considerable, albeit intermittent, staying power. Like a specter from the film *Ghostbusters,* it returns to slime me just when I least suspect it. This is because it's a colorful, provocative image for thinking about faith—even for a believer such as myself.

So even as college has become grayer and grayer in my memory, Marx's dictum has remained in bold color. It's taken me some time to puzzle out why,

1. Karl Marx, *Critique of Hegel's Philosophy of Right* (ed. Joseph O'Malley; Cambridge: Cambridge University Press, 1977), 131.

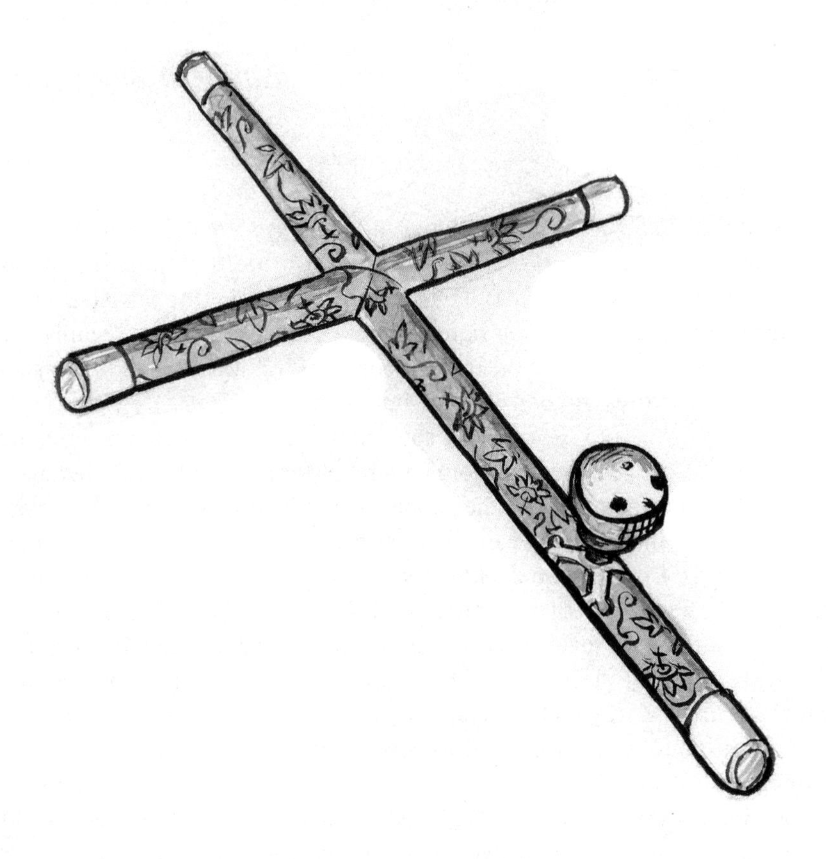

but I think I finally have a read on it: It stays with me because the content as well as the context of the quote give me pause. Marx wrote the passage specifically because he was concerned about religion's capacity to dull the pain of existence among the exploited working and lower classes of his day. This anesthesia, he thought, tempered their zest for overthrowing the forces that oppressed them, the upshot being that religious types favored apparent happiness over the real deal. As one generally opposed to oppression, and as one familiar with the phrase "Pay, Pray, and Obey," you can see why this strikes a nerve in me.

Better still, you don't have to be a Marxist to think he's right. I've met my share of tried-and-true capitalists who hold basically the exact same position, viewing religion as little more than magical thinking. Oxycodone for the soul. A little pill of false hope ingested to numb the pain of life with the promise of happiness eternal.

If Marx is right, then I—and a lot of people I know and love—long ago sailed past recreational usage into full-blown addiction. Probably because of the implication that I am accidentally drug addled, I have spent a good deal of time thinking about this analogy. And despite my initial resistance to the notion of religion-as-opiate, after pondering it I had to admit (reluctantly) that there may actually be a problem here. What if he was right?

There is one reason why I remain unconvinced that religion is primarily a means of soothing the pain of life, that by believing we become somehow inoculated against pain. It's that, if numbing the pain is what religion is supposed to do, I'm faced with a rather sharp question: What am I doing wrong?

I am a "Cradle Catholic," and a Jesuit to boot. I live a religious life, in multiple senses of the word. But religion has not been a duller of pain for me. Or at least not only so. And yet there's something in Marx's accusation that remains true. It's the persistent strangeness of this fact that has led me to think that Marx's metaphor possesses a rare trait: It's both transparently false and unwittingly true at the same time.

#

What do I mean, then, when I claim that religion-as-opiate is transparently false? Two things. First, I mean to recognize that, for every pain religion assuages, every ray of hope it offers, it also brings its share of coldness into our world.

This is a less-than-comfortable fact for those of us who profess to be religious. It should be.

I am not even talking about remarkable instances of hardship born of religion, the kind that eventually make their way into our history books:

Crusades, Inquisitions, coerced conversions. There is pain aplenty in much more anonymous sufferings: the suffering of the vulnerable youth whose trust in a minister of God is met only with the shattering betrayal of abuse and a possible lifetime of trauma. The suffering of a woman who feels called to ministry in a congregation and yet is barred from it. The suffering of those who, because of their support of the unborn and unwanted, feel dismissed by cultural elites and intellectual debutantes. The suffering of a gay person who discovers that the supposedly unconditional love of God comes with considerable fine print. The suffering of those who are persecuted for the sheer fact that they practice a religion at all.

Someone may wish to tell them that religion takes away their pain. I am not that person. All too often it does nothing of the sort. What kind of person, I want to ask the shade of Marx, has any use for an opiate that doesn't anesthetize?

The second transparent problem with the religion-as-opiate idea is that . . . how to put this . . . it *under-describes* what's there to be seen in the world around us. Put differently, even if religious belief can push people into a kind of "holy flight" from the world's troubles, the opposite is also the case. For many people, Christians among them, religion prompts deeper engagement *with* the world, and at places so staggeringly painful that there is no proper relief, medical or otherwise, from the trauma such engagement can cause.

A woman in Calcutta, moved by the plight of the poor and the love of Christ, who cares for the dying and orphaned, the crippled and destitute. A man who asks to go to the poorest parish in Los Angeles, sharing life and kinship with gang members trapped in spirals of violence. A college professor who leaves a tenured position at a cushy American university to replace one who was assassinated for standing with the poor in El Salvador. A religious sister in Philadelphia who stands at the bedside of a comatose young man, whom she does not know, because it is from that vantage point that the gospel makes sense to her.

You see what I'm driving at. The ideas that are the beating heart of Christianity—compassion and mercy, to say nothing of Incarnation—are as likely to throw believers headlong into the world as vice versa. And this world remains a place where pain and providence, suffering and salvation cohabitate.

Of course, this is not all of religion. Yes, it leaves out some nasty preachers and judgmental congregations who, no matter how tiny their numbers, become the faces of Christianity in an image-driven culture. It overlooks the ever-rising tide of historical atrocities perpetrated under the banners of religious faith. And it sidesteps a fair number of theologians who seem to think that God must be small enough to dance on the head of a pin.

Yes, it may not be all of religion. But is it not the best of it?

#

One of the properties of an opioid is that it is highly addictive, so addictive in fact that the person who stops using is consumed in a hell of withdrawal.

I took my first hit when I was twenty. It was just before my junior year in college, and I was on a silent retreat. If I could describe what happened more clearly I would, but precision fails me here. (Such are the perils of trying to write about the ineffable.) Suffice it to say that over the course of those few days I felt the immanence and embrace of an overwhelming love. It was a kind of love that, against all of my presuppositions and even preferences, touched parts of my life that I had long hidden. It named even these lovable.

I recognized this Love immediately and intuitively as the Mystery that we call God. And for as much as I craved this kind of acceptance—gasped for it, really—I also resisted it. Ever ready to set boundaries on God's love, especially for myself, I found it almost unseemly or repugnant to be embraced so wildly, unreservedly. Yet so I was. Lucky for me, God is far less zealous than I am in protecting his honor.

Did this hit produce a high? You bet your ass. But it was not sheer comfort. Conversion, even aided by grace, rarely is. This experience called me to more authentic relationships of all kinds. It did not so much pull me out of the world as thrust me into it. To repurpose a line by the poet Spencer Reece, "All I know now / is the more he loved me the more I loved the world."[1]

That high lasted for a long time, and in its wake I began to make some painful (not to mention important) decisions, most of which were another reminder that religion is a poor opiate. It was this experience that brought me back to the religious faith of my childhood, with all its beauty and blemish. It was after that moment that I first began seriously considering a Jesuit vocation, a call whose inklings I had long resisted. But all of a sudden it seemed a very practical way to incarnate the love I had come to know. Years later, here I am.

#

With time, the initial intensity of encountering the Divine has waned. In recent years, in fact, there have been times when God has seemed at best hidden and, at worst, notable only by absence. I have learned that what was once present as a stunning, scalding light can indeed be reduced to a flicker. There is a profound disorientation that accompanies this return to ordinary time, to say nothing of the hunger and almost visceral yearning for the absent to be present once more.

1. Spencer Reece, "The Road to Emmaus," *Poetry* 199 (October 2011), 14.

It is here, on the other side of this barren circle of dependence and withdrawal, that I've come to see more than falsity in Marx's analogy. He was right, in a way; there is something addictive about religion. Call it "spiritual," call it "mystical," call it whatever the hell you like, but it points to the belief that we can actually come to feel God's presence, to *know God*. To speak in the dialect of Ignatian spirituality for a moment, we can relate to God even "as one friend does to another." The flip side of this is that there is such a thing as spiritual withdrawal. I've seen it in others; I've felt it myself.

I don't use the language of addiction glibly. It really is the only analogy capable of capturing the experience of craving something that will destroy you, even though in this instance the "you" destroyed is the false self. What's remarkable, to me at least, is that it means that there are times when this God is known most acutely in absence—that feeling of something or someone once there, but present for now only as longing, desire, thirst.

Most likely Marx, at this point, would accuse me of speaking in riddles. I would like to assure him (and you, dear reader) that I am not. Those who have endured the loss of a beloved—to death or the breakdown of a relationship—know this present absence all too well. So does the poet Marie Howe. Though she might bristle at being called a "religion addict," her slight, four-verse poem "Annunciation" captures the experience I'm identifying better than my prose.[2] It begins,

> Even if I don't see it again—nor ever feel it
> I know it is—and that if once it hailed me
> it ever does—

It's in the aching that the absent one is present, sometimes even more vividly than when close at hand. And in the absence something is there, something real. Yet we sense it strangely, in the vacant contours of the space it once occupied.

Masters of the spiritual life have filled books reflecting on this experience, offering suggestions for how to handle times when the thousand-watt bulb of God's light seems to burn out with a pop and a hiss. Some are more helpful than others. Their focus is usually on regaining the high, on flooding the soul with light once more. Mostly the emphasis is on waiting and patience and persistence. On angling ourselves back toward God once more. Howe continues:

---

2. Marie Howe, *The Kingdom of Ordinary Time* (New York: W.W. Norton & Company, 2008), 43.

And so it is myself I want to turn in that direction
not towards a place, but it was a tilting
within myself.

The idea I want to contribute is simply this: even when the feeling's gone, and even if it never returns, it is still there. We know it by our longing, by the void left behind. It's in this sense that Marx was right: To be religious is to be a kind of addict, and forever.

as one turns a mirror to flash the light to where
it isn't—I was blinded like that—and swam
in what shone at me

only able to endure it by being no one and so
specifically myself I thought I'd die
from being loved like that.

An addict, that is, for whom nothing can ever be the same again.

28. Let History Repeat Itself: Finding Catholic Health Care's Future in Its Past

Michael Rozier, S.J.

For my money, there are few American Catholic lives more compelling than those of the women religious who built hundreds of hospitals across the United States. These are women who have the qualities the movies attribute to them—compassionate, generous, and charitable. But they were also, quite frankly, bad-asses. Take, for example, the seven Benedictine sisters in Duluth, Minnesota, who opened a hospital to care for a bunch of lumberjacks during a boom in the industry. Medical care was typically done in one's home, and, like men in a lot of frontier towns, these lumberjacks were away from their wives, who would have otherwise taken care of them when they got sick. In addition to offering medical care, Sr. Amata Mackett would darn their socks, bake them pies, and provide counsel during times of trouble. You may be thinking that this is exactly what you would expect from a nun. But when the lumberjacks tried to avoid paying their bills, she chased them through the forests of northern Minnesota with a fire poker to collect funds owed for their medical care.[1]

Thus, these men learned the same lesson I learned in grade school: Don't mess with a nun.

You might think Sr. Amata is the exception, but with the pioneering sisters of American Catholic health care, fearlessness seems to be the rule. Did you know that the world-famous Mayo Clinic was begun in the aftermath of a devastating tornado in Rochester, Minnesota, by Franciscan sisters and three Protestant doctors, a father and his two sons? Or that when Philadelphia was struck by a cholera epidemic in 1832 and everyone else refused to care for the sick, the Sisters of Charity responded to a request from the city Board of Health to step into the breach? Or that in the early days of Alcoholics Anonymous, another Sister of Charity in Cleveland amended hospital admittance policies to include alcoholism when no other hospitals would? And that of

1. Suzy Farren, *A Call to Care* (St. Louis, MO: Catholic Health Association of America, 1996), 140.

the four thousand women who served as nurses during the Civil War, over six hundred were women religious from twenty-one different congregations, sifting through fields of dead bodies to nurse those still alive back to health?

These women were not only at the forefront of health care; they were some of the most visible representatives of the nascent Catholic Church in the United States. When much of this country was skeptical of Catholic allegiance to a foreign pope, the heroic actions of these women were a significant antidote against anti-Catholic sentiments. To be sure, this was not their goal; their desire was to respond to the call of Christ. Still, their authentic response could not but win over the watchful public. That's the secret of the gospel: When it is lived well, it draws people in and makes the world a less divided, more joyful, more caring place.

Thus, a group of women who once needed special permission from the local bishop to attend a meeting at night ended up constructing an industry that now annually serves over 5.4 million patients and has revenues of over $100 billion.[2]

But for all the gripping history, I find the present far less compelling. Rather than being an obvious part of the church's witness to the gospel, Catholic health care often either gets mired in minutiae of moral controversy, or administrators allow the invisible hand of various markets to influence decisions disproportionately. It doesn't have to be this way, and I think we can find a way forward by glancing back.

#

You don't have to look too far into history to find a totally different world of health care, a world where, if someone could afford medical care, they got it at home. Hospitals, from their inception in monastic Europe up to nineteenth-century America, were essentially for the poor and isolated. Patients often tended to one another, the sickest receiving care from those whose ailments were less severe. Physicians visited when they didn't have private patients, but even then weren't terribly effective. And patients were there for weeks or months, often waiting to die of whatever disease ailed them. Moreover, like many Catholic parishes, ethnic hospitals arose in the United States to care for those who shared the same language and culture.

Compare this to hospitals today. No longer for the poor, now they are for those with insurance.[3] Hospital stays are usually brief—measured in hours

2. http://www.chausa.org.

3. The best estimate is that less than 2 percent of hospital expenses are related to charity care (those without insurance or those with insurance who can't pay their bills). Catholic hospitals do better than this, but providing this type of care is partly why they retain tax-exempt status.

or days rather than in weeks or months. Hospitals arc largely chosen based on insurance networks, not language, faith, or culture. High-quality care is rendered even at the simplest community hospital due to standardization and accreditation procedures. And could you even imagine one of your fellow patients—less sick than you, of course—helping with your care? ("This won't hurt a bit. . . .")

The health care of yesterday would be unrecognizable if implemented today, and the specific reasons women religious first began providing health care in this country have largely disappeared. The military now has full medical teams. Epidemics are handled by a well-trained public health service. Many nonreligious hospitals have very effective chaplaincy services. Language translation is legally required for all patients. And the poor must be given emergency care at any facility, even though they all too often still don't get decent care.

So, if the reasons Catholics first got into health care have disappeared, could it be that we no longer need Catholic health care? As more and more health care is paid for by government funding,[4] an increasing number of people will make a case for that position. Catholics, of course, can contend that we have a right to be engaged in the provision of health services. But I think that argument is unfit for the legacy we have inherited. We serve not because we legally can, but because it is who we are. I would much prefer that non-Catholics, upon seeing what we do, realize just by watching that our society still needs Catholic health care. My hope is that they can stand alongside us in the public square and help us make our case.

For that to happen, though, we need Catholic health care to be as responsive to today's concerns as the sisters mentioned above were to the needs of their time. And in the same way that they evoked the image of Christ for those who looked upon their faith and actions, in order to move forward we must consider what we can do to evoke Christ the healer for those who look upon Catholic health care today. The United States is in as much need of the gospel today as it was a century ago, and I trust when proclaimed well the gospel attracts more than it repels. So where do we start?

This is admittedly a difficult, open question. The United States Conference of Catholic Bishops offers *Ethical and Religious Directives*, a fairly comprehensive document, but one that is deployed in a very narrow way. If the only important element of being Catholic is not performing certain reproductive procedures, then we are quite simply not responding to the vast needs of our time. And the image of Christ evoked is just a shade less compelling than the one we encounter in scripture.

4. The Center for Medicare and Medicaid services project that the percentage of health care funded by the government will rise from 44 percent in 2009 to 50 percent by 2020.

The Catholic Health Association states in its profile, "Catholic health care is a ministry of the Catholic Church continuing Jesus' mission of love and healing in the world today. . . . Catholic health care is committed to improving the health status of communities and creating quality health care that works for everyone, especially the vulnerable."[5] That sounds a bit more like the Jesus I read about in the Gospels. But what does it actually mean?

The sisters' work flowed from who they were. Their faith preceded their actions, but their actions increased people's faith. Their love manifested itself in deeds more than in words. With due respect to the work of management consultants, these women built an unparalleled network that cared for the most vulnerable without ever sitting through meetings to craft a statement of mission, vision, and values. Perhaps if you have to go to great pains to describe the importance of what you are doing, it might not be that important.

#

I can't imagine the sisters serving during the Civil War sitting around a campfire with a tin of beans asking themselves if their actions were "Catholic enough." The sisters serving during the cholera epidemic didn't have to search far to understand that what differentiated their work from others is that the sisters actually showed up. None of them had to worry about explaining how valuable their work was because its importance was evident to anyone who had eyes to see. They were Mary *and* Martha, contemplation *and* action, inextricably linking who they were and what they did. They were believers in Christ who made Christ present in their actions. It is consoling to imagine how vivid it must have been for those who lived alongside them.

It's that vividly imagined scene, and the consolation it stirs up, that demands we learn to ask a better question than "What makes Catholic health care Catholic?" I think it's this: "How can Catholic health care today evoke the same awe and faith that were evoked by these women in the past?" Or, "How can Catholic health care evoke the image of Christ the healer for those who look upon it?" Our goal for Catholic health care should be that our love manifest itself in deeds more than in words, trusting that, once again, those who have eyes to see, will.

#

Who are the soldiers, the cholera victims, and the lumberjacks of today? Who is not being cared for in the way that Christ desires? To whom or where are others unwilling or unable to go?

5. http://www.chausa.org.

Without pretending that my vision is comprehensive, the answer to those questions certainly includes immigrant laborers, the addicted, the mentally ill, the elderly, the unborn, battered women and their children, the urban poor, the rurally isolated, and the many Native Americans living on reservations. Imagine if the Catholic Church put its vast network at the explicit service of these groups. Imagine if we did so with the same creativity, generosity, and disregard for self as the women religious who founded the movement in the first place. Consider the image of Christ we would be reflecting into the world.

Paul Farmer, the world-famous physician and anthropologist, famously adapted a catchphrase from liberation theology for use in the field of public health. He said, "Disease has a preferential option for the poor." All of us who work in the health sciences know this to be true. From Belize to Boston, every public health project I have taken on reinforces for me that those who bear the greatest burden of disease are those who are least able to afford it. Nearly every major disease affects the poor at a higher rate than it strikes the rich. Even worse, the poor are less likely to have insurance; they can less easily miss work; they have fewer options for child care; they are less likely to have transportation to hospitals or pharmacies, and so on. Both science and morality are telling us the same thing—turn your gaze to the vulnerable.

It is true that many Catholic hospitals do community outreach and use their suburban, tertiary care facilities to fund those services. Jesus, too, moved easily between different groups, whether Sadducees or Samaritans; he healed the nobleman's son (John 4:46-54) as well as a man who had been ignored by others for thirty-eight years (John 5:1-15). But there is a major difference between having your primary institution in the suburb with outreach to the poor and having your primary location among the poor with outreach to the suburb. The distinction carries with it a psychological and spiritual shift in emphasis, and both those on the inside and those looking upon them can sense the difference.

I am not unaware of the famous dictum, "No margin, no mission," the point of which is to emphasize that without a bottom line in the black, there won't be any chance for service to those on the margins of society. And the way funding works in our country, the least vulnerable have money to spend on health care and the most vulnerable do not. It seems to me that those who invoke this dictum imagine our institutions as modern-day Robin Hoods, shifting funds rather than stealing them. Indeed, the high profit margins from cardiac care facilities can and do fund a lot of free screenings for diabetes or breast cancer. And even in the early days, sisters provided private, more expensive rooms for wealthy patients so they could fund care of the poor elsewhere in the hospital. Still.

I have never carried the responsibility of keeping hospital doors open, but I don't offer this challenge naïvely: We must regularly—every day—ask ourselves what consumes our time, what is seen by the public who look upon us, and what image of Christ is being communicated—is it margin or mission?

#

As fewer women religious are health care providers and administrators, the charism of these women is being entrusted to others—women and men, lay and religious, Catholic and non-Catholic—and we should hope that the sisters' lives give a paradigm for *all* involved in Catholic health care. Handing over their works need not be a sign of diminishment if those who take the reins are as loving and fearless as Sr. Amata. If they—we—are, it will be only a magnification of the sisters' vocations. But it won't be a matter of simply maintaining what we already have or tinkering around the edges. The landscapes of health care and society are always changing, which means we must go where we are needed and leave where we are not.

The Alexian Brothers, in 1985, were among the first actively to promote a ministry for those affected by HIV/AIDS, an unpopular decision at the time but one rooted in care for the outcast. In 1995, several Sisters of Charity opened a clinic as a public–private partnership in El Paso, Texas, providing primary care to those who would otherwise go without because of distance to the nearest clinic, or because of their immigration status. The Sisters of the Holy Cross reorganized their operations in Utah, eventually merging with Mercy Health Services so that they could begin a new ministry, giving priority to the underserved.

The reasons women religious first entered health care in the United States have largely disappeared, but the reasons for the church to be engaged in such ministry have not. Hospitals, once refuges for the marginalized, are anything but today. It's not that the margins of society are empty; it's that we, the church, must go elsewhere to find them.

Health care can be an integral part of the church's mission, but if we must go to pains to describe how that is, we are doing it wrong. In one hundred years I hope someone like me picks up a book about Catholic health care in the early-twenty-first century and is as inspired by us as I am by the women religious of the nineteenth. It won't be easy, but if the stories of these women are true, it never was.

29. You Will Become Catholic

Joe Hoover, S.J.

It is mid-Lent and you stumble into a church, not because it is Lent or you have a habit of churchgoing but because you need a bathroom. You try to look like you belong there, bowing your head, making yourself a bit tense. They are just about to begin a service.

Something about the candles, the kid in the white gown holding the taper, the marble, the death, everywhere death and gloom and a lack of irony. This you want. Though you did not know it until now. Suddenly you can't make yourself leave.

You will stay for the entire Mass. And you will return, again and again.

One day you will sidle up to an usher in a green corduroy sport coat who frankly will be no help—who will not exactly fall all over himself to point you in the right direction to start becoming Catholic.

Which will only make you trust this place all the more.

You will go to a weekly class and they will tell you to find a "sponsor" (what is this, AA?), and every Sunday you will have to parade with your little group mid-service out of the church in front of the whole crowd, like a row of prisoners whose time in the activity yard is up.

Then one Saturday night you will put on a white "alb," which the harried woman whose smile you never believe and who is in charge of the whole thing has told you many many times "is your baptismal right to wear."

And the embarrassing and surreal totality of water. They drench you. Water as you have never used it before. Water without utility. You are not swimming, nor drinking, nor cleaning, nor cooking nor washing. You are doing what? "Symbolizing"? Is that a thing one does?

You just know the feeling, the way it is on your skin. As if no argument can be made against this, if someone would ever want to. If a charitable friend might tell you, for instance, that your Baptism is not really a thing that is happening to you—that it is a thing leveraged or constructed or something. But, no, it did happen to me. The water was really there. Damp towels to prove it. Why would I put myself through this bizarre pointless soaking if it wasn't real?

Your logic actually doesn't work that well, but for you it suffices.

And, truth be told, arguments are made against you, by people who know you, though they are never spoken out loud. You wish they would be! You want to hear them. Because really, you know better than this. You have no legitimate cover for taking such grievous measures with your life. There was no Catholic girlfriend, no pending wedding to become spiritually aligned for. There has been no vision, no astounding conversion story, no miracle of the internal organs. No Bible passage randomly flipped to, revealing the foul depths of your nonetheless sacred heart.

And so people will just think you are not that smart anymore. Or maybe you never really were that smart. And once they realize this, that you went off the mental rails somewhere—or never were on those rails—they can then consign you to a part of their brains that understands this quaint, even touching turn to old-time religion.

As for you, while you could cite doctrines, beliefs, and a bone-deep feeling, really it's this: You are in the game. That's all you really know. You're on the field, and you want to stay there.

#

For a while you will feel that to become Christian is to have taken on a kind of divine obligation to compliment people a lot. To say stiltedly, on car rides or at the tail end of breakfast at a diner, You are a good person, Jimmy. I have always really appreciated . . . the way you . . . work so hard on your lawn.

Every Sunday after Mass you will remain in the pew and with eyes closed pray for five minutes. But every time, rather than praying, you will simply become annoyed at all the people who are jingling their keys, shouldering their purses and chatting away as they leave the pews. It will take you an embarrassingly long time before you realize the futility of your devotion; that what you think is a practice drawing you closer to God is only making you loathe his people.

Though you don't think of yourself as some kind of fanatic, you will be drawn to Masses said by the priest who holds the host up a bit longer, stares at it a bit more fixedly. Eyes locked on the round wafer like a jeweler examining an unusual stone he can't quite fathom.

One day you will go to a pro-life rally even though you are pro-choice, pretty much. You don't tell your new Catholic friends this because you don't want to make waves or get into tedious arguments. You find the demonstration to be, well, pathetic. The only celebrities they could muster up were a Britney Spears back-up dancer and a woman who was once in a John Wayne movie? And one bishop? And no matter that your astute new friends tell you that the Catholic Church is not identical with the political entity called "the Pro-Life Movement," one or the other, you think, could dress things up a bit.

You will have moments, early on, when you wish everyone would just give the Catholic faith a shot. If only they would really stop and think about it! If they would just put all the pieces together. Get over all their hang-ups. If only you could talk to people, individually. If you could put something in your voice—a kind of pleading but not begging. An argument that is clear but not mechanical. Sensible but not wooden. If it's true that the Creator of the Universe (!) sent his only Son from heaven . . . and if it's true that this Son showed us how to live . . . through calm breaths merely stating facts, syllogisms leading to undeniable conclusions. If only you could tell them all over coffee how these seemingly oppressive Catholic things like "pontiff" and "dogma" and "hierarchy" are good! Because structure actually liberates and authority lends security and charismatics can be tested. . . . And you would go on, reasonably—charming even—and wouldn't they just melt into the arms of Rome.

But you never seem to get the perfect opportunity to make your case, and then over time it will all just seem less urgent and you will wonder if that is a loss or a gain.

You will drive through Madison, Wisconsin, and find yourself pondering why all college dj's in all college towns sound the same: the low halting monotone, the long silences, the sense that every record they are about to play (and it is always an actual record) is tucked away in some teetering stack just out of reach from where they sit.

This will have nothing to do with Catholicism. It will just be one of those things.

#

You will hear a really fine sermon at Mass approximately two, maybe three times a year.

The rest will float out there, and not land. They will bear little relation to your lived experience, nor move you emotionally nor call you to change anything about your actual life. You may never really notice this, though. You will just come to believe that this is how it is in the Catholic religion. In fact, you will vaguely believe that most priests probably have the ability to rouse their congregations with love, anger, and justice. But they are taught in seminary to humbly mute all of that, so as not to draw attention from the Eucharist. And that, truly, the only place one can expect to hear inspiring oratory is in a pregame college football locker room.

One day someone will point out to you that in Michelangelo's *Pietà,* the Blessed Mother is shown at the age she would have been when she gave birth.

The fourteen-year-old virgin holds her dead, grown child in her lap. She just gave birth to Jesus, and then he's thirty-three and crucified and then he's gone. All in an instant.

For the rest of your life whenever you see this statue, you just think—you can't even think. It's beauty and terror . . . this child holding . . . where do you even. . . . You realize that almost everything you could ever be taught about your religion is told perfectly and completely in this one block of marble. And though you do not consider yourself fervidly territorial, you feel a sort of wanton pride that this one, Michelangelo Buonarotti, lines up on your side.

#

At some point you will reconcile with the fact that there is a wickedness inside of you, as in all people, that will never go away.

Or you don't reconcile with it and you will always try to be better, to improve and perfect yourself in ways you can never achieve and you will die in ways you do not notice, slowly turning into a clutch of dry leaves on a rootless tree, crackling apart and scattering into the hot wind.

But you do, you do reconcile it, and something lifts.

You will get married and have three children, and they will all, of course, end up leaving the Catholic faith. One will do so outright, publicly, though not heatedly. She will come home from college and sit in the kitchen Sunday morning scrolling down a screen while you and her mother go off to church. Have a good time at Mass, she will say brightly, not looking up. She will be charitable. I respect your religion, Dad. Jesus was a great ethicist. Later that afternoon you will see her in the living room, draped in a plain gray smock or poncho, sitting in lotus for two straight hours meditating on the state of her ultimate emptiness: a feat that you will witness again and again for several visits home before you are able to tell her, without feeling like you are betraying your own religion, that you truly admire her endurance.

The younger daughter will leave the faith, but you will never know about it, not really. Because she will keep going to Mass with you when she comes home to visit. And because there is so little you actually know about her. This will be the source of a thin film of sadness at the edge of your life, for all of your life.

Every time she comes home her eyes seem a bit more hooded, darker, her body thinner. You wonder if she is on something. One day you finally ask her outright, and she just looks at you and says, Are you kidding? This clears up nothing. She sits next to you at Mass and says the words and does the gestures and where is she? All you can think to do is pray for her, but really, how do you pray for people? What does that even mean?

The third child, the oldest, will leave the faith by actually becoming more Catholic.

He will trade in faith for its opposite, certainty. Or the near occasion of. With votives, holy cards, novenas, rosaries, medals, prayer chains, adoration and several months of advance work hunting down precisely the right kind of Mass, he will conflate the shareholder ethos of late-modern American capitalism with the Holy Roman Catholic faith. He will have turned simple, poignant devotions into a network of annuities. If, say, the patella hits the marble and stays there longer than the time people conventionally allot before swinging into the pew, this small investment (when bundled with countless others) will likely pay off in future dividends. No, he's not simplistic, he's not dumb. He knows there are no guarantees. In either the financial world or the religious. But, honestly, the ticket is in his hand—it's his to cash in or not. If he just keeps showing up and punching his card, surely he will reap a healthy yield.

#

One day a member of the Knights of Columbus standing in the vestibule will hand you a little metal pin bearing feet the size they would be on a fetus in the womb. You take it, because he handed it to you.

One day you will start to wear this pin with the little feet on it. This does not mean that you have stopped becoming pro-choice. It just means you are wearing a pin that shows the size of the feet of a child when it is in the womb. But you will start to become more conflicted about being pro-choice.

You will never get beyond "becoming more conflicted about being pro-choice."

#

Each morning in the loamy hours before work you will sit down and pray. This feels like the responsible thing to do.

You do not realize that you pray every day out of fear that if you do not pray there will not be a God. If you do not by talking to him decide that he is there, he will not exist. This is a responsibility for holding together the entire universe that weighs on you far more than you know. It is only your ignorance that helps you get through it.

You will find yourself telling people that Mass is the best part of your day. And when they ask why, you will just look at them. As if they are out of their minds.

Where is your younger daughter? Where did she call from last? Philadelphia? Newark? (Newark? Why Newark? What happens in Newark?) Where is she sleeping, and with whom? Does she have a job? How does she eat? What courses through her body that isn't meant to be there? Or are you just overprotective, worrying too much. Is this how it just is with one's kids?

#

Every year on the Sunday before Ash Wednesday a priest will tell you, as if he were some completely revolutionary paradigm-shifting soft-hearted theocrat bestowing on the spiritually starved masses something they have never heard before: Don't *give up* something for Lent; *do something* for Lent!

Every year. How completely irritating. You like giving things up. The harder the better. And you will not let anyone, not even a priest, get between you and the serrated edges of your quietly self-induced suffering.

And speaking of priests—fine men, truly—but there will come into your life one day a cheery young cleric who tells you and all the men standing in the back of church at the 6:30 A.M. weekday to come sit in the front row! Take your jackets off. We're a community!

This will last about three days.

And then he will be told the way things work here. One or more of the men will take him aside, and gently clue him in as to the way it is. Maybe you will be the one to do it. Respectfully, of course. But telling him nonetheless that you were never taught in the Rite of Christian Initiation for Adults that there was a certain prescribed yardage from the altar within which one had to stand or sit for Mass to be valid and licit. At least not as far as you knew. Was there a new teaching on this, Father? No? OK. Well.

#

You will never think of leaving the church. No matter what gets said, or pronounced, or forbidden, or revealed, or never said at all. You just wouldn't. Sometimes more out of stubbornness than anything. Like a dusty film heroine yelling at her exhausted band of fortune seekers: We've already come this far!

If the temptation ever did arise to leave, you would probably stay because of the way Ted Nugent cleans the paten after communion at the Sunday 7 A.M. As the priest sits in the chair Ted (truly, he looks just like the great outdoorsman, everyone thinks so) stands in the corner of the sanctuary and carefully dusts the crumbs into the chalice, pouring the water in, gently swirling it around, biceps pressing through a lime-green sport shirt, fu manchu hovering over the holy vessels. Doing all of this as if it all means something. Means . . .what? Silence. And him dusting the paten, the last strains of *Now Thank We All Our God* still hanging in the air, and something is there. And whatever that thing is, you would not so casually leave it over . . . well, over anything.

#

One day you pick up a notice for a speaker on "Interreligious Dialogue," which includes this:

> Those who, through no fault of their own, do not know the Gospel of Christ or his Church, but who nevertheless seek God with a sincere heart, and moved by grace, try in their actions to do his will as they know it through the dictates of their conscience—those too may achieve eternal salvation. (*Lumen Gentium*, 16)

You look at this pamphlet every so often. Depending on your mood, you can't decide whether this statement is:

A. The most arrogant thing you have ever heard in your life. Who are we to decide to allow others to have their salvation? Do they really need our unsolicited blessing? They will be just fine, thank you, or

B. The most shameless example of Clintonian pandering you can imagine, unfit for a stately enterprise like the Roman Church. Why not just say, Here's the truth, here's the path, either get on board or good luck wading in the flood? But not this half measure, long as we all do our best—I mean, those people didn't have to go through Rite of Christian Initiation of Adults. They didn't have to knock on the door of the church in their white "albs" and say "Let us in!" or whatever it was. They didn't have to take a second job to pay for their kids' Catholic schools. They didn't have to avoid sex before marriage, or not really but at least feel pretty bad about it.

Worrying about this will take up approximately twelve minutes of your life.

Your parish gets a grant and hires a woman, married with a couple kids, who has a Master of Divinity degree and is very bright and holy. She offers spiritual direction to parishioners and frankly is supposed to be quite good. And the fact is you would never think of taking the caustic, unruly matters of your spiritual life to her. But if she were a nun you would. You don't even realize this about yourself. But if someone were able to point this out to you, you would say, Yeah. OK. A nun. That's probably right.

Your Buddhist will come back. She will come back as if she had never left: getting in the car to go to Mass and kneeling before the service starts and entering the communion line and kneeling afterward and when you look at her, bewildered, just looking back at you like, What?

You suddenly will find yourself wanting her to stay Buddhist. And go to Mass. Can one do this?

Your son will inform you that what the church needs is the same counter-intuitive medicine a recessionary economy needs. It must throw off, or simply stop worrying about, its regulatory framework (The Media, Theologians, Unchastened Public Opinion), and simply do "what it does best." It is undergoing a time of creative destruction, and it must become more itself by burning out the understory and popping out those conifer seeds that only germinate under extreme heat. If it becomes leaner, less cluttered, more streamlined, delivered back to its "core competency," so be it; all the better for confronting the hostile territory of the new "unchurched" century.

#

It is a Friday in Lent and you have been fasting all day to be in solidarity with Guatemalans, and now you hate Guatemalans. Your wife is away, the house is empty. You wander into your younger daughter's room. She long ago took down all the old posters and pictures. The walls are nearly bare. This happens to be a time in your life when the faith you once held so easily seems to be, not totally lost, just empty. The God whose presence was once felt is now just an idea "assented to." Truthfully, it hurts. Does it hurt as much as if, say, you lost your mortgage? Who knows? But it does hurt, more than you let on to yourself. It makes everything dark.

Maybe it has to do with your daughter. You sit down on her bed and wonder where you went wrong with her. Didn't you take her places? Didn't you take her fishing? Isn't taking a kid fishing supposed to be some kind of cold sealant on their character, and your connection? Why did your fatherhood (your work, your entire life) not turn out the way you thought it would? Or did it? What are you supposed to expect? Or does it matter? What would Jesus do? What a stupid question. Where is your daughter? You want to know her and talk with her and just have her around. Nothing in your religion can take this—her life, your relationship, your confusion, your nightmares—into its stony hands and solve it.

If you had enlisted that spiritual director she might tell you that you are feeling so distant from God because you are moving absolutely close to God. And so from this new, up-close angle you don't recognize him anymore. Your fears, your doubts, your "dark night"—it is causing you to turn away from your usual bag of tricks and rely on God and God alone.

And maybe that would be on target. Or maybe it wouldn't. Maybe that is what spiritual people say to comfort themselves. You have tried to talk about all this at confession, as if you have been doing something wrong. Your priest has encouraged you to pray more and maybe just kind of lighten up. He didn't really say that, but it came through.

So, why? Why did you enter this way of life in the first place? What was it all for? You can say the things everyone says. My faith is my "rock." The church is what I "fall back on." And you would mean it. It would be true. That *Pietà* is followed by a resurrection. Even when God is distant, you just continue. You believe because you want to believe.

But your faith doesn't take this little girl into itself and make her decisions for her, care for her, feed her, or tell you exactly what to do about her.

Why did you go into that church that first day, then? What was it all about? Is it like that story Christopher Plummer tells? About drinking all night in a bar on Broadway with Jack Lemmon? The morning finally comes and they're still down there going strong and finally Jack stumbles up the stairs and out into the morning sunlight.

Plummer isn't ready to call it quits, and he asks Jack where does he think he's going. Lemmon mumbles as he goes out, I gotta get to Mass. Gotta go to Mass.

Plummer looks confused and tells Lemmon, You don't go to Mass.

Gotta get to Mass.

Plummer runs up the stairs and out the door and watches as Lemmon weaves down the street. Finally he yells after him, But Jack, you're not even Catholic!

Did you stumble with the mysterious instincts of a superb comic actor into the faith? Well, what then? Because frankly the comedy is getting a little black.

You can't even really weep about any of this because it's all so formless. You don't know where she is, and you don't know where you are. You are hungry, annoyed, vacant, helpless. The only answer is to mow the yard. You start to get up from her bed. And then you notice something on the wall, down by her pillow.

It is a small framed picture, one that has been there so long you never even see it anymore. An angel rising above a bridge being crossed by two barefoot nineteenth-century children. A little country girl with billowy clothes and a blue ribbon in her hair, her arm around her plump, scared, effeminate little brother. One plank of the bridge is gone, the water rushes below. The angel with fat red cheeks hovers behind, arms outstretched, looking tenderly and a bit hungrily at the kids.

It was a gift on her fourth birthday. You remember when she got it. Like yesterday. Her little dress, her green shoes. The darkness roils around the bridge, night sweeping in, the kids crossing. Not yet on the other side. And the white presence looming. Long ago, every other picture was taken down, thrown away, you realize, but this one.

Contributors

Brendan Busse, S.J., was born and raised in southern California. His love of narrative and social justice led him to pursue degrees in English (B.A.) and Theology (M.A.) at Loyola Marymount University. Before joining the Jesuits, he taught high school and served as a Jesuit Volunteer in Belize for two years. Brendan is currently a faculty member at Seattle University. For the record, he hasn't shaved his face in its entirety since October of 1994. The precision of this date is due to the fact that facial hair was a "Senior Privilege" at his high school; welcoming the privilege, he has never looked back.

Ryan Duns, S.J., hails from Cleveland, Ohio, and has studied at Canisius College, John Carroll University, and Fordham University. He currently studies theology at Boston College. When not studying, he pursues his dream of being a rock-star accordion player and provides music at Irish dancing competitions across the country. In addition to teaching a YouTube course entitled "A Jesuit's Introduction to the Irish Tin Whistle," Ryan also blogs at "A Jesuit's Journey."

Quentin Dupont, S.J., was born and raised in Lille, northern France. His undergraduate studies brought him to Concordia University in Montreal, and Santa Clara University in California. After bachelor's degrees in economics and accounting with minors in finance and law, he pursued a master's degree in finance and banking at the university of Paris. He entered the Jesuits in Los Angeles in August of 2003, and presently studies theology at Boston College. Quentin is a fan of baseball and football, and loves music, movies, and playing golf.

Paddy Gilger, S.J., is an amateur sociologist and philosopher but a professional Milwaukee Brewers fan. He lived and worked for a few years at Red Cloud Indian School on the Pine Ridge reservation. Ordained in June of 2013, he is currently associate pastor of St. John's Parish at Creighton University, which is his alma mater. Paddy is the founding editor-in-chief of *The Jesuit Post.*

James Hooks, S.J., is from Tampa, Florida. Before entering the Society of Jesus in 2001, he worked as a radio announcer, studied Spanish Literature at Florida State University, and taught English in Japan. He was ordained in June of 2012, and recently completed an advanced degree at the Jesuit School of Theology in Berkeley, California. His thesis focused on the cultural roots of unbelief and religious disaffiliation among youth in the United States. He is now associate pastor at Immaculate Conception Church in Baton Rouge, where he also works part-time in campus ministry at Southern University.

Joe Hoover, S.J., is a Jesuit brother who works in the fields of acting, writing, and Ignatian spirituality. He also works at *America* magazine and is a part-time teacher at St. Ignatius Loyola School, a grammar school in New York City.

Jeffrey Johnson, S.J., is originally from Chattanooga, Tennessee. Jeff graduated from Vanderbilt University with a bachelor's in English before serving as an officer in the Navy. After entering the Jesuits, he studied at Fordham University and Boston College, where he earned a master's degree in English and a license in sacred theology (STL). His STL thesis was on the relationship between theology and literature. He is the assistant principal at Strake Jesuit High School in Houston, Texas.

Paul Lickteig, S.J., is a Jesuit priest who has just finished his licentiate in sacred theology at the Jesuit School of Theology in Berkeley, California. His interests include Christian theology, theater, studio and visual art, experimental (or "really bad") music, odd martial arts, rigorous honesty, not lifting weights, comic book heroes, and writing simple things in alternately opaque or incredibly ambiguous ways. He currently serves as associate pastor at St. Francis Xavier Church in Cincinnati, Ohio, where, if luck favors him, he will also learn how to bow hunt.

Vinny Marchionni, S.J., joined the Society of Jesus in 2008 and currently teaches history at Cristo Rey Jesuit High School—Baltimore. He relishes being back on the east coast after a three-year stint in Saint Louis, where he fell in the love with the study of liturgy, served the homeless and Greek life at Saint Louis University, promoted the Jesuit vocation, and actually managed to complete the mission entrusted to him by studying philosophy. He loves all things Philadelphia, especially its food, its history, and its Eagles.

James Martin, S.J., is a Jesuit priest, editor at large at *America*, a Catholic magazine, and author of several books, including *Jesus: A Pilgrimage*, *The Jesuit Guide to (Almost) Everything*, and *Between Heaven and Mirth: Why Joy, Humor and Laughter are at the Heart of the Spiritual Life*. Father Martin is a frequent commentator in the international and national media on matters religious and spiritual, and has written for, among other outlets, *The New York Times*, *The Wall Street Journal,* and *Slate.* He is also the "Official Chaplain to The Colbert Nation." (He's also about twenty years older than everyone else in this book, which the editors point out to him as frequently as humanly possible.)

Timothy O'Brien, S.J., met the Jesuits while studying political science at the College of the Holy Cross. He entered the Maryland Province in 2008 after a stint as a copy editor for the federal government. A graduate student in theology at the University of Chicago Divinity School, Tim moonlights as an editor at *The Jesuit Post.* He desires God's love and grace, and to win the New Yorker's cartoon caption contest (in that order). Tim also served as co-editor of this volume.

Perry Petrich, S.J., once played in a children's band in New York City where he also earned degrees in theater and theology from Fordham University, writing his thesis on "The Hold Steady." Originally from Tacoma, Washington, his false idols include the Mariners, Seahawks, and Washington Huskies. He now coaches middle-school football in Phoenix while teaching ninth-grade English to boys at Brophy College Prep on the side.

Nathaniel Romano, S.J., is a scholastic of the Wisconsin Province who is currently working as a staff attorney at the Milton R. Abrahams Legal Clinic at the Creighton University School of Law. He has a Juris Doctor degree from the University of Wisconsin Law School and is a member of the state bars of Nebraska and Wisconsin. (Nothing in his articles is intended as legal advice or to solicit or otherwise establish an attorney–client relationship.)

Michael Rossman, S.J., an Iowa native, joined the Jesuits in 2007 just after graduating from the University of Notre Dame. After studying abroad in East Africa during college, he now teaches at Loyola High School in Dar es Salaam, Tanzania. Obsessed with checking LeBron James's stats but not blessed with his skills, Michael enjoys coaching basketball at Loyola. Moving to the coast of the Indian Ocean has not changed his addiction to *The Atlantic* (magazine).

Michael Rozier, S.J., has a degree in international health systems from Johns Hopkins University. He taught global health and public health ethics as he served as the founding director of undergraduate education at Saint Louis University School of Public Health. He currently studies theology at Boston College School of Theology and Ministry.

Sam Sawyer, S.J., a Bostonian by choice since undergrad days, is back in Boston for his theology studies. A software engineer before he was a Jesuit, he keeps *The Jesuit Post*'s site up and running, and tries to find time to write for it as well. He spent his two years of regency in Baltimore, teaching philosophy at Loyola University Maryland, where he insisted that students have things called "reasons" for their answers. He misses the teaching, but not the grading.

Chris Schroeder, S.J., hails from St. Louis, a setting that instilled in him a quasi-religious love of baseball and a truly religious love of God and Catholicism. Places he has been proud to call home during his Jesuit career include Belize, El Salvador, and, most recently, Denver. His hobbies include late-night jaunts, rambling philosophical discussions, and recreational beard growing. Currently he studies theology at the Jesuit School of Theology in Berkeley, California.

John Shea, S.J., studies theology at the Jesuit School of Theology in Berkeley, California. Before entering the society in 2003, he earned his Ph.D. from Ohio State University in evolutionary biology, focusing on parasites and host behavior. He enjoys swimming, skiing, hiking, watching *Doctor Who,* listening to novelty songs, eating gelato, and hugging trees.

Joe Simmons, S.J., teaches philosophy at Creighton University in Omaha, Nebraska. He studied classics and Spanish at Marquette University, and pursued his master's degree in philosophy at Loyola University in Chicago. His thesis was on religious epistemology and Ignatius Loyola. He has taught at several Jesuit high schools, and loves when students ask the big questions. Joe's favorite writers include David Brooks, David Foster Wallace, Saki, Dostoevsky, Augustine of Hippo, C.S. Lewis, and Catherine of Siena.

Matt Spotts, S.J., is a native of Cincinnati and entered the Jesuits after graduating from Fordham University. He has a master's degree in early modern European history from Saint Louis University with a concentration in the religious and cultural life of the Reformation era. Near associates report that his actual areas of specialty have much more to do with period dramas, obsessive sports fandom, and hot caffeinated beverages. He lives in Indianapolis, where he teaches courses in history and religious studies at Brebeuf Jesuit Preparatory School.

Jayme Stayer, S.J., holds a double degree in music and literature from the University of Notre Dame, and an M.A. and a Ph.D. in English literature from the University of Toledo. He has held faculty posts at Texas A&M University—Commerce, Universidad Centroamericana in El Salvador, and John Carroll University, where he currently works in the English department. His recent publications include a co-authored rhetoric textbook, *Think About It* (Cengage, 2013), an edited volume, *T.S. Eliot, France, and the Mind of Europe* (Cambridge Scholars, 2014), and a work in progress, *Becoming T.S. Eliot: The Rhetoric of Voice and Audience in Inventions of the March Hare* (forthcoming). A professional singer, he has performed with the Chicago Symphony Orchestra, the Cleveland Orchestra, and the Boston Symphony Orchestra. He joined the Jesuits in 2003 and was ordained in 2013.

Eric Sundrup, S.J., a native of Cincinnati, Ohio, and graduate of Xavier University, is an M.Div. student at the Jesuit School of Theology in Berkeley. During the last few years he has split his time between Bolivia, Peru, and the Pilsen neighborhood of Chicago, where he taught at Cristo Rey Jesuit High School. He enjoys running and creating new projects that then take up all of his free time.

Jason Welle, S.J., born and raised in southern California, attended a high school seminary before going to the University of California, Santa Cruz, to complete a B.A. in community studies. He worked nine years in the travel industry, including seven as a flight attendant. In the midst of his high-in-the-sky career, he took a leave to do something more down-to-earth: serving as a Peace Corps volunteer in Malawi. Jason is now studying theology in Berkeley, California.

George Williams, S.J., currently resides in Berkeley, California, and works as the Catholic chaplain of San Quentin State Prison in California. Having completed fifteen years of prison ministry in Massachusetts before moving across the country, George considers his work at San Quentin to be his "dream job."